The Stories We Carry

A memoir about finding your voice and re-writing trauma into triumph

JAS RAWLINSON

First published by Ultimate World Publishing 2022
Copyright © 2022 Jas Rawlinson

ISBN

Paperback: 978-1-922828-77-4
Ebook: 978-1-922828-78-1

Jas Rawlinson has asserted her rights under the Copyright, Designs and Patents Act 1988 to be identified as the author of this work. The information in this book is based on the author's experiences and opinions. The publisher specifically disclaims responsibility for any adverse consequences which may result from use of the information contained herein. Permission to use information has been sought by the author. Any breaches will be rectified in further editions of the book.

All rights reserved. No part of this publication may be reproduced, stored in or introduced into a retrieval system, or transmitted in any form, or by any means (electronic, mechanical, photocopying, recording or otherwise) without the prior written permission of the author. Any person who does any unauthorised act in relation to this publication may be liable to criminal prosecution and civil claims for damages. Enquiries should be made through the publisher.

Cover design: Ultimate World Publishing
Layout and typesetting: Ultimate World Publishing
Edited by Karen Crombie from Exact Editing, and Jas Rawlinson.
Cover photo: Louise Wright

Ultimate World Publishing
Diamond Creek,
Victoria Australia 3089
www.writeabook.com.au

Praise For "The Stories We Carry"

"Raw, unapologetic, and so incredibly hopeful. Trafficking, domestic violence, and trauma are experiences that many women face, and I know many will relate to Jas' words, her experiences, and her triumphs over extraordinary adversity. We need books like The Stories We Carry; books that are honest, heartbreaking and real. Stories that are our own. Thank you Jas, for your courage and perseverance."

Jonty Bush – Australian MP &
former Young Australian of The Year

"Jas has such a way with telling stories – I couldn't put this book down. Through her life experience vignettes, I learned so much more about sexual exploitation and abuse, and how they intersect with many other social issues; and I say that as someone who works on these issues full-time! This is a great book for those interested in understanding women's issues better, and for those working for years already in this space."

Dawn Hawkins – CEO,
National Center on Sexual Exploitation

"This book gives readers critical information, knowledge and wisdom about what abuse and trauma look like in real life…and generously shares the tools needed to transform pain into purpose, and hopelessness into healing."

Sherry Lukey – International EFT Tapping Expert for Heart-Centered Entrepreneurs & Leader

"Moving and courageous. The Stories We Carry provides valuable insights into the reality of domestic and family violence, and its long term impacts. Above all else, it is a celebration of the power of choice, of courageous acceptance, and the joy of shining light into the lives of others."

Nadia Bromley – CEO of Women's Legal Service QLD

"The Stories We Carry is a book that will change the way you think about mental health, trauma, and the stories we tell ourselves. This book shows us that acknowledging and integrating trauma experiences into our life can help guide a personal life journey, rather than serving a life sentence."

Matt Newlands – Speaker, Counsellor, Mental Health Advocate

"The Stories We Carry is an open insight into facing and overcoming types of trauma that can debilitate the best of us. Reading of these experiences and the ability of oneself to rise above them invokes hope for those that may feel there is none."

Glen Hulley – Founding CEO of Australian Registered Charity, Project Karma.

Dedication

To Rhys, my little love. Never forget that you have the power to re-write your life at any moment.

Content Warning

This book contains discussions around domestic violence, bullying, human trafficking, sexual assault, and suicide, and as such, some names and identifying details may have been altered where necessary to protect the identity and privacy of the people mentioned. Please be aware that the information contained in this publication (including the resource section) is not recommended as a substitute for professional support. Should any of the content in this publication trigger feelings of distress, please seek professional support from your GP, or call Lifeline on 13 11 14.

Contents

Author's Note 1

PART 1: The Stories We Carry 5
PART 2: Resources to Help You Thrive 345

About Jas Rawlinson 363
Connect With Jas Rawlinson 373

Author's Note

*I*n another life, this book would never have been birthed. There were many times in my adolescent years where I came close to removing myself from this world completely, and from the age of 10 until 21, I felt as though I were constantly treading water. As a young woman, I believed that suicide was my only way out of the despair that I was experiencing, but in reality, I just wanted the pain to stop.

At such a tender age, there was no way I could have ever known – or believed – that I would go on to live such an extraordinary life. There wasn't space within my brain to even think about life outside of school – let alone to picture myself speaking on global stages, travelling to human trafficking destinations overseas with undercover rescue agents, spotting myself in magazines in supermarkets, and earning a fulltime living as a book coach and best-selling author. It didn't seem possible, and yet, it was all waiting for me.

Many times in the last 15 years, I have thought about writing a book, but it wasn't until late 2021 – in the midst of ongoing lockdowns and uncertainty – that I finally realised that this was my calling. Even now, I can still remember the exact day that this book switched from being a dream to a rough first draft. I was sitting in a cafe, overlooking the ultramarine waters of Moreton Bay in Queensland, and as I typed away on my laptop my mind kept circling in an endless loop. *How many children are out there right now, experiencing the same fear, isolation, and despair that I did as a child, in a home with family violence? How many women are living in cities with lockdowns, where they feel trapped and unable to leave?*

As I stared out the open window, images of myself as a young girl sprang to life. I thought about the nights spent lying in bed, praying that my dad would leave forever. I remembered the powerlessness that swamped me, as I heard his thunderous footsteps coming down the hall to scream at me. And I felt the fear inside my chest, as I considered saddling my horse and leaving in the middle of the night.

Decades had passed, and I was now safe. I had a life that was filled with purpose, love, peace and fulfillment. But how many children were out there right now, crying for someone to help? How many lay in bed, too afraid to make a sound and already learning to numb their emotions while waiting for the abuse to end, and a new life to begin?

The knowledge that our most vulnerable were being trapped behind closed doors, their abuse kept hidden, made my stomach feel like a bag of rubbish slowly shredding and rotting under the blaze of a hot summer sun. *I want it to stop,* I thought to myself, as I stared out at the ocean. *But what can I do?*

That was when I started writing 'The Stories We Carry.' Not for me, but for all those children I couldn't help. For the young women currently going through increased violence during lockdown, who weren't yet able or ready to seek support. For the men and women – like so many of my book coaching clients – who were still carrying physical manifestations of past trauma.

I knew that one day, they would be ready to begin the healing process, and when they were, I wanted this book to be there. I

The Stories We Carry

wanted these words – my stories – to act as a light; one that may help guide them toward their first steps of freedom. A life raft, that may just keep their head above water long enough to recognise that there are so many reasons to live, even when it doesn't feel that way.

So if you find yourself reading this book, feeling that no one understands and you're walking this journey on your own, know that I am with you. When you question if anyone cares, know that I am thinking of you. And if you wonder if you could possibly ever live free from the trauma you've been through, know that it is possible.

I believe in you, and I see you. This book, my words, these stories… they are all for you.

PART 1

The Stories We Carry

"I decided that the single most subversive, revolutionary thing I could do was to show up for my life and not be ashamed."

—Anne Lamott

Chapter 1

The forest was quiet, an eerie silence spilling across the riverbed. Nothing but the tranquil sounds of trickling water moving down the mountainside and the occasional call of a whipbird. Then, there was a small squeak of leather, my saddle squeaking softly and my stirrups clinking as I removed the toe of each boot, allowing them to hang loosely alongside the horse's body.

'Which way, Buddy?'

In front of me, a long pair of dark, chestnut ears twitched back and forth, thinking, listening. I leaned forward over the 14-year-old gelding's neck, shortening the reins and clicking my tongue as we followed the worn lines from the small collection of motorbikes that had zipped through over many years.

On we went, through thickets of lantana, the poisonous pink and yellow buds brushing softly against my legs and face. Up here, on the side of the peak, I felt I could finally exhale. It was my happy place; a secret world that only a few of us knew about.

When I was younger, I used to run through these mountains with one of the local kids in the neighbourhood – a slightly older girl named Kylie. Like me, she was horse crazy, and since neither of us had one of our own, we spent our weekends lying on her bedroom floor flicking through copies of 'Horse Deals.' As we did, we clipped pictures from each magazine, gluing them carefully inside a scrapbook. Each horse had its own special name and a list of details about its temperament, skills, and strengths, and the two of us would spend afternoons picking through this list of treasures until we found the perfect horse to take 'riding'. Then, as young girls do, we saddled our imaginary pets and took off into the paddocks and hills alongside our houses, crawling through fox holes and exploring the valley.

There were no mobile phones in our pockets in those days. No streetlights to give us an indication of passing time. Just the sky and the wind. Here in the mountains we never felt unsafe. Well, almost never. Snakes, leeches, and eels were commonplace, and sometimes, we'd even find a left-over claw from a freshwater crayfish. But the only thing that really bothered me were goannas; the sight of their grey, leathery, prehistoric-looking skin wrinkling as they crawled stealthily towards one of the chicken sheds. 'Never stand still if you see one,' my father had said. 'They'll climb you like a tree and rip your skin off!'

At the time, we had no idea if he was joking or not but we still ran anyway.

Now, as I rode up the mountain on my real horse, I thought of my friends from school and how different some of their lives were. Like Anna, who was bullied and beaten by girls at her bus stop and lived next to a rough community housing area where people regularly threw beer bottles over the fence, sometimes just missing her head.

I'm so lucky I don't have to think about anything like that, I thought, as a light shower of brown and green leaves dropped around my legs.

Yes – but you have so much more to worry about, whispered the wind.

I shook it off, riding through the forest and then doubling back to the country road on which we lived, trotting in the direction of the highway. As one, Buddy and I made our way past hundred-acre properties and long wooden fences until we arrived at a clearing; a patch of hillside where thick trees surrounded the edge, sheltering me from the road and opening up to an uninterrupted view of the sunset-streaked sky.

'Isn't it beautiful?' I whispered, scratching him behind one ear. 'Look at that view!'

I thought again of my friends and how jealous they'd be if they could see this view from horseback; the gentle brushstrokes of pink, purple, and navy lines that graced the horizon. I stared at the sky and thought about all the things that I had to be grateful for. Yet, as I sat there for some time, I couldn't find a single one to focus on.

Instead, a heavy sensation of dread began to fill my bones, followed by a barrage of questions. On and on they went, like a race track filled with adrenaline-hungry drivers.

What will tonight be like?

Is he going to be okay?

I hope he has to work late.

Please, God. Please don't let him come home.

The crickets began to chirp as the sky began to darken. All the while I tried to ignore the truth, but I knew I couldn't put it off any longer. I had to go home.

As I rounded the corner into our road, I pulled Buddy to a halt, knotted my fingers into the lengths of his wiry, silver mane and then allowed him the treat he'd been waiting for – one last wild gallop. Like a greyhound he shot forward, adrenaline soaring through every inch of my skin as I moulded my body expertly to his. As one, we rocketed down the road, swallowing up the distance between us and the small brick house on the hill. The one that I called home. But the closer we got, the more my dread intensified. The truth was, I didn't want to rush. If I could, I would have dragged out the time forever. But I needed the adrenaline; the short-lived sensation of joy and freedom that came with being alone on horseback. I needed to feel safe and free and alive, even if just for a few minutes. Then my mask would go back on.

With every slash of his mane against my 14-year-old arms I wondered how much longer I could keep living this lie. How much longer I could keep hiding in my room, walking on eggshells and pretending to my friends that everything was perfect when it so clearly wasn't. How could I tell them, though? I barely understood what was happening myself – how could I expect them to?

Outside the thick metal gate of our property, I paused and looked upwards, allowing my eyes to travel past the thickets of lantana and towering silver ghost gums. Up, up, up past the lower ridges of the mountain, until I found the highest peak. And all the while, I wondered: *What would happen if I just kept riding? What would happen if today I finally left home and didn't come back?*

'So, in closing, that's why I think that Coffs Harbour should have a David Jones store.'

With a broad smile and a flourish of her hands, my classmate confidently sauntered back to her place and took a seat. She had absolutely aced her public speaking assignment. As for me? Well, I'd spent most of the time staring at the paper in my trembling hands and wishing I could be anywhere else.

Over lunch, I sat by the edge of a small lily-filled dam with my friends – April, Anna and Chloe – as we talked about our newest crushes and who was going to host the next sleepover. As the only girl with a horse – and the only one in our group who lived out on a country property – my place was a hot favourite.

'Wanna come over this weekend and we can do a tent sleepover?' I offered. 'I asked my mum and she said we can camp out in the paddock and you guys can take turns riding Buddy!'

Beside me, April lit up. 'Oh my gosh, yes! I bags having the first go!'

'No, I do!' yelled Anna.

'I'll bring the chips,' offered Chloe, her dark green eyes glimmering. 'What movies are we going to watch?'

'What about 'Toothless?'' I offered.

Instantly Anna's eyes brightened. 'Oh my God, I love that movie! Kirstie Alley is the bomb.'

She was right. Toothless – a movie about a dentist who dies an untimely death and then finds herself in 'limbo', agreeing to take on a job as a tutu-wearing Tooth Fairy in order to get her life back – was one of our favourite movies, and although we'd already seen it, we were happy to watch it again.

'Maybe I can ask Mum to take me to the video store this week and I'll pick it up? I think it's only a 24-hour release though, so fingers crossed we can get it.'

The girls grinned and nodded, all of us looking forward to a weekend of camping, movies, cake, and lollies, and we quickly got to work planning our epic sleepover.

What I didn't tell them, however, was how much a sleepover meant to me. How much I *craved* the chance to have other people in the house so that Dad would have to be on his best behaviour. Whether it was shame or confusion, I wasn't sure – but I knew I didn't feel safe talking about these things.

Everything was so complicated when it came to my dad. Once upon a time he had been my hero; a stocky, handsome man with dark blue eyes and thick brown hair just like mine. A man who carefully fitted a motorbike helmet over my tiny seven-year-old head, popped me on the backseat, and held my arms tightly around his leather jacket as we tore away from the front of the school yard, the wind whipping at our hair as we snaked through the quiet streets of Coffs Harbour before heading south, weaving in and out of country roads until we reached the mountain ranges that surrounded our small brick home. He was a man who had bought me a Little Mermaid nightgown at the age of four – one that still fit well into high school, even as it slowly shrank and my body grew taller. A protective father who, upon hearing that an older boy from a local school had touched my tiny developing chest on the school bus, had bundled us both into the car and followed the vehicle until it pulled over, demanding that I point out the guy so he could tell him to 'keep his fucking hands to himself.' (As a sensitive kid, I was so terrified of confrontation and seeing my dad go to war for me, that I may have picked the wrong boy!)

The Stories We Carry

Even though my dad had been in and out of the picture between my birth and the age of six, I always felt that I was the apple of his eye. Even on a night where I heard the smashing of glassware, as he threw a plate across the room while I was tucked in bed. The sound terrified me, but it seemed to be a one-off, so I didn't worry too much at the time. That is, until things began to change.

Without warning, he seemed to morph from being my protector to being someone who flew off the handle every time I made the smallest mistake. He spiralled into fits of rage, screaming at my mum, controlling our movements, and demanding to know where she'd been.

There was a time when I was around 11 or 12, where my mum had asked him to drop us outside Video Ezy in Toormina Gardens while he went to do some other shopping. With only one car – an old 1980 Toyota Celica – we often had to work around Dad's plans, and so, we'd arranged for him to meet us outside the store in 15 minutes. Instead, he left us there for hours. What made things even worse was that my friend Helena was with me.

For two hours we walked up and down the carpeted aisles, looking aimlessly at VHS covers before sitting down at a brightly coloured toddler's desk, where we sat colouring in the lines of a children's scrapbook with crayons and chalk, until Dad decided he was ready to come and get us. I was absolutely mortified.

The key factor here, as I would learn years later, was control. In Dad's mind, he was the 'head of the house,' and he wanted to ensure we knew it. When he said 'Jump', we jumped. When we wanted to go somewhere, he needed to control the parameters around it; and most importantly, we never went anywhere without him knowing. Sometimes, as the years wore on, he also began to hide the keys to the Celica. Often, he'd do this when he knew that Mum was planning to take us to church, or had something important scheduled.

Slowly, my hero began to disappear, his easy-going smile and warm laughter lines transforming into a hard, calloused canvas. He became a man who would stand at the head of the table and snap, 'That's *my* chair. What are you doing in it?' if I accidentally sat at the far end. A man who would teach my baby brother, in subtle ways he could not yet understand, that anything he said was to be believed, regardless of whether it was true, while everything I said was to be questioned.

Why? Because to be female was to be inferior.

All of this took a toll on me, filling my young body with anxiety, confusion, and an ever-present sadness. But I had no words for what was going on, either at home or inside my head. Everything felt so invisible, so hard to describe. *If only this pain inside my heart showed as a bruise,* I thought. *If only his words cut our skin, so that we had something to prove what's happening.*

'Hey Jas, can your mum make some of those banana muffins again?'

Suddenly, April's voice cut through my head-noise, bringing me back to the present. I forced a smile and looked down at my hands, twisting a piece of bread from my sandwich and throwing it to one of the nearby sheep that was eyeing me off. 'Sure. I'll ask if she can make us that cob bread dip for dinner as well.'

'Yesss,' breathed Anna ecstatically. 'Your mum's cob bread dip is the bomb!'

The Stories We Carry

'Everything is 'the bomb' to you.'

'That's true.' Ripping a piece of paspalum grass from the ground, she placed it in her mouth and grinned toothily like a crazed pirate.

To the outside world, everything seemed fine. I was a young girl who was privileged enough to go to a private school, I had a small group of loveable friends, and I lived on a five-acre property with my own horse, a dog, and a couple of chickens. And while I did have a few bullies – two guys who coincidentally had the exact same name – I never had to worry about things like 'stranger danger'. In so many ways my life *was* privileged.

Yet, there was also another version of my life that existed in tandem. One that was anything but perfect, safe, and privileged. One where I hid in my cupboard. One where I felt the constant flutter of anxiety and devastation because I couldn't protect my mother. One where I never knew what version of my dad was going to arrive home that day.

But no one saw that side. No one asked. So instead, I kept my increasingly anxious thoughts to myself.

Through it all, my mother did her best to keep us safe. She managed the unmanageable; she problem-solved the unsolvable. She was the one getting us through each day. The silent hero in a world that was becoming increasingly fearful. A dangerous world that none of us quite yet understood, but would one day become too great to ignore.

Chapter 2

Be strong. Be strong. Be strong.

My fingers worked quickly, tearing the small rectangular item from my bag and tossing it toward the bin. Like a scratch on an old vinyl record, I felt my heart skip a beat, my eyes darting around to check if anyone had seen. If they had, they didn't react. The school yard was the same as always – a cacophony of screams, laughter, and shit-talking.

As I heard the *thunk* of my tomato, ham, and lettuce sandwich dropping into the trash, an unexpected thrill rushed through my body. *Like one of those buzzers on 'The Price is Right',* I thought to myself. *Ding, ding, ding! Congratulations, Jas! You are the winner!*

My prize? The self-congratulation that came from choosing willpower over food.

Quietly, I re-zipped my school bag, hunching into the now slightly emptier backpack and walking toward the small dam where my friends sat. Already my mind was working overtime, coming up with excuses as to why I wouldn't be eating with them. It made me anxious – the thought of all the lies I would have to tell. It felt as though the dopamine rush I'd just felt was already being washed away; overshadowed and stamped out by all the invisible Jenga pieces I'd have to layer in order to keep my secret safe.

And then, there were all the lies I'd have to tell myself in order to try and wash away the guilt.

Mum worked so hard to provide food for us. It had been many years since she'd had full time employment, and during that time things hadn't gotten much better in Coffs Harbour. She'd been a school teacher for over 20 years, but since giving birth to me, she'd struggled to find anything permanent. Thankfully, she managed to hop from one casual contract to another without too much time in limbo, but it was always a guessing game and I knew that the anxiety of never having secure, permanent work weighed heavily on her – particularly during the school holidays, when she had to ride out anywhere from two weeks to two months without pay. Only days earlier, I'd seen the extent of her distress when my little brother accidentally dropped a brand-new jar of mayonnaise on the floor. On that morning, I'd heard the high-pitched shriek of her screams and had run down the hallway to find Jason – his bare feet planted firmly on the cold black tiles of our kitchen – surrounded by shards of glass and lashings of creamy white goop. As he too began to cry, I looked across to my mother's face, her eyes streaming with tears that ran down each cheek into a puddle of despair.

'No!' she'd cried, trying hopelessly to scoop up the thick, creamy dollops of mayonnaise that now lay ruined on the floor. 'No, no, no...'

I knew the weight of responsibility and anxiety that my mother carried about providing for us. How much work had been required to buy that special jar of Soy Mayonnaise; a treat, amidst the normal scrimping, saving, and sacrificing of everyday items. And here I was disrespecting all that hard work by throwing my food away. Still, I couldn't stop myself. I *had* to do it. I had to be thin like the senior girls that I looked up to; the ones whose lives seemed so perfect.

The Stories We Carry

Maybe if I look like them, I won't feel the way I do, I wondered hopefully. *I might not be able to control what's happening at home, but I can control this.*

I congratulated myself again, willing my body to stop thinking about food as I sat down with my group. Across from me, Anna sat on folded legs, one hand stretching out toward 'Sweety Pie', one of the tall, white sheep that we often shared our food with. Then, suddenly, she stopped.

'Hey, where's your lunch?'

'Oh, I forgot to pack it,' I shrugged. Then, quickly, I changed topics. 'Hey guess what? I called into Star FM last night for their CD competition and I won!'

The three girls stared silently, their faces lit up like a Christmas tree. Then they all began shrieking.

'No way!'

'Holy crap, what did you win?'

'Don't tell me it's the new Backstreet Boys album – I will literally kill you.'

'Even better,' I smiled, stretching out on the soft grass. 'I won a pack of, like, ten CDs. Including the new Britney album.'

Anna dropped her lunch, her two wide brown eyes staring into mine. 'Ugh, you suck.'

'You can have the Human Nature ones though,' I teased.

'Umm, no thank you.'

We chattered on, gossiping about things we'd heard and seen, how hot Devon Sawa and Jonathan Taylor Thomas (JTT, as he was called) were, and the latest pop culture news from TV Hits. But soon, the school bell rang out across the fields and it was time to head back to class.

All throughout the day my stomach rumbled, turning in on itself as it begged for food but I wouldn't relent. When I felt hungry, I'd think of the glossy images in my Billabong surf magazines; photographs of long, perfectly tanned limbs and cardboard thin stomachs. Of happy smiles and ice-creams that dripped down their smooth, thin legs (ice-creams that probably never got eaten, but made for pretty photographs). Then I'd walk out to the bus stop and stare hungrily at the older girls; the ones with tiny waists and blue-checkered skirts that clung perfectly to their curvy hips; spreading thinly over washboard stomachs that never wrinkled, rolled, or creased when they sat down. *If only I could swap bodies with them*, I thought enviously. *Then my life would be perfect.*

My attempt at starving myself didn't last long, much to my despair. Though I was able to avoid dinner that night by pretending to be sick, there was no way to get out of the house without Mum knowing I'd skipped breakfast in the mornings, and so I tried to re-start my 'diet' from the moment I got to school. I made it through recess, but by lunch I was so starved that I had to call it quits. As a 40 kg girl with an overactive thyroid – and an inability to keep weight on due to stress – this shouldn't have been a surprise. But to me, it meant only one thing: *Failure.*

You're so weak! screamed my inner mean girl. *You couldn't even last two days without food.*

The Stories We Carry

All I wanted was to have control of my life; to feel beautiful and worthy and loved. And to me, the way to achieve that was through thinness. To be like the girls in my surfing magazines. *If I can just be skinny like them, I'll be happy*, I thought wistfully. *I just need to be thinner.*

Every day, from the moment I woke until the time I went to bed, I thought about my weight. Every time I stood on a set of scales and saw the flickering of the little black arrow, I'd wish and pray for it to go lower. At my 'heaviest' I was a mere 40 kg. Yet, the version of myself that I saw was something very different.

As a teen in the '90s, no one talked about things like 'body dysmorphia'. I had zero understanding of mental illness, or that there was a real, diagnosable reason behind many of the things I was going through. I thought that my constant mirror checking – and the extreme emotional distress I felt every time I looked at my body – was simply normal. I thought I was inherently flawed. Didn't everyone else see it, too? How ugly, fat, and disgusting I was? To my young mind, it seemed impossible that they wouldn't.

Unfortunately, my body dysmorphia was only reinforced by particular girls at school, one of whom told me point blank, 'Hey, just so you know, all the guys call you "the ugly one" behind your back. I really wanted you to hear it from me, not them.' Decades later I would discover through one of my peers that this was a lie, but at the time I took her cruel words into my heart, sinking further into self-hatred.

So deep was this self-loathing that some days I refused to even speak. That was how much I hated the sound of my own voice. Most of the time, I scrawled angry, suicidal words in my diary, drawing horrifying images of what I wished I had the mental courage to do to myself. Amidst long journal entries about boys I liked and who my favourite boy band was, I wrote poems about how much I hated my dad and what I'd give for him to disappear forever. Then I'd go to sleep, where I'd dream of all the ways I could leave this world so that I never had to feel this pain ever again.

Resilient is a word that often gets thrown around when it comes to kids. 'Don't worry, they're resilient! They'll bounce back. Just wait and watch – she'll forget about this sooner than you expect.'

It's true, to a degree. But sometimes, what people see as resilience is thinly cloaked survival. In my case, I'd become so used to the heavy emotional load I was carrying, that people around probably didn't realise. After all, I was the high achiever. The scholarship recipient and Student Leader. The conscientious, people-pleasing, good girl. People saw all the things I achieved and how I excelled, but they didn't see the multitude of invisible plates that I was carrying; the ones jammed under my armpits while I balanced another stack on my head. They didn't see the ones I was gripping between my knees and underneath the crook of my chin. It was an almost impossible act to keep up, but to the outside world I looked like I was on top of it all.

I never felt resilient. I felt like I was drowning – constantly.

On top of everything going on at home, I was also being bullied at school. It had first begun at the age of 10, when a boy named Trent had started picking on me. At the time I'd been told by various people to 'just ignore it', because 'it obviously means he likes you.' It was a bizarre logic that had never made sense to me. Not in the beginning, when he took sick delight in pulling on my ponytail, not months later, when he mocked my school work and announced to the class how much my project 'sucked,' and definitely not years ahead, when he'd chased me – aged 12 – into an empty toilet block after school where he'd sneered, 'Got you! You're going to get it now, bitch.'

On that horrifying day I'd cowered atop the closed toilet seat, willing myself to breathe as I tried desperately to work out how to escape. How to possibly get out of there without him attacking me. In the end, however, I'd realised the painful truth. No one was coming to save me. *I have to do this myself,* I thought resolutely. With adrenaline pumping through my tiny limbs, I set my jaw, stood up, and rushed through the door. Instantly, pain radiated through my right shoulder and I crumpled forward in shock. Beside me, something round and green fell to the ground.

'Got ya, bitch!'

Just metres away, Trent stood laughing, the apple that he'd just hurled into my body now lying on the ground between us. With tears streaming down my face and my bravado a distant memory, I sprinted back across the school yard. With every step, my heart broke more and more. Why did I have to be terrorised at school, as well as at home?

Sadly, Trent didn't give up as the years stretched on – not even when he finally got expelled (or 'voluntarily' moved on, whichever you want to call it). Instead, his best mate simply picked up where he'd left off. This boy, who coincidentally had the same name, liked to make my life miserable by taunting me in class, pulling my hair, or finding other ways to upset me. Trent 2.0 was more of a nuisance than anything. He didn't physically scare me, like 'Original Trent.' But he knew exactly what to say to cut me down emotionally.

Some teachers told me to 'just ignore it,' while a male staff member actually advised me to 'punch him in the face.' Neither seemed like good ideas to me – particularly the latter. I'd spent years travelling up and down the coast for dental work in Brisbane, and after surviving the *ordeal* of owning multiple thick, nerdy dental plates – including an infamous dental device that hooks into your plate and then straps around your head like something out of a horror film – I most definitely did not want to lose my precious teeth to Trent.

Eventually, though, I couldn't hold back my anger, and on that day I snapped.

I was sitting in Mr P's class when it happened. I was staring at the blackboard, listening intently to the discussion on Geography, when I felt a spidery sensation working its way through my hair. Whirling around, I looked straight into the eyes of my bully, my gaze flickering down to his smarmy lips. *Ignore him, he's just looking for attention*, I told myself. *Remember what adults always say? They're just doing it for attention.*

A few minutes later I turned around to get something from my bag, and that's when I saw it. He'd stolen the book I needed for class. I could see it peeking out from his own backpack.

'Put it back,' I demanded.

'I don't know what you're talking about.' Trent stared at me, a repulsive, aggravating grin worming its way up the left-hand side of his face.

Before I knew it, I was on my feet, my hand shooting out from my body. My vision blurred and I heard the sharp clap of my palm

– felt the heat of flesh upon flesh – as I slapped that stupid smirk right off his face.

For a moment we both stared in stunned silence, his mouth a perfect 'O'. No one spoke a word; in fact, my sudden breakdown was so swift that some students didn't even seem to notice. But in one gulping, rushing force, reality caught up, sending a flood of nervous energy through my veins.

Crap. What did I just do?

Trent began to quiver, his voice returning in a burst of anger. 'Mr P! Mr P, Jasmine just hit me!'

Quickly I returned to my seat, cheeks flushed with embarrassment, just in time to pick up my pen before the teacher turned around. I held my breath and waited. *Shit, how much trouble am I going to be in now? Why the hell did I do that? Why didn't I just suck it up and ignore him?*

Mr P's eyebrows drew together, his own face twisting into disbelief. For a moment he let his hand drop, the thick white chalk that had been writing lines of text across the board now hanging loosely from his index finger and thumb. Seconds passed, feeling like hours. Then he switched his gaze from me to my bully.

'Don't be ridiculous Trent, Jasmine would never do something like that,' he snapped.

'But... but Mr P!'

In one swift motion, the teacher swivelled back to the board and continued on with the lesson, leaving Trent 2.0 sputtering and shaking in anger.

I didn't dare look back; I couldn't even begin to think about pushing my luck. Instead, I picked up a pen and continued with my notes, gripping it so tightly it left an imprint on the inside of my index finger. After class I held my head high and left for lunch, hoping that my random act of violence would be enough to send a clear signal: *Stop fucking with me. I'm done.*

Though violence has never been something I condone, my actions that day felt appropriate. It had taken years of mental abuse from two different boys – alongside everything I was enduring at home – to reach that breaking point.

I was done with being a passive victim.

'Sing for me. Come on, I wanna hear you sing!'

From the doorway of my bedroom, a short, thin girl with dark brown hair and pale skin stood staring at me. 'Come on, hurry up,' she pushed, placing her hands on her hips, two greenish-blue eyes staring me down.

'Fine,' I exhaled. 'But turn around. I don't want you to watch me while I'm singing.'

'Can do. But don't chicken out – I'm waiting.'

Gosh, she really is bossy sometimes, I thought. *Why do I have to do this again?*

Out of all my friends, Rachael was the one who surprised me the most. Unlike the rest of my group, she couldn't care less about

The Stories We Carry

horses, and wasn't that fussed about boy bands. She'd rather spend weekends hosting a Murder Mystery card game than trekking through the bush, and she always made chicken tacos instead of mince (everyone's usual favourite). She was also a theatre-obsessed extrovert who'd been performing in eisteddfods and shows since she was practically a toddler.

I like to joke that Rach saw me as her newest 'student in waiting'; someone to mentor and help come out of her shell. But all jokes aside, that's exactly what she did. On weekends we'd spend hours coming up with whacky improvisations that made us burst into laughter, or re-writing the lyrics to Christina Aguilera's 'All I want is you' (which became 'All I want is food') while dancing around in her room, and it was through Rach that I began to bloom. She pushed me out of my comfort zone in a way that no one else would; a way that terrified me at the time, but was exactly what I needed. It's also thanks to her that I ended up choosing Drama as one of my Year 9 electives – a decision that, undoubtedly, helped save my life.

Amidst the stomach-crunching anxiety and depression, self-hatred, obsessive weighing and loneliness, performing arts was the thing that gave me a voice. It was the place where I found a sense of worth and excitement and an opportunity to express myself. The theatre was a new home away from home.

Unfortunately for me, once Rachael found out about my secret dreams of becoming an international pop star (hilarious, given that I was so shy I had to bribe my way out of public speaking assignments!) she was unrelenting in her pursuit to hear me sing. Like a drug-detection dog in the middle of a baggage claim area, she zeroed in on me and refused to give up. She was bossy, and she didn't care.

'Come on Jas,' she repeated, standing now in the doorway of my bedroom, back turned at my insistence.

With nervous energy racing through my body I leaned against my cupboard – its doors plastered with N'Sync, Hanson and Backstreet Boys posters – and racked my brain for a song. Eventually I settled on a random Christian anthem that we'd sung at school recently, repeating the words while I silently willed my voice to stay steady. Eventually, she turned around and stared at me, somewhat surprised.

'You're actually good, Jas,' she said. 'Why are you so hard on yourself?'

'I dunno. I mean, I'm not that good.'

'You could be *really* good. You just need more practice.'

'Maybe…'

Eager to move the focus off myself, I changed topics and began blabbing about something random, the two of us sitting cross legged on my bed gossiping about other kids at school. Though incredibly ordinary, that day was also momentous, because it was the beginning of so much more.

Over the next few months I began stepping out of my comfort zone in small ways, making friends with a few of Rachael's theatre friends from outside of school and finding hidden talents that I'd never known existed. By the time I was 17 I'd been cast in a major role for two of our school's annual performances, with both of them stretching me to go far beyond what I thought I was capable of. In one role, I was cast as Sophie Wender, the six-toed 'fringe dweller' from the post-apocalyptic, science fiction novel 'The Chrysalids.'

The Stories We Carry

This role was particularly challenging – not only in terms of the number of lines, but also the emotion I needed to show. After the performance, I lay in bed wondering how I'd been able to immerse myself so fully in an imaginary world. *How did I do that? How did I connect so deeply that I was able to cry in front of an audience of 500 people?*

There was something about art, about creativity, that had the ability to awaken an entire world within me that I'd never known could exist. When I wrote, I disappeared for hours into blue-lined pages and small black and white letters. When I had a camera in my hands, I entered a flow state that not even hunger could break. And when I was on stage, I was both terrified and ecstatic.

It was something I needed; a lifeline that kept me going throughout the next few years as Dad's mental state began to worsen. I had no idea what was happening, but his mood swings were becoming more frequent and volatile; his swearing now turning to physical outbursts of rage. One night, while he was carrying on, swearing and screaming, Mum raced to the back door and clicked the lock shut. Her hope was that it would give him some time to calm down. That Dad would take off to the shed to work on his bike, or go for a walk.

Instead, he smashed a 60 cm crack into the back laundry door.

That night, I lay still as a stone beneath the covers of my bed, my entire nervous system on high alert. By now, Mum had worked to calm him down and only the soft, filtered sounds of the TV could be heard but I just couldn't relax. I lay wide awake, terrified. *If he can crack a door in half that easily, what hope do we ever have of protecting ourselves if things get really bad?*

For weeks afterwards, I had to stare at that almost broken – not quite hanging on – back door. A diagonal splintering that if I'd pushed gently, would have folded in on itself, revealing a close view of the mountains behind our home. Every time I stopped by the fridge to get something to eat. Every time I ran my hands under the laundry tap. Every time I walked up the back steps, the fragmented door was waiting for me.

A grim reminder of what could happen next time.

A silent warning of how much worse it was going to get.

If anyone had ever asked me to explain what it was about my dad's abuse that made it feel so devastatingly damaging, I would have struggled to put it into words. Unlike so many other children, I never experienced physical or sexual abuse at the hands of my father – instead, he relied on all the things that went unseen by the general public. Coercive and financial control, verbal abuse, gaslighting, mockery, bullying... anything he could use to destroy my self-esteem and break down my identity. In many ways, this felt more destructive than if he'd just slapped me across the face.

Constantly, I felt like I was losing my mind. If I forgot to feed the dogs at night or accidentally left the back door open, I'd receive lashings of verbal and mental abuse; streams of words about how worthless, lazy, and stupid I was. However, the real punishment would come the next night, when he would wait until 8 pm to feed the animals, leaving them whining with hunger, or fail to do something that, if I had done the same, would have led to a barrage of verbal abuse. He was illogical and irrational, and the deliberate double-standards he wielded only reinforced his superiority.

The Stories We Carry

On the rare occasions where he did smack me for doing something wrong (up until the age of 11 or 12), I at least had some warning that it was coming. I could brace myself for the pain and know that it would soon be over. But with mental and emotional abuse, there was no way of telling when the pain would end. It was insidious; it followed me into my bed at night and woke me up with horrific nightmares. It embedded itself in my perception, clouding the way I saw myself. It wrapped itself around my brain, and then endlessly replayed his words back to me. It was a never-ending, constant, malicious loop.

You might be smart when it comes to books, but you're dumb in every other way.

Wow, look at how fat your gut is!

Geez, it's true what they say about driver's license photos. You look so bad.

You'll just be a dole bludger when you grow up. You're too dumb to do anything useful.

Any animal you have will just die, you'll never be able to look after it on your own.

You should be in a girl's home. That'll teach you some manners.

You're a bitch.

You're stupid.

You're stupid.

You're stupid.

One night, I opened my journal and tried to work out what it was about me that made him so repulsed by his own flesh and blood. Why he hated me so much. In minutes, I came up with an exhaustive list, my tears dripping onto the pale pink paper as words grew longer and more expressive. I ended it with the words: *Because I'm a girl. Because I won't be silenced.*

Over time, I withdrew further and further from him, squashing down my love for the man who was meant to be my hero and forcing it into a small container in the back of my mind. One with an airtight lid. I thought back to a day earlier that year, when I stood in the driveway, my voice clogged with emotion. 'You said you'd change! You promised!' I screamed desperately. 'Why do you keep hurting me?'

He stood motionless, one side of his lip raising into a snarl. Then, in a flat, steely voice, he replied. 'You don't do anything *I* want you to, so why should I do anything *you* want?'

Now, as I lay in my room, I wondered again how he could hurt me so deeply with just the power of his words. How could he make my desire for him to be a loving father seem as though it were something I had to earn by constantly jumping through his hoops of blackmail and manipulation? Laying back against my pillow I stared up at the small collection of glow-in-the-dark stars on my ceiling. *Does anyone else feel this hopeless?* I wondered. When I thought about my friends, I saw nothing but perfection. Fathers who hugged them tightly and drove them to sporting games or theatre performances. Dads who were quietly spoken and confident without being controlling. Men who treated me as though I were their own daughter, speaking with such softness that the ache in my chest grew so strong that I could hardly breathe. This ache, however, was nothing compared to what happened when I watched these men hug their own daughters; the desolation I felt as I realised just how different our family was to everyone else's. In hindsight, I can see that nothing is ever as perfect as it appears – not even my friends' fathers – but at the time, my perception was this: *I am alone with this pain.*

In the safety of my room, with my parents asleep on the other side of my wall, I began to daydream. *I wish I could press a button and make the police come and take him away,* I thought wistfully. *Or maybe a little device that records him without him knowing, and sends that audio to the police. Then we'd be able to finally prove that this is real!*

But there was no secret button. No magic device. Only four walls that housed hurtful secrets no one else knew about.

Instead, I turned to the next best thing – my cassette player. Soon, the sounds of Destiny's Child's 'Survivor' began to fill the room, their voices taking me away from the pain. As I lay there, drowning in my loneliness, an unexpected thought pushed its way forward. A question.

You can't stop what's happening right now, but maybe one day, you can do that for someone else. Maybe you can find a way to help other women – to make sure no one ever has to feel this hopeless and alone.

In the background, my stereo clicked loudly, the cassette tape reaching the end. I sighed and switched it off.

Don't be so stupid, I interjected, replying back to the thought. *As if I could ever do anything to help anyone else.*

But still, it wouldn't leave.

What if...? it persisted. *What if one day you can use all of this to help someone else?*

Chapter 3

'Um, I don't know how to tell you this – but I think I just found your perfect match.'

Rachael spun on the spot, her wide blue eyes fixing on the lacy red material in my hands. Then she took a step backward, lips curving into a wry smile. 'Oh yeah, that's totally my style,' she laughed, pushing the G-string back onto the clothing rack.

'Well, you know what they say, don't knock it 'till you've tried it!'

'You wear it, then.'

I scrunched up my nose, shoving my hands back into the baggy pockets of my green cargo shorts. 'Eww, gross.'

Rach and I skipped off through the aisles, laughing to ourselves as we headed toward the bright red doors of the Reject Shop. Once there, we rifled through the wigs and accessories, taking turns to model our wackiest finds. It was only a few weeks until our school's annual Mufti Night, and I'd decided to go as Daria, the MTV legend. As an introvert, it felt like a close enough fit. After all, I'd much rather hang out in a corner and make sarcastic remarks than strut around as the centre of attention.

'What about this?' Rach asked, picking out a Hula Hoop. 'I can go as Australia's first Hula Hooping champion!' She turned sideways, skimming the pink and green ring around her hips. 'Come on! What could be more aspirational than this?'

I raised an eyebrow quizzically, watching as the hoop spun in slow circles toward the ground. 'Nah girl, you need some edge,' I added. 'Something to really make you stand out.' I scanned the shelves, searching through rows of strange accessories until I found the right fit. 'This!' I said, pinching a thick black wig from the wall. 'Now you're set. You can be the only Hula Hooping champion in Australia to win the championship while wearing a mullet.'

'Yes! Totally!'

Weekends with Rach were my favourite. I never had to pretend to be anything other than myself when we were together – in fact, the weirder we could be, the better. Like many teenagers we spent nights dressing up in strange costumes, hosting murder mystery parties, hanging out at the shops, and hogging all the dial-up internet on her computer to make Mad Libs or chat with guys on MSN. We were normal teen girls growing up in the early noughties, and that's what made it so great. We were carefree – and carefree was something I was learning to appreciate more and more, given the tension going on in my home life. I made plans as often as possible to be out of the house, regularly having sleepovers with Rach, Chloe, or April, or inviting them to mine in the hope that it would force Dad to behave himself. Sometimes I got lucky, but mostly, it was just easier for me to go elsewhere. Having fun in my own home only seemed to unsettle him further, leading him to make sure that my joy was quickly swallowed up by misery. There were many ways he did this. Extra chores. Countless cruel remarks, as he berated and micromanaged everything I did. Nights spent constantly walking on eggshells. I don't know if he was even aware that he reacted in this way – I only know that he made sure, every time, that I was punished for my 'crime' of happiness.

The Stories We Carry

That afternoon, as Rach and I hugged goodbye and I strapped myself into the back seat of the car, I felt a heaviness descend. A sense that something wasn't right.

'Where's Dad?' I asked, peering at the empty passenger seat. When we'd left that morning, all four of us had been in the car. Now, it was only Mum and Jason.

'He's back at the garden nursery,' she explained. 'He wanted to stay longer so I told him I'd pick you up and come back.'

For a few minutes we drove mostly in silence, savouring the peace that existed when it was just the three of us. It was something I couldn't explain to my girlfriends – many of whom thought my dad was 'cool' and 'kind of cute' – but even when the terrifying Mr Hyde had gone on holiday and Dr Jekyll was back in charge, I couldn't relax. His happy smiles and jokes only flared my anxiety further, because I knew how quickly things could – *and would* – change.

Outside the local nursery, we sat and waited. In the backseat, the hands on my watch slowly ticked by, the minutes stretching from five to fifteen, until eventually, Mum decided to go into the store to look for him. She talked to the owner – to customers – asking if anyone had seen Dad leave, but the answer was always the same. 'Sorry! Haven't seen anyone by that description.'

In the end, my mother made the decision to begin driving towards home, all of us scanning the sides of the street in search of my father. It was only a minute or two later that we spotted him, his stocky frame sweating and striding along the pathway. A frozen pineapple icy-pole hung from one hand, but his ocean-blue eyes were as hard as concrete. Instantly my stomach dropped. I knew.

I just knew. The rigid set of his jaw; the way he walked. Things were about to get ugly.

Mum pulled up to the curb, calling out to him through the window. 'Shane, where have you been? We were looking for you all over the nursery.'

He turned, eyes ablaze. 'You absolute bitch,' he spat. 'You fucking bitch. Stealing my car and taking off! Who do you think you are?!'

In the back seat I stiffened, wishing I could disappear. I pictured my favourite '90s TV character Alex Mack, and instantly wished I could turn myself into liquid like her, sliding away to someplace safer.

From the driver's seat, my mother lowered her voice. 'Shane, you told me to pick you up, and I came to pick you up,' she said, placating, searching for his rational side. 'But you weren't there. I asked around everywhere. What else was I meant to do? Please, just get in the car and we'll all go home. I'm here now.'

Dad turned away, continuing to storm along the path outside the Coffs Harbour Show Grounds. 'Just fuck off!' he screamed. Then, in one quick motion, he coiled his arm and flung it forward, a chunk of frozen pineapple smashing against the open window. My brother and I flinched, the cold ice and paddle pop stick narrowly avoiding our heads. 'Fuck off!'

It was my brother's ninth birthday.

That afternoon, the three of us sat in silence in our living area, feeling like sitting ducks awaiting the hunter. *How long until he gets home? What happens* when *he gets home? Will he have calmed down, or are we all going to cop it for leaving him behind?* Alone in my room I paced in circles, my stomach heavy with worry. With my nervous system tightly coiled and no idea what to do with the adrenaline coursing through my body, I flung open the heavy wooden doors of my wardrobe and crushed myself into a corner. Clothing draped over the back of my ponytail, and a thick plastic box filled with books scraped against the edge of my shin. There I stayed, one with the darkness. Shallow breaths cycling in and out, in and out. Mentally I counted the time that it might take him to walk the distance from town to home. *A good few hours, at least,* I figured. *That is, unless he hitch-hikes.*

Tentatively, I crawled out from the cupboard. Jason and Mum were sitting in the living room, my brother playing a video game while she frantically made cups of tea and paced. Desperate for distraction, I grabbed the phone and dialled my boyfriend's number. We had barely begun talking when, suddenly, a noise caught my attention.

The sound of the front gate opening.

Oh no. No, no, no.

As we later discovered, someone had given Dad a lift home. At first, he was calm – walking around the backyard and going in and out of the shed like nothing had happened. Mum figured he was trying to blow off steam and told us not to worry. 'I think he's okay,' she whispered. 'Just give him some time.'

I went back to my room; but then, suddenly, I heard a different sound. Dad's car roaring to life, the engine revving loudly as gravel crunched and flew through the air.

"Jason, get out of the car! Please, get out!" It was my mother's voice, her words growing with volume as she begged and pleaded for my brother – who had been coerced by Dad to get into his car – to come back to the house. As I later discovered, he'd read the worry on her face and leapt from the car, jumping toward the safety of her arms.

And now, Dad was on a warpath.

In an instant I was on my feet, running along the hallway and searching for my mother's face. 'What's happening?! Mum, what's happening!' I screamed, the phone now hanging limply from my hand.

Before she even had a chance to speak, I heard his footsteps and instantly, I knew; I just knew.

Get out! screamed my intuition. *Run. Now!*

I lurched for the back door, snapping it shut. But at that very moment Dad burst through the laundry entrance. *Forget the locks*, screamed my head. *Go to the front door. Get out, get out fast.*

Together, our heartbeats thundering as one, we ran for the front verandah, narrowly avoiding my father as he stormed through the kitchen. Like wild animals, we skidded and leapt, fleeing along the deck, down the thin steps, and straight toward the boundary fence. We knew where to go. We knew what to do. There was only one place where we would be safe, but we had to move fast.

My mother reached for a rung of barbed wire, forcing a gap for us to slide through. It was something I'd done a million times before, pulling apart the two middle strands so I could slip between and make my way to Kylie's house. It was second nature, but it had always been done with such care and precision; never while running for my life.

My father flung himself down the steps, his voice booming ever closer. 'Jason! Buddy, where are you going? We're going to the beach, remember? It's your birthday!'

Jason and I plunged through the gap, Mum the only one still on the other side. 'He's not going anywhere with you right now,' she yelled back. 'Not right now.' She stepped forward, easing under the wire. Then, she stopped. Her dress had snagged on the razor teeth of the barbed wire. It was stuck.

My mouth suddenly turned to sandpaper. My heart almost leaping out of my chest. Dad stormed closer, still calling out to my brother.

Then, *ripppp*. Mum's dress, tearing free. Her feet bounding forward, carrying her away from the fenceline. The three of us heaving and puffing as we ran, our feet frantically pounding up and down, down and up. Forcing our way through the long grass. Up and over a thick metal gate. Then, finally, past the macadamia trees toward the front door of our neighbours' house.

Thank God, I thought, spotting their cars. *They're home, we're OK.* Frantically, we knocked on the front door, the seconds feeling like hours.

No response.

Knock, knock, knock.

Still no answer.

We stood on the front step, our skin crawling like live electrical wires. 'They must be out,' Mum puffed, trying to catch her breath. 'Could be up the back. Working… in the shed.'

She reached up and tried the door, the knob twisting freely. With overwhelming relief we surged inside, locking it shut behind. Cathie and her husband were close friends of ours and we knew they'd understand once we had a chance to explain, but right now every second counted.

Only then, as we sat in the lounge area – tucked away from any windows – did I look down at my right hand and feel the tightness of my knuckles. In shock, I realised that my fingers were still locked tightly around the cordless phone.

How much did my boyfriend hear, before the signal cut out? I wondered. My stomach clenched, a fresh wave of anxiety rolling over me. *What must he think of me? What will other people think of me, if they find out the truth about my family?* It felt so shameful, the thought of people knowing how 'unperfect' my life was.

Right now though, I didn't have time to worry about all of this; because Dad's car was barrelling up the driveway. I knew from the noise of the spinning tyres and crunching gravel. There was no one else who could possibly be coming for us.

'Jason! Where are you?'

My father's footsteps travelled closer, his voice focused on my brother. Suddenly, a bedroom door at the back of the house creaked open, and out slipped our neighbour Cathie. She rubbed her eyes – having clearly just woken from a nap – and looked at us in confusion. Then, she heard Dad's voice. From the couch, we stared in terror, our eyes pleading. *Please. Please don't answer the door. Please don't make us go back to him.*

Cathie walked toward us, encircling my mother with her arms as her husband – appearing from behind – walked to the entry way to confront my father. I huddled closer, terrified. Both Mum and I feared what might happen if he got hold of Jason; if he took him in the car and left. None of us wanted to think about it. For the next hour he tried his best to coax us out – sometimes pretending to leave, in an attempt to lure us into a trap. But never did his car engine start, and so, we stayed put.

Eventually, as dusk began to fall, he gave up. 'I'll go home first,' Mum said, hushing our cries. 'I'll make sure everything's okay and then I'll come back for you.'

'No!' I sobbed. 'Don't go. Please, don't go home. What if he...?' I couldn't bear to finish the sentence.

'It'll be okay,' she soothed. 'He knows that Cathie and her husband have seen everything, and he knows they are keeping an eye on him. It will be okay, I promise.'

An hour later she returned for us, letting Jason and I know that Dad had calmed down and we were safe to come home. Suddenly, we were back inside the four walls of our house, acting like nothing had ever happened.

That afternoon, I saw once again the mental tightrope my mother walked. The courage it took to face the monster that was Mr Hyde, and talk him down until Dr Jekyll could return. It was a delicate act; one that terrified me. *How do you do it? How do you make the monster disappear?* I wanted to ask.

Jas Rawlinson

I climbed into bed that night with a head full of worry. Questions of *What if?* and *What happens next?* pestering me as I tried to sleep. Outside, all was quiet, but my mind was on hyper-alert, seeking out the smallest of sounds. Searching for the slightest threat of danger. For the millionth time, I wondered how much longer I could keep going – if tonight was the night to saddle my horse and quietly slip away under a blanket of darkness. Was there anywhere I could go where I'd feel safe?

I realised there wasn't.

And so, I had only one option. To keep treading water.

Chapter 4

'Hey Jas, what are you doing at lunch?' Rachael's voice was a whisper, just audible above the excitable chit-chat of our English teacher. As usual, Mrs E was gallivanting around the room with the energy and excitement of a small, frantic chihuahua, and as normal, we were all wondering just how many Red Frogs she'd consumed. They were, after all, her favourite lolly. That, and 'those little cakes from the canteen that make me lose *all* self-control.'

Yep. When it came to weird teachers Mrs E was on a whole other level. But secretly, she was one of my favourites.

Ducking my head, I turned to Rachael and shrugged discreetly. 'Nothing much. Just sitting with the gang on the front basketball court. Why's that?'

'I need to talk to you,' she said, her voice uncharacteristically serious. 'Meet me by the bubbler in ten minutes?'

I nodded, packing up my stuff and heading out with the lunch bell. As we made our way down toward the back paddock, Rachael's greenish-blue eyes searched mine, a line creasing itself between each brow. 'Jas, I'm worried about you,' she began.

I pulled to a stop, pausing by the senior toilet block and staring at my best friend like she'd just told me the sky was green. 'What do you mean?'

'You're withdrawing more and more. I'm really worried. I just... you're not YOU anymore,' she said gently. 'What's been happening at home?'

I felt my skin begin to crawl; the familiar choking sensation that overcame me whenever I thought of telling the truth. There was a part of me that longed to let it all out. To be free. But the greater part of me knew that doing so was futile. Why scare people away? Why let people in on the ugly truth? My friends would never come over again if they knew what Dad was really like. Or at least, that's what I told myself. It seemed easier to shut up and suffer in silence.

By now, I'd been holding these secrets for six years and even though I'd let a few things slip to Rach (and my boyfriend, who had heard the shouting through the phone on the day we fled next door), she didn't know much. I was an expert at keeping everything under lock and key. I was proud of it – proud of my ability to rely only on myself. But as I was quickly learning, there was one part of me that wasn't cooperating – my body.

Increasingly, I was turning up to school feeling like I had a stomach bug or some kind of illness. My insides would tremble and a groggy, nauseous wave would overpower me, threatening to send me to the Sick Bay. *Is this what it feels like to come off drugs?* I'd wonder, as my fingertips trembled uncontrollably. *What's happening to me? Why do I feel so sick?*

What I didn't realise was just how much my body was suffering from the constant fear of threat or harm. It was as though I were always on high alert for a wild animal; my ears pricked to discover any unusual sound, my eyes always scanning and interpreting situations for danger. This happened every moment of the day – causing me to jump with fright at loud noises, or become overwhelmed and tearful the moment I heard aggressive or argumentative voices. My mind and body were always searching, searching, searching, and no matter how much I silenced my words, my body could not keep up with suppressing the lies.

That afternoon, I realised that I had to come clean. I had to tell someone. And so, slowly, carefully, I gave myself permission to tell Rachael the truth.

'Jas, I'm sure if your mum went to the police you could get your dad to leave,' she said gently. 'You could fight to keep the house. There are people who know – me and my parents would stick up for you.'

'He won't go,' I said bitterly. 'Mum already asked him to leave and he refused.' *If only it were that simple*, I thought.

Rach continued, trying her best to be helpful. 'You just need to show the police proof,' she reasoned. 'You know, like, tell them what he's done. Once they have the proof – '

'There *is* no proof,' I cried, my voice rising higher than I'd expected. 'Mum never went to the doctor when she had bruises, so we've got nothing!'

Shit.

Instantly I looked away, wishing I could mentally 'Command Z' and backspace over what I'd just said. *Why did I just tell her that? Maybe she didn't hear me properly*, I thought hopefully. *Maybe she can pretend she didn't.*

Rachael fell deadly silent. 'Jasi. You never told me it was that bad.'

'It's not that bad,' I said flippantly. 'He only does that stuff occasionally. He knows if he hurts her too badly, we'll have proof.' I looked away again, my stomach now buzzing like a cage full of angry bees.

Stop talking Jas, screamed my mind. *Why are you telling Rach all of this stuff? This isn't okay. You're meant to keep this private.* No matter how hard I tried, though, I couldn't stop, because now that I'd opened up the words just wouldn't stop flowing; everything pouring out in a traumatised, garbled mess of rage and fear and despair.

'I'm just so scared and I don't know what to do,' I sobbed, my hands nervously shredding a thin strand of grass. 'This morning he kicked mum in the leg and she was in so much pain, crying so hard, and he just didn't care. He knew she was having problems with one of her hips and he was so intentional about it. All he said was, "You deserved it."' My lips curled in disgust, the evilness of his words overwhelming me as I spoke them. 'I'm scared of staying and what he'll do to us – and I'm scared of leaving and losing our home,' I admitted. 'I'm scared of what will happen if I leave home to save myself and leave Mum behind. Because then she'll just be even more vulnerable.' The words rushed out, a long, heavy stream of sadness. 'And I just can't deal with this anymore. *I want it to stop.*'

Sitting on the short, clipped grass, our feet stretched out in front, we talked long into the afternoon. Rachael didn't try to fix anything. She just sat in that space with me. She loved me. She let me be. She let me exhale.

It was only when the bell rang that I realised we'd been out of class for the entire afternoon. School was over. *How have I talked for so long?* I wondered. Instantly, a feeling of fear and guilt swamped me. *Did I do the right thing? Should I have shared that much?*

The Stories We Carry

I didn't need to worry. If there was one person I could trust in this entire world, it was Rach. She was my lighthouse, my rock. We were two teen girls going through our own shit, navigating feelings of despair, imposter syndrome and uncertainty, but together, we were like the twisted roots of a giant fig tree, roots that wrapped like limbs around each other, weathering whatever storms were to come. Somewhere, deep inside, I felt that maybe with her support I could make it through. It was a small spark of hope; it was what I needed.

'This one.'

My mother's finger tapped on the colourful square, her eyes scanning across a skyline of pink-purple sunsets and silhouetted palm trees. 'What do you think, kids?'

I leaned over, reading through the print out that the travel agent had given us. *Go to sleep and wake up in paradise every day at one of Coolangatta's favourite resorts. Winter special: six nights for only $349!*

'Really? You mean it?'

'Yep. We'll go together – just you, me, and Jason.'

'What about – ?'

'I'll figure it out.'

Mum looked down at the sunset photograph, handing it back to the travel agent. 'Yes, let's book this one. Thank you.'

Jas Rawlinson

By now Mum was starting to see just how much of a toll Dad's abuse was taking on me and she needed to get us out – even if only for a week. The trip was planned carefully, with Mum hiding the truth by telling him we were spending a few days with one of her family members. Instantly, however, Dad was on his best behaviour, begging and pleading with us. 'You don't have to leave. You can stay here. It's all going to be okay,' he lied. But the more that Mum insisted on us leaving, the harder it got for him to keep Mr Hyde in check. 'You WITCH!' he barked, stalking down the hallway as we packed our bags. 'Tell me right now where you're going! How dare you sneak around trying to steal my children from me?! Tell me now!'

Your children. The words soaked through my mind like acid, lighting fresh fires of hatred in my heart. *You only care about us when you want to control us. We are not 'yours.'*

The next few days were filled with anxiety and Dad very nearly found us out – when he turned up to my elderly grandfather's house where we were staying, and hid in the side garden – but on a cool winter morning, we took our bags and disappeared north. Arriving in Coolangatta, we walked up a steep headland path until we reached our hotel, marvelling at the faint outline of Surfers Paradise on the horizon and the way the buildings jutted upwards like jigsaw pieces. Jason and I were especially excited, taking turns to jump on the hotel beds or lay back in the hot tub until our fingers resembled wrinkled prunes.

One afternoon, while skipping and laughing in the ocean, my little brother suddenly ran screaming from the water's edge. 'Oh my God! It's a great white pointer!' he screamed.

Instantly I jumped on the spot, swivelling to scan the horizon. 'Shit. Really?' He was right – there it was. The unmistakable triangular shape of a fin sticking out of the water. I, too, was just about to run screaming from the ocean when suddenly it dipped out of view before gracefully arching upwards. To the left and right, three smaller fins also surfaced.

It was a pod of dolphins.

I doubled over, laughing until I couldn't breathe. 'Great white pointer!' I screamed, between fits of laughter. 'It's a *dolphin*, dumb ass!'

Jason's lip jutted out, his brow furrowing. 'Whatever,' he sulked. 'How was I supposed to know?'

That day, Mum, Jason and I all stood on the sands of Coolangatta Beach, laughing like we were the only people on the planet. It was such an unremarkable moment. Something so casual, it shouldn't even remain in my memory.

It was the freest I'd ever felt.

Over the next few days, I lived life to the fullest, exploring the local surf shops, hunting through bargains at the Supre Factory Outlet, and spending hours swimming and rock-hopping along the boulders below Greenmount Point. I'd look in the mirror and smile, thinking about how free and peaceful I felt, and strangely, even my body dysmorphia seemed to have taken a holiday. It was as though we'd stepped inside a gigantic bubble, safe from everything and everyone. A place where Dad couldn't reach us.

I was picking up my towel, getting ready to go to the beach when suddenly a noise broke the silence. The unmistakable shrill of the hotel phone. Mum and I froze, staring at each other in confusion. Who could be calling? No one knew we were here... right?

Cautiously, she picked up the receiver. And then her face fell.

Pop! Just like that, my bubble burst. The peaceful serenity that I'd felt only moments beforehand seemed like nothing but a cheap façade; like it had never really been there at all. He'd found us.

My heart hammered fast, my eyes searching for clues on Mum's face. Mostly, she stood silently, speaking only a few hushed words. Then, she hung up. 'Come on, let's get to the beach,' she said, reaching for her brightly coloured towel.

'But Mum, what happened? What did he say?'

My mother started to speak, but then thought better of it. 'Don't worry,' she soothed gently. 'It's all going to be okay.'

'How can it be okay if he knows where we are?'

'Come on, let's go.' Mum rushed us out the door, leading us through a back entrance that led toward Rainbow Bay. Not much was said, but as I later discovered, it was only too easy for a perpetrator of violence like my father to find his family. Hotels were relaxed, easily connecting callers with very few questions asked. All they needed to know was the correct name. In my Dad's case, he'd taken a calculated guess that we'd probably headed up the coast, so he'd started calling around hotels that he knew Mum had stayed in when she'd holidayed up north in her twenties. It took only two calls for him to strike the right match.

This is so wrong, I seethed. *How can he find us so easily?*

The Stories We Carry

Now that my bubble of peace had popped, I no longer felt safe and at ease. Once again my mind was on high alert, searching for invisible tigers and lions, always on the ready in case I needed to flee. My stomach clenched up into its old knots. How long would it take Dad to get to us, if he were to leave right now? Three, four hours max? He could arrive at any moment. He could arrive during the night and come straight to our room. Who would stop a 'loving father and husband' from 'meeting up' with his family?

No one.

I realised, right then, that it's never as easy as 'simply leaving.' If your abuser wants to track you down, they'll do everything they can to make that happen. And if you have children, or you're on your own, with most people in your life oblivious as to what you're going through, it's easy to feel that it's all too hard. That it's better to stay in a situation that you can try to manage, than leave and face the unknown. I know that's how my mother felt, most of the time.

As I walked the beach, I thought of the Queensland Border monument just metres away from where we stood. How easy it was to step from one side to the other. I suddenly realised that nothing we did – no intervention order – would stop Dad. A piece of paper would be as flimsy as that border. All you had to do was step across, or swim around the edge of the Bay. No matter what you did, a person who was determined to step over your 'border' would find a way.

We needed to be free of him. But how would we ever find that kind of freedom?

Chapter 5

Despite my promise to never settle for an abusive relationship, I found myself in one that mimicked exactly what I was experiencing with my Dad. For at least a year, everything in our relationship was just like a fairy-tale. Kurt treated me with an abundance of care, kindness, and patience. He was never late when meeting up with me and made me feel, for the first time in my life, like an absolute princess. I was so connected to him that he became my entire world. It was only after our first 12 months together that things began to change – and just like my dad did to my mother, he began to constantly accuse me of flirting or having feelings for other boys I knew. Initially, these accusations were fleeting and rare and quickly eased with reassurances of my love. But soon, nothing I did or said seemed to help. We were forever on-again/off-again, and there was always some issue that I had to 'fix.'

One night, while sleeping at a friend's house with a couple of other teens from school, my boyfriend decided to crash the party. He'd seen me swimming in the pool, laughing and joking around with two of my best mates, and he didn't like it one bit.

'You flirt with Benji 24/7!' he spat, as I stood by the side of the pool, trying to reassure him of my devotion. 'You need to understand *what* you are. You need to understand what *you've* done.' Then he stormed off, leaving me bewildered and heartbroken. I was so self-conscious that I didn't want to speak to any of my male friends for the rest of the night.

That evening, after hours of tossing and turning, I crawled from my bed and tip-toed to the balcony. With my back pressed firmly against the cold brick wall, I sat there for over an hour, crying and berating myself for what I'd done to make him so upset. Finally, at 3.30 am, I returned to bed. I was so frozen from the chill of the winter air that I could no longer feel my feet. Sometime later that day, while writing in my journal, I tried to pinpoint what it was that had made me feel the need to sit on the balcony for so many hours; why I'd been unable to remove myself from the cold concrete floor and return to the warmth of my blankets.

I think I wanted to punish myself, I wrote.

Unconsciously, I was beginning to repeat the patterns of my parents' relationship. Now, I was the one who was constantly apologising, placating, and jumping through mental hoops to allay my partner's unfounded fears. Now, *I* was the one who had to feel the push/pull of wanting to spend time with other male friends, but knowing what would happen if I did. Suddenly, I was the one being berated and belittled. 'Bet you wouldn't pull away from me if Benji was the one with his hand on your leg,' my boyfriend jeered one afternoon. 'He always has your attention. I just suck at everything, don't I? How can I compete with him?'

'Are you serious?' I snapped. 'I love you so much – I tell you that all the time! What more do I have to do to prove it to you? You just told me that you were over it. Why are you bringing this up again?'

'What are you talking about?' he replied, staring at me with manufactured confusion. 'I never said anything about Benji. I said, 'You *drive* me round the *bend*."

The Stories We Carry

It was textbook gaslighting. The most reliable weapon when it comes to manipulating victim-survivors into doubting their own reality. But I was a teenager and this was the early noughties – no one talked about things like domestic violence, much less psychological manipulation techniques. So, unsurprisingly, I wrote it off as typical teenage jealousy. This only allowed the abuse to thrive, and over the coming months I began to experience deeper emotional cruelty. When he flew into a rage, swearing at me over the phone, he'd make me out to be the one with a problem. 'Oh you want me to stop swearing? Of course, of course,' he laughed bitterly. 'You're perfect, aren't you! You'd never swear. Not like me. Little Miss *Perfect*.'

On another occasion, Kurt rang a friend of mine and told her – in graphic detail – that we'd slept together. 'Running total, 16 goals,' he bragged. Not only was this demeaning because of the way in which he did it, it was humiliating because we talked regularly about waiting until much later in the future to have sex. (We were, after all, Christian kids who'd had abstinence drilled into our heads at every waking moment.) Even then, I found myself wondering how someone who claimed to love me could take such sick delight in lying behind my back and intentionally upsetting my best friend. But as always, I pushed it away and forgave him.

I was so afraid of hurting his feelings that I found it easier to just focus on doing everything I could to make sure he was happy – even if it meant going back on my own promises. Sometimes I'd call him out on his behaviour, telling him that it wasn't okay, and that we were done. But just days later I'd be back in his arms. 'There's no one in the world like you, Jas,' he'd sob on the phone. 'I don't know how to live without you.'

And with that, I'd run straight back to him.

The reality, as is true for many survivors and victims, is that amongst all of the crying, fighting, and jealous accusations, there are many moments of laughter, kindness, and joy. He was one of only two people who knew what was happening in our home, and often we'd spend hours on the phone as he listened thoughtfully and reassured me that the awful words that flew through my dad's lips were ugly lies. That I *was* beautiful. I *was* smart. And most importantly, that he would always love and protect me. So, despite the cruelty and jealousy and times where he sounded more like my father than I cared to believe, I kept chasing and running back to him, hoping he'd rescue me from the pain bubbling inside my mind.

To be honest, I didn't believe that anyone else in the world would ever love me as much as he did. I was a girl starved of male validation and all I wanted was love. So how could I even imagine giving up the only guy who'd ever expressed true interest in me?

It was unfathomable.

'Jas! Dinner's ready.'

'Coming!' I yawned and rolled off my bed, leaving my notebooks spread haphazardly across the bright yellow sheet. I was in the middle of rehearsing for a major school play and I was determined not to be the person who forgot their lines. Mrs H, our drama teacher, had selected me to play the part of Sophie Wender in the cult classic 'The Chrysalids,' and not only did I have a large number of lines, but I was also in charge of creating a soundtrack for the entire performance. It was huge and exciting and I didn't want to mess it up.

The Stories We Carry

Padding down the hallway, I walked around to the end of the table – knowing better than to sit in 'Dad's chair' – and tried to keep myself small. This is what I did, most nights. When he was at work I'd chat away with Mum about anything and everything, but as soon as I heard the crunch of his tyres on the gravel outside, I clammed up. Like a typical teen, I was quiet and sullen, never giving away too much information, whether it was about me, my boyfriend, or stuff at school. I'd told Mum very explicitly that I didn't want him coming to my drama presentations or award nights. Not only would it put me off my game, but it was insulting. Why invite someone who cared so little for me? Why let him into a piece of my soul that he would only weaponize against me?

I flicked a quick glance his way, eying him off as I waited for dinner. He seemed calm. At ease. I felt my chest begin to relax, my breath flowing a little easier. *Everything's fine*, I told myself. *Tonight is going to be okay.*

As Mum began to prepare dinner, my brother began talking with Dad about something inconsequential and as the seconds passed, I noticed a shift in the air. It was as sudden as flicking a light switch; as instant as turning on a tap. Only, in this case, it wasn't light or gushing water that sprang forth – it was Dad's anger. Out of nowhere he began laying into Jason with harsh words and verbal abuse, his hands flying and his eyes ablaze. But it wasn't until my mum stepped forward to defend him that everything turned sour.

'You think you can tell me what to do and say to my son? You're really going to get it now,' he growled, stepping forward.

In terror I watched as he moved closer to my mother, his hatred raining down on her. I'd lost count of how many times I'd seen him speak to her – and to me – this way. But tonight, in this moment, I was done.

I flew across the room, placing myself between the two of them. Then I levelled my eyes straight at his, forcing the anger solely on me. 'Get away from her!' I screamed. 'Leave her alone!'

'Fuck off,' he snarled.

I stood still, shaking and trembling. But I'd gone too far to retreat. 'Get away from her,' I repeated. 'Touch her and I'll call the police.'

The moment the words left my lips, I saw a side of Dad that I'd never before witnessed. An ice-cold hatred ran through every inch of his face, a snarl lifting the corner of one lip. Then he lunged. His hand smacked across my arm, his body growing almost impossibly larger before me. A chair fell to the ground and I staggered backwards, my heart racing wildly as I side-stepped his grip and kept moving.

Oh no, what have I done?

He lunged again, one hand wrapped around the cordless phone, holding it away so that I couldn't call for help. And then he came for me. I ran, fear choking me as I flung myself through the front door. To this day I have no idea how, but by some miracle, by the time my feet had carried me outside, the cordless phone was tucked safely in the palm of my hand. I'd somehow managed to snatch it from him; I'd managed to evade his grip.

Now there was only one thing left to do.

Hiding behind a mango tree, I mashed my finger against the keypad three times. Zero, zero, zero. Seconds bled into what felt like hours, tears spilling down my cheek as I waited in desperation for the words that would make everything okay. The words I'd heard so many times on television shows, never before imagining that I would ever have to hear them myself.

'Police, Fire or Am – '

'Police!' I screamed. '*Police*! Now! You have to get here now!' In the darkness, my tears fell harder, great globs of salt choking each word as I struggled to speak. 'You have to get here now. He...' I paused, my ears tuning in to the sound of screaming and shouting erupting from inside the small three bedroom house up the hill. 'Oh no,' I sobbed. 'He's laying into her. He's laying into her. He just won't stop. Make it stop!'

Through hysterical shrieks, I tried to explain what was happening. The depth of his emotional and verbal abuse. But I couldn't. All I could do was to stare out into the ebony night sky, waiting for the flashing sirens and red lights that would make everything okay. I paced back and forth, hoping and praying that they would soon arrive so I didn't have to go back inside alone, but no one came.

'Jas. Jas!'

My mother's voice cut through the darkness, calling me forward. My heart thudded in my ears, my head questioning whether it was safe to return. Slowly, one step at a time, I crept from my hiding place, wondering just how much I was going to pay for what I'd done.

'He's gone out the back,' she said quietly, as if reading my mind. 'He's gone to cool off.'

I stared at her, the cordless phone hanging limply from my hand. My voice was flat, a haunted echo. 'I called the police. I'm sorry. I had to.'

Mum only held me close, tucking Jason and I into her arms as we all waited. Waited for whatever was now going to happen.

It may have only been an hour or less before the police arrived, but to me, it felt like hours. Sadly, by the time they did pull up outside our back door, charming Dr Jekyll was back and he'd had plenty of time to perfect his story. Watching him pander to them and perform an act that was as routine as ordering a coffee was excruciating. It made me feel as though not a single person could see what was truly going on. That the accusations I was making were all in my head.

'Officer, the person you should be investigating is my daughter,' he said coldly. 'She abuses her little brother. She's always hitting him.'

My jaw fell open, all speech leaving me.

He said this with complete sincerity. Without a shred of shame or hesitation.

The casual cruelty of it killed me.

'That's... I've *never* done that!' The words lodged in the top of my throat, suffocating me from the inside out. 'I wouldn't ever do that!'

In the end, the police left without laying any formal charges. What I didn't know, however, until much later, was that one of the officers knew my mother. His daughter had been one of her students over the years, and he recognised her instantly. While my father was busy speaking with his partner, he leaned discreetly toward her. 'You don't have to live this way,' he said quietly. 'If you need help, let me know.' My mother's head nodded subtly, her movements as discreet as possible.

Sadly, there was nothing more they could do at that moment and so they left. No formal charges; just a note in the system about what I'd reported.

This, to a man like my father, was like taking a sharp stick and poking it straight into the soft underbelly of a bear's stomach. He was humiliated, and now that I'd 'tarred his reputation', the risk of harm against us was higher than I could have ever imagined. After all, what did he have left to lose?

It was at this point that things could have gone one of two ways – one of those ending with all of our names, ages, and faces listed in the 'deaths and notices' section of the Coffs Harbour Advocate newspaper. As a 16-year-old, I wasn't aware that what was happening in our home was a textbook example of 'Coercive Control.' I didn't know that this form of abuse, which uses threat, coercion, manipulation, and fear rather than physical abuse to control a victim, is the number one factor leading to domestic homicide.*

As a teen, I didn't recognise any of this. But I know without a shadow of doubt now that what happened next was a miracle.

One that quite possibly saved our lives.

---

* Source: Report of the NSW Domestic Violence Death Review Team for the period 1 July 2017 to 30 June 2019 (parliament.nsw.gov.au)

Chapter 6

On a quiet afternoon in April, we packed our bags and left. Our possessions were limited; small, thoughtful collections of clothing, toys, and school textbooks. My favourite posters, photo albums, and essentials. With a lump in the bottom of my throat, I kissed my horse goodbye, and wrapped my arms tightly around my gentle giant of a dog, Bundy. 'Bye, boy,' I whispered sadly, stroking his thick navy coat and holding out a hand to shake his orange paw. With his tongue lolling happily to one side, he nudged his massive head under the crook of my elbow and nestled in. I scratched him under the jaw, making his eyes narrow in pleasure. 'Why do I have to leave you behind? I really wish you could come with us.'

Deep down, I knew that if we were to get out, we'd have to make sacrifices. And he was one of the hardest.

We climbed into the car and left; down the rocky driveway, along the bumpy road full of potholes and then out toward the highway. Ten minutes later, we were standing on the driveway of what would be our new home for the next three months.

It was humble; a small three bedroom building on the side of a hill. It was nothing special, but it afforded us freedom and privacy, and that, to me, was priceless. The best thing, however, was its location. Sitting smack-bang between mine and Jason's schools, it was close to town and only 10 minutes from the beach. Best of all, no one had any clue where we were.

In reality, the house sat just back from the Pacific Highway – the very road my dad drove along every day for work – but it was wrapped protectively by the dark green folds of a banana plantation, making us feel completely incognito. It was an oasis of peace; a wonderland of magic and mystique where we could gain some space from my father – and it was all thanks to a generous-hearted woman named Ada.

Like my mother, she attended the same church in West Coffs, and over the years the two of them had become friends. She was tall, with light reddish hair and kind eyes, a woman who walked the talk when it came to faith. She wasn't one to offer meaningless platitudes or 'thoughts and prayers', instead, she embodied what it meant to genuinely show God's love to others. Over the years she and Mum had talked on and off, though I don't think she really knew the extent of what was happening in our home; that is, until one Saturday afternoon in early 2002 when my mother, no longer able to cope with the threats, abuse, and fear, picked up the phone and made a call that changed our lives.

'I just can't cope,' she sobbed. 'I can't deal with this anymore, Ada. We're always walking on eggshells; he's always screaming at me. Nothing we do is right and I just can't take it another minute.'

Tears and vulnerability were a rarity from my mother. Even now, many decades later, I can probably count on one hand the number of times I've seen or heard her cry. My mother is fierce. My mother is strong and resilient. My mother is a warrior. When Dad flew off the handle she wouldn't scream back – yet she also didn't back down or cower in a corner. She knew when to hold her words. She knew when to counter the illogical rants with quick wit and sarcasm. She knew when to speak up and defend herself. She was never the 'battered woman' stereotype that is often portrayed in advertising campaigns for domestic violence, and yet, she was still a victim of abuse. For so long she had shouldered all of our burdens, but finally, on a random day in 2002, her resilience bucket had run dry.

She'd been in the garage, wrangling our ancient washing machine to connect the hose to the tap, but as often happened, the two parts just wouldn't marry up. Dad frequently did taps up too tightly for any of us to release, and when Mum had asked for some help, he'd exploded into a fit of rage. 'What do you mean, you can't do it?' he sneered. 'It's the simplest thing in the world. How many times have I shown you how to do it? Go and fucking do it yourself!' he shouted, storming off across the paddock.

Surrounded by piles of dirty laundry, my mother's body began to heave and tremble, tears of frustration and pain slipping down each cheek. And that's when she cracked. When I asked her about the conversation she had with Ada that day, she said, 'I didn't expect anything. I just needed someone to talk to. I didn't ask for help. Everything that happened came because of her kindness.'

As Ada listened to my mother's pain, she spoke the words that changed our lives. 'Robyn, I have a place for you and the kids.'

'What?' Mum held the phone closer, stuttering as she tried to understand.

'My husband and I have a property,' she continued. 'We're developing it into apartments later in the year, but right now there's no one in it. It's a vacant lot with a small house. I want you to take it for the next three months. Get away from your husband and focus on yourself and your kids. Get some space.'

Those words were an extraordinary gift; a box laden with small, gorgeous, intricately wrapped parcels of hope, freedom, and peace. Gifts that we'd yearned for until our bodies and minds ached, but felt would remain on a shelf, tucked away from our reach. But now, they'd been handed over to us. For at least three months we would have space from Dad; space that we hoped would give him time to acknowledge that he needed help, and to commit to seeing a counsellor with Mum. She still believed he could get better, she still loved and wanted him to change, and he'd promised he would. But she knew that as long as we were all under one roof, there was little chance of that ever happening. For me, personally, I didn't want to go back. I didn't want three months. I wanted forever. I didn't trust that he would – or could – change, and I couldn't get his nasty words out of my head; the ones that told me how useless, stupid, fat, and lazy I was. But if a few months was all we could get, I'd take it with both hands.

'You're a good kid, Jas,' Ada said to me, not long before we moved in. 'No matter what your dad says to you, never believe a word.' I'd moved my head, nodding softly, staring at the floor shyly. It was the kindest thing anyone other than my mother had ever said to me.

Now, as night fell and I stood in my new room, I peered through the window to the dark green banana trees whose fronds bobbed softly in the breeze. I listened, hearing the soft whoosh of cars as they sped along the highway below, their lights illuminating the darkness. I wondered if Dad was out there right now. If he was searching for us. Mum had told me that he'd already called her mobile that afternoon, absolutely livid at arriving home to find us gone.

'I warned you,' she'd replied. 'I told you if you didn't stop abusing us all the time, one day you'd come home to find us gone.' Then

The Stories We Carry

she told him to stop calling, and to give us some space until she was ready to talk.

Even though he had no idea where we were, I couldn't help but worry. How long would it last? How long would we have this place to ourselves? What happened once the three months were up? Would Dad commit to getting help? All of these questions buzzed within, as I tried to sleep. In the end, though, I realised that despite all the uncertainty, I still felt safer than I had in so very long.

Right there and then, I decided that this house would be our Peace Home.

Our oasis of freedom came at a time when I needed it most. Rachael had recently moved away to the Gold Coast to pursue her acting career further, and I was in the thick of Year 11 studies. The loneliness of being apart from my best friend, coupled with the hectic schedule of drama performances and major exams, meant that I was in desperate need of stability and peace, and this wonderful house gave me the respite I needed.

Some days I'd lie on a towel in the paddock, my hair soaked in lemon juice as I thumbed through pages of Cosmo, trying to bleach my naturally dark hair to fit in with the latest fashion trends. From my sunbaking spot I'd sit and watch the highway traffic go by, feeling a strange sense of delight that Dad may be driving past right now, with no idea that I was sitting in this secluded field. On weekends, friends came to visit and we held parties in the old banana shed out back, getting high on sugary lollies and listening to the Top 40 Countdown. At the back of the barn was a large wooden table top that could be spun in circles, and we'd sometimes load it up with bowls full of salt and vinegar chips, Maltesers and fizzy drinks, delighting in spinning the wheel to pass around food. It was a period of innocence and exactly what my teenage years should have been.

During this time my mother continued to meet with my father in public spaces, where they talked about what would need to happen in order for us to reunite as a family. Years later, I would ask her why she still held hope; why she always planned for us to return, instead of searching for a permanent new home for the three of us. To me it just didn't make sense, but decades later I came to understand the complexities of domestic violence much more intimately.

As many survivors know, there are many reasons as to why victim-survivors struggle to leave, particularly when children are involved. Financial stress, poverty, fear, love... The reasons vary, and often, a victim-survivor can feel that it's easier to stay and try to help the person they love to change.

As my mother explained to me only recently, Dad was the epitome of the characters Dr Jekyll and Mr Hyde, and she was deeply worried about what he was truly capable of. 'I was concerned that if we moved out and left permanently, he might... he might take that really badly.' Her voice grew dark, heavy with unsaid words. 'I'm worried he would have taken us all out. I had to take things slowly; to manage him the way I always had. I knew who he was at his core – who he could be when Mr Hyde was gone. I loved him and I just wanted him to change. I didn't want to leave my marriage, I just wanted him to get help.'

While Dad made some changes in those first 12 weeks, they were too far and few between, and so she refused to return home. This was only possible due to the extreme generosity of Ada and her husband, both of whom called to offer us another three months rent-free in the Peace House. I remember being overwhelmingly relieved, the knots within my belly gently untangling as I processed the news. Six months without Dad? It felt like a gift greater than any birthday present I could imagine.

As we approached the four-month mark, Dad finally agreed to start seeing a counsellor with my mother. This was huge, as prior to this, he'd only ever seen one therapist – a female practitioner who had booked us in for a series of family sessions. Those hadn't gone well. Not only was Dad uninterested in listening to her – as a woman – but he'd also completely disregarded my feelings when I admitted for the very first time that I was suicidal. His cold reply? 'So what? We've all felt that way at times.' Once the female therapist discovered that violence was occurring in our home, she was no longer able to see us as a family, and requested to see him alone. Unfortunately Dad had refused, and as a result, he'd had no one to hold him accountable.

Now, though, for the first time ever, he was making some small changes. My mother had been referred to a male counsellor – a very kind and no-nonsense Christian man by the name of Bob – and despite being retired, he agreed to see my parents for regular sessions. In an act of kindness that I still struggle to understand, he offered them a rate of just $5 per hour. Somehow, this man was able to get through to my Dad and connect with him in a way that no one else could. One day at a time, my father slowly began to listen and take steps to work on his anger and control issues.

As always, though, I was sceptical. While my parents continued to meet semi-regularly and my brother often spent time with him on a weekend, I stayed away entirely. I didn't want to see or speak to him, and in the entire time that we stayed at the Peace House, I can barely even recall seeing his face.

On the night of my 17th birthday, as I celebrated with friends, I suddenly noticed a small white envelope lying gently across my pillowcase. It had been placed there by my mother, but I knew – instantly – that the handwriting on the front was not hers. Nervously, I picked it up, flicking open the back and instantly feeling the twist of my stomach. It was from Dad – he must have passed it to Mum when they'd last seen each other.

Slowly, I slid the card out, my eyes coming to rest on an image of a light-skinned girl with bright blue eyes, and a glamorous trail of red hair falling across her clam-shell bra and green scaley tail. Instantly, a wave of nostalgia washed over me. The Little Mermaid had been one of my favourite Disney movies as a young girl. So much so, that Dad had bought me a pyjama dress with an image of Ariel on the front, her tail curled majestically around the edge of a rock as she sat staring out at the ocean. I'd cherished that soft fabric, wearing it night after night, even when it became too short to be a nightie. At that point, I'd tucked it into the back of my wardrobe, occasionally wearing it as a bed shirt.

But that had been then... back when I still believed in magic and fairy tales and men who loved their daughters. Back when I still called him my father, instead of using his first name.

Now I stared at the card, consumed by a sudden flash of anger. *What's he playing at? Is this his attempt at 're-connecting' with me? Does he honestly think this is going to make up for everything he's done?* I picked up the card and shoved it into the back of my wardrobe. Somewhere I didn't have to look at that stupid picture and be reminded of all I'd lost.

Tonight, I'd focus on my friends. On joy and freedom and laughter; celebrating with the people I could rely on. If Dad was truly going to change, he was going to have to prove it to me. He was going to have to try harder.

―

October 25th.

I flipped the page of the calendar over, my eyes zeroing in on the large circle that had been drawn in red biro. Instantly, I began counting the days, my jaw clenching harder with each box.

No, that can't be right, I thought. I drew a finger back across the squares, restarting my counting. But there was no mistake – the truth was clear as day.

Only four weeks to go until we move back home.

Six months had flown by, and we were nearing the end of our time at the Peace House. I was elbow-deep in exams and drama performances, and on top of it all, my boyfriend and I had just broken up. Suddenly, my depression was back, and it was back with a vengeance. Everything in my brain just wanted to slow down, but instead, my thoughts were erratic and flighty, my nervous system overwhelmed with constant bursts of cortisol.

That morning, I ran into Kurt while we were on our way to school. *Maybe he wants to get back together?* I prayed hopefully. *Maybe this is just another rough patch?*

'Hey, what's up?' I greeted.

'Hey fatty,' he replied coolly.

Instantly I felt my stomach tense, an ache spreading out across my chest. 'Can you not call me that?'

'What, it's funny,' he jeered. 'Get over it.' Turning his back to me, he began gossiping to another male friend, his demeanour instantly changing. 'Hey, guess what, I met this chick called Candice and she's *so* amazing,' he gushed loudly. 'She started at my work the other day, and let's just say, I had a *very* pleasurable dream about her last night.' He turned and looked straight back at me, his eyebrows raised, face twisted in a sickening smirk. 'Know what I mean?'

My entire body went cold, the barbs from his words cutting me to the core. It had been only days since we'd broken up. Only a week since I'd said no – again – to his increasingly coercive requests for sex, after which he'd decided things 'weren't really working out' for us. And now, just like my dad, he was revelling in the chance to upset me.

I thought back to a conversation I'd had with Rach a few weeks earlier, one where I'd cried dramatically about how much I was in love with Kurt and how no one else could possibly love me the way he did. Over and over she'd told me that I would get past this, that one day I wouldn't even remember him. But nothing she said got through to me.

'He's my whole world, Rach. I can't live without him!'

'Do you really think so, Jas?' she asked, her voice thick with sadness. 'Do you *actually* believe that?'

'I do,' I stated simply.

The Stories We Carry

Now, as I stood listening to Kurt rave about his new crush and her body, I couldn't believe I'd ever been so stupid. That I'd ever believed he truly loved me.

The misery that rolled over me in this moment was so severe that it drove me to do something I'd never expected. Like the swell of the ocean on a cold winter day, it crashed over the top of my walls, consuming me whole in an instant. *It just never ends*, I thought to myself. *The pain, the rejection, the degradation... I can't take this anymore.*

As my friends rushed toward the basketball court, eager for lunch, I slunk out through the school's open driveway and turned right. Without a clear idea of where I was headed, I let myself be carried along by the numbness within. Down the road. Toward the train line. Somewhere that no one would find me. A place where I could let myself fall apart.

A place with a rooftop.

The roof was warm, its gunmetal grey panels barely moving as I hoisted myself upwards onto the top of the agricultural shed. From there, I could swivel my view to the right, taking in the sight of the paddocks that ran all the way to the train tracks at the end of the road. Beyond them stood a vast expanse of dense, woody forest.

Here, in the solace of the school's livestock yard, I broke down. My voice shrieked high and low like a wounded animal; one long stream of angry devastation. A torrent of salt water ran down both cheeks, snaking its way along my skin and then falling with silent splashes to the hot tin sheeting below. In silence, I begged the animal in my head to stop. To make the pain go away.

Jas Rawlinson

I just can't do this. I just can't do this anymore.

For an hour I sat there, the roof shuddering underneath the weight of the sobs that racked my thin, tiny body. I cried for the girl who, at the age of 16, had had to leave her home, her horse, her dog, and the forest that felt like paradise, to move to a safe house. I cried for the girl who had spent so much time loving a guy who treated her so callously. I choked and gasped and held my arms tightly around the 17-year-old girl who no longer wanted to live.

From further up the road I could still hear the laughter of my peers; their voices slicing through the air in an occasional whoop or shout. As the tears eventually dried up, my thoughts turned back to Kurt. How much I loved him, and how it just wasn't enough. The way that he'd managed to turn several of my male friends against me, each of them siding with him over jealous accusations and lies.

I peered over the edge, staring blankly at the ground below. *Is he right?* I wondered. *Am I the one who's the problem?*

Somewhere deep within, the Black Dog of my depression began to stir. One at a time, her jet-black paws stretched out, her intense eyes pushing me to conjure up images that made me want to weep. All the ways I could make her stop. All the things that would free me from her bleakness.

You know what would make this all go away, she nudged.

Yes, yes I do.

Oh, how I knew. I'd been treading water now for more than eight years – half my life – and my ability to continue holding on to hope was diminishing by the day. It was naïve to think that going

The Stories We Carry

into a temporary safe house would make the pain go away. That it would wipe the slate clean, erasing the trauma as easily as a cloth swiping across a blackboard. As I was coming to learn, that's not the way that life works.

On the roof, I began walking. Pacing from one end to the other, each step conjuring up more questions. Then I walked to the edge and looked down one last time.

You know what to do, she nudged.

Yes, yes I do.

Chapter 7

'Jas!'

Shit. Shit, shit, shit!

As I stood on the roof, a tall, burly man walked towards me, his bearded face creased with lines from the sun as he squinted upwards. He swung the gate of the agricultural yard open, a small group of students trailing from behind. Silently I cursed again. No one was meant to see this. No one was meant to find me.

I scrambled down from the roof, overwhelmed by embarrassment and shame around what was now going to happen, and the fact that my breakdown had become a public event – something the kids and teachers would all be aware of. I dug my fingers into the side of the building, lowering my legs until they touched one of the beams below and then vaulting onto the soft dirt. *What now? How do I unfix this? Shit, why didn't I see them coming earlier?*

I busied myself with one of the horses, walking around the corner of the shed and running a hand along its neck as the group of students approached. *Maybe*, I thought hopefully, *if I just act as though I'm a stupid teenager climbing on buildings for fun, I can brush this off.*

It was wishful thinking, really. There was no way to undo what I'd done or sweep away the reality of what had been seen. One look at my face – tear-streaked cheeks and red rimmed eyelids – gave it all away. There was no going back. Everyone was going to know now.

With great concern and tenderness, Mr S quickly arranged for two younger girls to escort me back to school and make sure I saw the counsellor. Yet, all I could focus on was how embarrassing and unnecessary their actions were. 'Everything's fine,' I sniffed, trying to dismiss him, tears still welling in each eye. 'You don't need to help me.'

Mr S looked at me quietly. 'Jas, I'm worried you're going to harm yourself.'

A small scoff burst from my lips, my eyes darting away in embarrassment. 'If I was going to kill myself I'd pick a higher roof,' I quipped.

No one laughed.

I couldn't tell you what I said, or what happened during the walk back toward the open gates of my high school. Only that I felt the whole experience had been blown way out of proportion. I never breathed a word to my friends. What I do remember is the total lack of empathy my ex-boyfriend showed when – that afternoon, as I ran into him at the bus stop – he continued to talk incessantly about the new girl he was seeing, while taunting me about how 'rubbish' my feelings were.

When I arrived back at the Peace House I pulled out my diary and began writing down everything going on in my head. The conversation with the school counsellor (where I'd sat for an hour, giving her occasional answers of 'Don't know. Maybe. Yeah. Dunno,' until the time was up) and the reaction of my teachers. *I don't know why they all care so much*, I wrote, furiously scrawling my thoughts across the pages of my diary. *They think I'm going to kill myself. Come on!*

The Stories We Carry

Then I flicked the page over and went to sleep. Had I thumbed backwards only a few pages, I would have seen the many paragraphs where I detailed in angry red pen lines about wanting to end my life. It wasn't hard to see. Yet, somehow, it felt as though I was ensconced inside a world of my own private pain. One that others couldn't understand.

They could – but it didn't feel that way.

In the end, I knew that I couldn't act out the words in my diary. Not because I cared about myself or my future. Not because of my friends. Not even Rach could convince me to stay. In the end, it came down to only one person. My mother.

I can't hurt her in this way, I thought. *She doesn't deserve that. I can't leave her with this burden.*

And so I stayed. Even if just for one more day... I told myself I would stay.

'Hey Boy! Oh, I've missed you so much!'

Instantly, Bundy raised a paw to my knee, his warm hazelnut eyes looking into mine as he pushed his broad head under the crook of one arm. I smiled and pulled him closer, nuzzling into the thick, navy fur of his coat. Close to a year had passed since we'd left our mountain home – much longer than we'd first anticipated – and all I'd wanted was to feel the softness of his gentle face against my skin. It felt like so long since I'd been back home, since I'd been able to hold him close. But now, finally, I was here. We were here. All four of us once again in the same house. It was our first day back in the bush after nine months in the Peace House, and I was nervous. Though Bob had advised my dad to give me space once I returned home and not to put any pressure on me while I was studying for my final year of school, I wasn't sure if I could really trust him. Sure, he seemed to be doing well. It really looked as though he was in control of his anger, and thinking about how his decisions impacted us... but would it stick?

That day, as I sat on my bed re-tacking all of my favourite photographs to the wooden wall where they'd once been, I heard a gentle knock on my door.

'Can I come in?'

I looked into my father's eyes, instantly surprised by the timidness I saw. His whole demeanour was different; from the way that he walked across the room, to the softness around his jaw. It was so unfamiliar, and yet it was unmistakable.

'I wanted to ask you something,' he began slowly.

'Yes?'

Dad lowered himself onto the edge of the bed, my heartbeat quickening in response. He paused, drawing in a breath.

'I'm sorry. I'm really sorry for everything,' he said. 'And I want you to know that.'

I sat in shock, not knowing what to do with this unexpected display of vulnerability.

'I want things to go back to how they were... when you were a kid,' he continued. 'I want things to be different from now on. *I* want to be different. But I need to ask you something first.'

The Stories We Carry

'Yeah?' My heartbeat was thundering in my ears now, my mouth dry.

'Can you forgive me?'

I looked into his dark blue eyes and was instantly brought to tears. They were so warm. So open. *Has this tenderness always been there?* I wondered. *Is this how they looked back at me when I was a two-year old, sitting underneath the kitchen table tying his shoelaces to the dining chair to stop him from leaving for work?*

A lump rose within my throat, and before I could stop myself, I threw my arms around his neck and began sobbing. In an instant, I was his little girl again. He was my dad. The dad I so deeply wanted and needed. Like a child I sat on his lap, sinking into the warmth of his strong arms. *Everything's going to be okay,* I thought quietly. *We're going to be okay.*

It took so much courage to allow myself to believe him, but when I looked in his eyes I knew he meant every word.

Looking back, this moment still haunts me to this day. Because I know how sincere he was. There was no malice or acting as he sat there, asking for forgiveness. That was my dad – my real dad. The man that he was, deep, deep down. The one that existed aside from any jealousy, rage, or need to control. The version of himself that was Love.

Maybe that's why this memory hurts the most. Because for reasons I will never understand, Love wasn't enough. Much later – almost twenty years to the day – my mother revealed to me that in his final counselling session, my father had been given an ultimatum of sorts from the therapist that he'd grown to trust. 'Shane, you need to understand that your anger has nothing to do with your daughter, and nothing to do with your wife,' Bob stated. 'They are not the cause. This is about you.' He'd levelled his gaze at my father, and as my mother sat alongside, requested that Dad begin coming for solo sessions. 'I'd really like to talk to you more about your early life. Your childhood,' he prompted gently.

My father had recoiled, his face turning to stone. 'No.'

'I think it's important, Shane.'

'No. I'm not doing that.' My father was resolute; immovable. There was no way anyone or anything was going to change his mind. Dad never returned, and it was the last time he and Bob ever spoke, or that he had a strong male role model to hold him accountable. To this day, none of us know what happened to my dad during his childhood, but I know that if only he'd allowed himself to be vulnerable and to receive the support he so desperately needed in order to address those dark parts of his mind, everything could have been so different.

In the end, whatever Dad was dealing with – mental illness or otherwise – he simply wasn't able to hold back the demons that lay inside. It took just weeks for Mr Hyde to return, and in no time at all we were right back where we'd started.

It was the last time I ever put my trust in my father and for years afterwards I asked myself: *How could I have been so stupid?*

Chapter 8

So many times I was saved by the love and care of good adults. People who, once they saw what was happening, held out a hand to help me through. By now, it had become impossible to hide the truth from my teachers – especially after the 'roof incident' – and despite my shame and embarrassment, I realised that all they wanted was to help me succeed. There were so many acts of extreme kindness that my teachers carried out, from my Drama teacher Mrs H who allowed me to come to her house late at night to print an assignment, because my printer had run out of ink, to Mr Q, who lent me $50 from his own pocket when I forgot spending money for an excursion trip to Sydney.

But the teacher I think about most fondly is Ms K, my art teacher. Tall, with thick brown curls and a scattering of freckles across her nose, she was one of the youngest staff on campus and could have easily been intimidated – but that simply wasn't her style. She was tough; a 'take no shit' kind of woman, but at the same time, she had that effortless 'cool older sister' vibe. In her class we were transported into a space where we could be ourselves; whether it was slashing paint across a canvas, or commandeering the small black CD player in the corner of the room and loading it up with our favourite mix CDs. We were free to express everything we felt and loved. 'Get this,' I said one night as Rach and I talked over the phone. 'She let me play Linkin Park and a whole CD full of rap and hip hop. I mean, what other teacher would let us do that?'

Jas Rawlinson

Ms K was cool, strong, and compassionate, and while I respected her as a teacher, I couldn't help but feel at times as though she were a big sister. One afternoon while going through my assignments I found a bright pink Post-it-note taped to the front. On it, was a tiny little sticker of a bear, along with four lines of small black print.

'To a beautiful girl, Jasi. Here are some notes that should help with your assignment. Take as long as you need and remember I am always here to help.'

I pulled the sticky note from my workbook and tucked it away into my bag, determined to never forget these small acts of kindness. To me, they were anything but small. They were gigantic; strong and grounding, like the long, thick roots of an old tree. They tethered and held me down when stress and anxiety threatened to knock the breath from my lungs. They pulled away the panic that weighed heavily throughout the stress of Year 12 exams and assignments. Ms K's kindness showed me that – despite the days that I had an overwhelming desire to die – the world could be a beautiful place. Almost twenty years later, I still have her note.

Alongside the love of good adults, the other life-raft that kept me afloat was the healing power of theatre. Drama gave me something that I didn't get from anything else. It allowed me to find my voice and to tap into creativity, resourcefulness, and other gems lurking deep within. Sometimes, I wonder if perhaps this is how I found the strength that year to begin pushing back against my father's verbal and mental abuse, to no longer accept everything he said at face value, and instead, to question and counter it. To use and *raise* my voice.

Later on that year, I was selected to perform at Coffs Harbour's 2003 Annual Eisteddfod, and I threw myself headfirst into the challenge.

The Stories We Carry

Though there was nothing healthy about the level of chronic stress and adrenaline I was living under, it did give me one advantage – thriving under pressure. With only two days to choose a story for my performance, edit and adapt the original script, and learn the new version, I was a bundle of nerves. But instead, I focused all my energy into my goal: to do my absolute best.

When the night came, I took a deep breath, followed the directions of the backstage assistant as she ushered me forward, and stepped onto the stage. Every eye flickered upwards, a room full of strangers and other competitors all focused on the patch of light where I stood. I was only three lines in when, suddenly, a man in the front row yelled up at me. *Keep going*, I told myself. *Don't let him put you off.*

Then I realised who it was – the head judge. I faltered and stopped.

'Excuse me,' he called out again. 'I'm so sorry... sorry to stop you. We haven't called you yet.'

What?!

The audience stared in stunned silence, eyes fixed to the mortified girl standing centre stage.

'We hadn't called you yet,' he continued. 'But we'll call you shortly.'

I nodded in apology, my face turning the colour of a beetroot. *Just kill me now*, I lamented. *That's it. I'm done.*

As I hurried back out to the side of stage, I shot a murderous look at the stage assistant, who slunk away into the shadows like a dog with its tail between its legs. As soon as I had left the wings, I heard the sound of my name being called, and for the second time in the space of 60 seconds, I walked onto the stage and began all over again. Did I feel like an idiot? Yes. Did I let it stop me? No.

That night was a true test of resilience, one that showed just how far I had come. The young woman who walked onto stage (twice!) was entirely different to the broken, defeated girl who refused to talk for days on end, or pulled out of auditions at the age of 15 due to panic attacks. She wasn't perfect by any means, nor had she discovered her true potential. But she was no longer silencing herself. She was no longer quitting before she'd even tried.

A short time later I sat in the auditorium with Mum, her face beaming with pride, as the judges tallied the results. They began listing the name of the winners, reeling off their scores along with their school. And then, suddenly, I heard it – my name.

What? No, that can't be right, I thought.

The judge continued, his voice booming from the stage. 'In second place – only half a point behind first place – is Jasmine.' Then he repeated the name of my school, cementing the truth that I had, indeed, just placed second.

Mum screamed, her hand coming up to her mouth. 'Congratulations darling,' she grinned. 'Now go get that award!'

That night I sat in the passenger seat of our old Celica and looked down at the small silver and gold trophy in my hands. I realised then that no matter what Dad said about me, I *was* smart. I *was* capable of achieving hard things. And although I didn't yet understand the significance of this moment, there was a whole world within me that I hadn't yet tapped into.

The Stories We Carry

'Give it up for the class of 2003!'

In the centre of the school's auditorium, my friends and I threw our arms around each other with tears of laughter and disbelief. We'd done it. We'd actually finished school. It was momentous for each and every one of us, no matter our popularity or social standing, because let's be honest, no one breezes through Year 12 – even the super-smart kids. It's overwhelming and confusing, stressful and uncertain. Everyone just wants it to be over.

For me, I was thankful to have made it to graduation. It was only through the support of my mother, teachers, and the family of a friend – who'd allowed me to stay with them for several weeks during my final exams – that I graduated with fairly good scores. It was more than I could have hoped for, given the incredible stress I was under, and I was thankful to now be one step closer to freeing myself from Dad's constant abuse.

That night, we all headed to Urunga to enjoy a night of drinking and laughter together – one final hoorah with the humans who had been part of my life for the last years of High School. Unsurprisingly I got a little drunker than expected, and when I started swaying tipsily on the boat ramp, it was clear that it was time for me to go. Luckily, my friend Drew had promised to take me home and made sure I was safely tucked inside the car.

We were only a few minutes from home when, suddenly, dread began to swamp me. The night had been filled with so much fun and I was desperate to hold on to it; to stay in this bubble for as long as possible.

'Do you have to be home by a certain time?' I asked, a lilt of hopefulness tinging the end of my sentence. I turned toward the silhouette of Drew's face, hoping he understood what was going on inside of me.

'Nah, not really,' he said, shaking his head gently.

'Do you think we could go somewhere for a while?'

'Sure.'

Swinging the car around, Drew headed back toward the highway, the two of us singing along to the radio as we made our way to Sawtell Beach. Now that the alcohol had well and truly worn off I was freezing, and though it was spring, the night air was laced with a bitter chill. We sat with our backs against the hard wooden fence of the headland and he pulled his jacket around my shoulders, keeping me warm as we sat in silence. I savoured those peaceful moments on the hill with Drew. Cold winds whipping frosty tears from my eyes, his arms safe and secure against my chest. He was a thoughtful guy; the kind who once walked to the opposite end of the school to deliver my jumper – after classes had already started – because I'd left it on the basketball court. He was warm and gentle, and I loved him as a friend.

When we'd finally spent enough hours staring at the ocean, he took me home. And as I quietly crept into the house and crawled into bed, I said a silent prayer of thanks for the good men in my life; boys who were barely adults, yet modelled the kind of love that I needed to know existed. The kind of positive masculinity that had the power to counter the toxic jealousy, control, and superiority that my dad relied upon.

The Stories We Carry

Now that I was 18 and had finished school, it was becoming harder and harder for me to sit quietly and be the 'polite, good Christian daughter' my dad expected. To live under his rules and submit to the control he wanted to wield over Mum, Jason and I was increasingly suffocating. Though still terrified by my father, I was empowered by the hatred running through my veins; the kind of anger that made it impossible to take his abuse silently. Now I fought back, screaming until my throat was hoarse, or storming into the room to defend my mother's honour.

I was an angry, defiant young woman – and that was a very dangerous thing to be in this house. Christmas had been particularly scary, with Dad nearly killing us all with his erratic driving. We'd been on our way home from church, and as my mother revealed to me over a decade later, 'It was then that I thought, *this is how he's going to do it. He's going to take us all out.*' I knew I needed to get out of home fast, but with my casual retail job I didn't have the funds or the credibility to get a rental house. What I did have, however, were connections. So, just after New Year's Day in 2004, I picked up the phone and called the number I'd been saving for an emergency. The only person I could possibly think of who knew and understood the ever-present danger within our four walls.

'Hello?'

'Hi!' I cleared my throat and tried to hide my nervousness. 'Ada, it's Jas.'

An instant warmth filled the space between us, her voice bright and welcoming. 'Hey, beautiful girl, how are you?'

I made some small talk, filling her in on how I'd just finished school and my plans for the holidays, before turning to the truth. The real reason for my call.

'I was wondering if you had any houses that you were developing that hadn't been sold yet,' I said, trying to keep my voice steady. 'I just... I *really* need to get out of here.'

'Oh Jas...' She paused, suddenly understanding the gravity of my request. 'I'm so sorry. We sold the development earlier this year.'

'Oh.' My bubble burst, all my hope fluttering away like confetti falling to the ground. In its place was nothing but cold emptiness. 'That's okay, it's fine,' I mumbled, trying to rush past the awkwardness of the moment.

'Jas, I really am sorry.'

'It's fine, don't worry about it.' A tear fell from the corner of one eye and I turned my face toward the ceiling, blinking rapidly to stop the flow. 'Have a great night. Bye.'

In the silence of my room I turned to my diary, the only place I'd ever been able to honestly express the depths of my depression, and let it all out. The hopelessness. The despair. The anger. The betrayal. It was all there between the purple covers of that A4 journal.

As I wrote I pictured my dad's face. The way he'd sneered at me the day before, his middle finger raised in disgust. The way I'd screamed across the driveway, my voice cracking as the words travelled into his ears. The cold, unflinching stare of his eyes as he'd heard my words and thrown his own back.

The Stories We Carry

I hate you.

I hate you too!

I paused, fingers wrapped so tightly around the pen that my fingertips bruised. Then I snapped my diary closed, staring angrily at the cheerful collection of blue, orange, and green stars bursting from a background of bright purple. *If only he'd disappear forever,* I thought hopelessly. *If only I never had to see him again.*

There was no way I could have known what was to happen. That only 48 hours later, my wish would come true. If I could go back in time I would have told that young woman that what was to come wasn't her fault. That there was no way she could have known. In the moment, though, I didn't have the mental capacity to see the truth.

Years later, all I could do was to ask myself the same question over and over.

How could I have written that note? How could I have done that?

Chapter 9

Something's wrong.

That was my first thought, as I stood by the automatic doors of the Palm Centre, my bag slung over one shoulder as I stared at the woman before me. It wasn't the woman herself that made me uneasy, but rather, the stark lack of warmth in her usually joyful eyes.

In the entire time I'd known her, I'd never seen our neighbour Cathie without a smile on her face. She reminded me of a mother hen, all warmth and comfort and protection. She was the mama who gave you your personal space but always had your back; the one who knew when to deliver a stern peck of love, and when to draw you reassuringly under her wing. To me she was like a second mother, someone I was comfortable to sit alongside on a Friday night as our families laughed around a roaring fire in her back shed, the sounds of Van Morrison filtering through the air.

Today, though, that warmth was nowhere to be seen. Not only that, her eyes were focused firmly in my direction – almost as though she were waiting for me.

Was she?

I waved and smiled, and Cathie returned my gesture with a small raise of her hand and a quick glance towards the car park. But she stayed planted to the spot as I approached. Yes, she was definitely waiting for me. My heart rate began to quicken once again.

Something's wrong. Something's very wrong.

As I drew level with her in front of the automatic glass doors, she finally moved toward me, briefly smiling. 'I'm taking you home, sweetie,' she said quietly. 'I'm parked out here.'

I felt my eyebrows draw together, my brain struggling to make sense of what was happening. 'What's going on? Where's Mum?'

No answer.

Gesturing toward the car park, she turned and walked slowly, almost as though in a fog or a trance. I followed behind, my ears now filled with the thundering sound of my own heartbeat. By the time we arrived at her car I was beginning to slip into blind panic, but then, suddenly, I saw her. The unmistakable bounce of her thick black hair and dark blue eyes. The weathered resilience. The face of my mother.

Relief swam through my system, calming my heartbeat as I climbed into the backseat. But it was temporary; the sweet sensation draining away quickly like rain down a drain pipe.

'Mum, what's going on?'

In the dim lighting of the underground car park, the two women I trusted most looked numbly at each other, both lost for words. Seconds passed like hours, the air heavy with a feeling of dread. Cathie looked at me sadly. Finally she spoke, her words robotic.

The Stories We Carry

'It's about your dad, honey.'

Panic began to envelop me, images of horrible situations bursting forward. 'What did he do? Did he hurt you, Mum? Are you okay?'

Mum just shook her head quietly.

'What happened?' I repeated.

Then, she spoke.

'He's dead.'

For at least a second, one precious second, everything was still okay. Then, an overwhelming rush of intense feelings barrelled up and over me. Just like that day on the horse shed. A strange, wounded laugh shot out from my lips. A sound that felt so wrong, but was the only one my body could produce. *No, that's not possible. This is a sick joke.*

In the silence someone spoke, but by now I couldn't tell who. My mother? Cathie? Nothing made sense anymore.

All I heard were words, distorted by the rushing in my ears. Sounds. Awful, awful, sounds.

'He killed himself.'

Suddenly, I lost all ability to process or to understand. All I could do was sit like a marionette; my mouth opening and closing dumbly, random syllables colliding with sobs that choked out everything else.

Jas Rawlinson

The time was 1 pm. The date, just three days before my little brother's 11th birthday.

And with three words, our entire world had been forever changed.

Chapter 10

Jasi, are you okay? People at church were asking us to pray for your fam. What's happening?

Seb came into my work asking if you were okay – what's going on???

Jas are you okay? I just heard the news.

It was 4 pm, and – just like my life – my phone was blowing up. One after another, they kept coming – a torrent of questions cloaked in the familiar beep of a message tone. Questions about what was happening. Platitudes and thoughts and prayers. Messages filled with statements about how 'sorry' they were to hear about my 'loss.' But all I could think about was how I wanted it to stop. The messages, the empathy, the assumptions. All of it. They were all wrong, and with every message my guilt grew larger.

This is all my fault. I wanted him to disappear and he did.

Ignoring the texts, I clicked through to my contact list and moved the cursor until I came to the letter K. Then I called the name at the top of the list.

'Jas, are you okay? I heard something happened.'

Kane's voice was unusually quiet, his words steeped in concern. With the phone pressed to my ear I paced outside the back door, my eyes drifting across to the garage; the place where Dad had ended his life. Both of the roller doors were closed, locked up. The police had already been out. They'd already taken care of everything that needed to happen. Now, all that was left was a memory; the dreadful words that my mother had recounted.

Mum had been the one to find him. She'd been the one to place her hands on each side of his face and – despite the overwhelming shock – call for an ambulance while beginning CPR. There had been no time for her to scream or cry or collapse in disbelief. She had to try – even when it was clear that her efforts were not going to bring him back – and she never gave up. Under the instructions of the emergency operators on the other end of the phone, she kept going, one breath at a time, until the paramedics arrived.

My mother performed those breaths and compressions for 20 minutes without stopping even once. Only when the ambulance arrived did she allow herself to come to terms with what was really happening. And even then, she had no time to fall apart. She had to make sure I got home from work; she had to pick Jason up from his friend's house. She was on autopilot, numb and frozen.

Now, I looked across at the place where my father had taken his final breaths and wondered how this was happening. Was this real? Or was it a crazy nightmare?

Standing by the back deck, I told Kane the truth, blurting it out in a wounded sob. 'Can you come and get me?' I asked tearfully. 'I don't want to be at home right now. I just want to get out. Anywhere. Somewhere.'

'I'll be there in 30,' he said. 'I'll come straight over.'

The Stories We Carry

True to his word, my friend Kane, the guy who was undoubtedly the most annoying boy in our friendship group, drove straight to my house, bundled me in his arms, and held me together. Then, after promising my mum that he would have me home safely in a few hours, we headed into town.

Almost twenty years later, I struggle to understand how I could leave my mother after such a horrific tragedy. I look at my own son – only five at the time of writing this book – and think to myself, *How insensitive could I be? How would I feel if he up and left in a moment like that?* As I have since learned, logic is not always present in the face of trauma, and we never know how our body or mind will respond. At that moment I didn't want to be anywhere near the place my dad had died. I was in shock, and struggling to process the tragedy that had just happened. All I wanted was to escape it all.

That night happened to be the birthday of one of our good friends from school, and since I'd already been planning to go, I asked Kane to take me in. I wanted to pretend – for a few hours at least – that everything was normal in my world. To make the most of every precious second before the whole of Coffs Harbour knew the truth; before their entire perspective of me changed.

Because I knew it would. I'd no longer be 'Jas.' I'd be 'that girl whose dad killed himself.'

Kane and I made our way through the front doors, his hand resting protectively around my shoulder. Then I pasted a fake smile across my face and started the rounds, talking with mates from school and pulling my friend in for a birthday hug. For a while I kept up the act, but eventually it all caught up. One moment I was fine, the next, I completely fell apart.

'Jas, are you okay?' Allan paused, his deep brown eyes growing serious as a small crease pressed between his ginger eyebrows.

'I...'

I tried desperately to think of a lie, but it just wouldn't come. Allan was a good friend – and for the last two years our families had even holidayed together (initially by accident) in a seaside town named Yamba. Sometimes we'd catch up for a walk along the beach, telling stories and laughing at the fake 'tramp stamp' I'd given myself with a sticker tattoo. Only a few weeks ago we'd hung out for dinner one night, our families meeting up at a small restaurant in the town's main street as we celebrated our HSC results. What he didn't know, however, was that my dad had gone completely off the rails an hour before that dinner, emotionally and verbally abusing me to the point that I'd erupted into tears. Dad had recently gone for a job interview, applying for a senior management position at his landscaping job, and he'd been delivered the news just before dinner that he'd missed out. As a result, he took his anger out on me. What was meant to be a wonderful night of celebration turned into a nightmare, and I spent the entire evening holding back angry, bitter tears of hatred as Dad sat laughing and swapping jokes with Allan's family as if nothing had happened.

Now, I looked into my friend's eyes and wondered if there was still time for me to salvage this moment; to stop the train before it fell off the tracks. To make him believe that everything was okay, even if just for a few hours. In the end, though, I just didn't have the energy.

'My dad... my dad killed himself.'

The Stories We Carry

The moment the words left my lips I felt myself shatter. Like a glass vase falling to the floor, my soul splintered into a thousand pieces, each one breaking into smaller shards. It was as though my brain finally put together the missing puzzle piece; the one that said, 'He's gone. Your dad is gone.'

Allan quickly pulled me into his arms, waves of grief pulling me deeper and deeper until I couldn't breathe. Like the ocean at low tide, my lungs inhaled sharply, sucking inwards until they were so tight I thought they might burst. Pressed against his chest, I sobbed and sobbed, choking on all the words I couldn't say. All I could think to myself was, *This doesn't feel real. This can't be real. This must be a movie.*

To this day, I still remember the vivid sensation of feeling as though I were watching a film. The detachment – even within such heightened emotion – that made me think of myself as a character. As if this were an episode of a dramatic soap opera. It felt embarrassing to have such little control over my body, and yet, there was nothing I could do.

The hysteria flowed through me like dangerous rapids, careening down my cheeks and dripping onto my friend's shirt. Taking me by the hand, Allan led me through the cafe and out to the cool night air, where he sat quietly by my side, his jacket draped around my shoulder.

'Go back to the party,' I wept. 'You don't want to be around me right now. I'm just going to ruin everything. Please, I'll be fine.'

'Jas, I'm not leaving until you can look me in the eye and tell me you're okay,' he said softly. 'I want to make sure you're going to be able to get home safely. I'm not going to leave you out here.'

Why? I thought. *Why would you care?*

No matter how much kindness I was shown, I never believed I deserved it – not from Allan, or Drew, or Kane, or anyone else. And yet, there were so many people surrounding me, ready to venture into the darkness in which I sat and to compassionately hold out a small candle that allowed them to illuminate my pain. Not so that they could fix it, or tell me how to make it go away. Simply to hold space for the truth of what was going on. To sit and listen and wait. Even now, I think back to some of these friends – young men, barely out of boyhood – who displayed such compassion, gentleness, and kindness. Young men who showed me that masculinity didn't have to be synonymous with 'superiority'. It didn't have to be used as a shield to keep the world from knowing that you were drowning in depression. It was okay to cry. It was powerful to be sensitive. It was normal to comfort a woman when she was vulnerable, without using it as a weapon against her.

That night, Kane drove me home – one hand on the wheel, the other holding my palm tightly – and made sure I was safely in bed. There I lay, numb and in disbelief, waiting for this nightmare to end.

Praying that when I opened my eyes, I'd find it was all a terrible dream.

Shit, he's going to kill me!

Panic consumed me as I ran through the front door and down toward the water tank, my heart pounding wildly with each step. It had been two hours since I'd walked outside to fill Buddy's drinking trough – telling myself that I'd just take a few minutes to do something inside while it filled – and in that time, I'd completely forgotten to return. Now, a river of water flowed down the side of the hill, transforming the paddock into a slop of mud and sodden grass. *I'm going to be in so much trouble when he finds out*, I thought. *Dad's going to –*

Suddenly I stopped, my thoughts coming to a halt as reality caught up. *Damn it*, I cursed. *When is this going to stop happening?*

Dad had been gone for four days, and yet, my brain still couldn't accept the truth. Every morning when I awoke I was confronted by reality, but somewhere throughout the day I'd forget. I could be anywhere when it happened. Making lunch in the kitchen, talking on the phone with a friend, feeding the dogs. The only thing that was consistent was the feeling of always being on edge; waiting to be in trouble, or to hear his screams fill the air as he berated and belittled Mum.

Every day I had to tell myself that he was gone and we were now safe. That I'd never again have to hear that deep hatred in his voice as he branded me 'lazy', 'stupid,' or a 'little bitch'. Never again would I have to hear my own father tell me he hated me. Knowing and remembering, however, seemed to be two very different things.

I thought back to an afternoon a year prior, when I'd been called into the school counsellor's office to talk about what was going on inside my head. Since I wasn't fond of talking, I'd been asked instead to draw a picture that represented the life I wanted to live. With my eyes focused on the paper, I'd drawn an outline of three people with their hands linked together. Then, I'd scribbled an image of a fourth – a stick figure who was banished to the far left-hand side of the page.

Now, I realised that life had delivered me exactly what I'd asked for. Not only that – Dad was no longer even 'in the picture.' I was living the life I'd dreamed of and silently screamed for on so many lonely nights – and yet, happiness had never felt further away.

Chapter 11

Trying to describe how I felt in the wake of everything that happened on that day in January 2004 remains incredibly complicated, even after so many years. For a decade, all I'd wanted was to be free from Dad's abuse, but now that it had happened, I found myself stuck. Guilt followed me like a dog and my head was a sticky web of complex emotions. Questions ran through my mind constantly; an endless loop of thoughts that started with, *This is all my fault,* and ended with, *– but I don't miss him. Why do I not miss him?*

Dad's death hadn't freed me like I thought it would. Instead, I remained trapped in a void of hopelessness. I guess it should come as little surprise, then, to reveal the truth about where this trauma led me. After all, I was an emotionally damaged young woman with a toxic mixture of trauma, unhealthy coping strategies, and an unwavering need to be loved. On top of all of this, I was also incredibly naïve. Up until this point I'd had only two boyfriends, and after twelve years in a private Christian school, I'd well and truly perfected my role as the 'good girl who plays by the rules.' I'll freely admit that I was also the stereotypical judgemental Christian kid; the kind who felt morally superior to people who didn't live the way I did. In my friendship circle this was considered somewhat normal, but as the months slipped by and I became more enmeshed in the social circles of my retail job, everything began to change. Now I was surrounded by co-workers who openly dealt or purchased drugs, and spent their weekends getting 'shitfaced;' eating McDonalds every Sunday morning as they re-lived the regrets of the night before. Suddenly, I was hanging out with people who chatted casually about sleeping with two different people on the same weekend, and although I was shocked by the life some of them were living, I slowly began to integrate myself within these circles. There was a raw and gaping hole within my soul, one that longed for love, acceptance, and freedom, and despite not being interested in many of the things that my co-workers were, there was one thing we did have in common; a love of alcohol and the 'escape' that it offered.

Soon, I began spending every weekend with my new friends from work (or who I'd met at the pub), and every Friday and Saturday was filled with a blur of alcohol, club entry stamps, and the constant stench of smoke. There were no rules back then about having to smoke outside and so both smokers and non-smokers partied together, beer bottles and durries in hand on the middle of the dance floor. Sometimes I'd be mid-dance move when I'd feel the searing pain of a menthol light burning into my arm, or the foul, sticky sensation of beer sloshing down my back. It was like a jungle; one where wild animals prowled around under the cover of darkness, searching for their next thrill. Some found their escape on the dance floor, their limbs swinging in all directions as they danced off their nervous tension. Others drank and smoked, disappearing into the heavenly oblivion of apathy. And then there was another kind – the kind of creatures who came to the jungle *purely* to hunt. The type who liked to go after the vulnerable and weak – specifically young women – who were easily manipulated.

Though I had no idea at the time, I can see now that I was a clear target from the start. Like a pack of wolves, these men quickly sought me out – cloaking themselves in sheep's clothing to gain my trust. 'Wow, you are *so* not like other girls,' they'd croon. 'Honestly, I've never met anyone like you. How are you so sexy *and* funny?' I'd roll my eyes, pretending these phrases were the stupidest thing I'd ever heard, but deep down, their flattery only made me hungry for more. These words were like honey to me. I drank them in, allowing the sweet nectar of their compliments to wash over me like liquid gold and soak into the darkest corners of my mind, momentarily easing the self-loathing and suicidal thoughts that plagued me every single day. The more I experienced the thrill of being in the jungle, the more I began to distance myself from my old friends. *They don't get me*, I'd think to myself. *They all sit around judging me, as if I'm falling off the rails, but I don't even drink that much!*

In hindsight, my friends never rejected or abandoned me. But they did express how worried they were. Often, I'd get emails from April, who was working in America at the time, begging me to look after myself and stop drinking so much, or texts from Rachael asking me why I was making certain decisions that went against my values – but they were statements and questions made out of love, not judgment. To my mind, however, I was a misfit, an outsider. Too wild to fit in at church and too innocent for the new people I was hanging out with.

In much the same way that my body dysmorphia caused me to see a different version of myself in the mirror, it became impossible for me to see the truth about my own behaviour. My diary was filled with contradictions; lines where I admitted to being scattered from too much drinking, followed by statements like, 'I don't know why Kane was giving me such a hard time. I barely drank anything!' Then, only a few paragraphs later, 'I threw up so much last night, I can't remember what happened after we got home.'

Often, I felt the disconnect between these two parts of me; the Jas who was quiet, sensitive, and loved deep conversations with friends, time in the ocean, and the thrill of cantering her horse over home-made jumps. Then there was the 'new' Jas, who loved to drink herself into a void of escapism. The problem was, many of the people who were now part of my inner circle loved and encouraged this second version of myself. They all knew where I stood when it came to drugs and sex, (the former was a 'never' and the latter was a 'waiting for the right person' kind of situation) but they got a weird thrill out of seeing me write myself off in other ways. 'Let's corrupt Jas!' they'd joke. It was always said without any particular malice, but no matter who I befriended, they always seemed to get a rise out of seeing me step into the wild character I'd created for myself; the version who got blind drunk and then busted out her best Christina (X-tina) Aguilera moves on the dancefloor.

There were many mornings when I woke up sprawled on a mattress at a friend's house with a feeling of deep unease and shame about the choices I was making, but with nothing to replace the high that came from alcohol, it was impossible to pull myself away. As a result, I continued to put myself in risky situations, both with predatory men, and life in general.

There was a night that I narrowly escaped what, in all likelihood, was an orchestrated and coordinated plan to kidnap me. I'd just been to see a friend's band play a gig at 'The Planto', one of the most popular venues along the main street of Coffs Harbour, and since my other friends were all working, I'd gone alone. I was the kind of girl who 'teamed with the theme' (as Kath and Kim would say) when it came to events, and since I was off to a punk show I'd decided on a different wardrobe option that night. Unlike my usual mini-skirts and backless tops, I'd opted for a black and grey striped shirt and a pair of black, three-quarter length cargo jeans. I must have looked at least three years younger than I actually was.

After the show I walked down past the kebab shop toward the Mall where my friend Sharon worked behind the bar of a new nightclub. I'd made plans to swing by and grab her keys so that I could let myself into the spare room of her house, but as I arrived at the front of the venue, I felt my stomach drop. It was just past midnight, and in Coffs, that meant one thing: Lockout. Though I tried over and over to explain to the burly security guard that I needed to come inside to get the keys from my friend, he wouldn't budge an inch. 'Look,' I pleaded. 'My friend works behind the bar, her name is Sharon. If you can just ask her to come down, I'll grab the keys from her and leave.'

Chewing on a wad of gum, he stared at me through narrowed eyes. 'Nope. Can't let you in,' he repeated dryly. 'Sorry.'

For another minute I tried desperately to change his mind, even asking if there was a staff member who could escort me up and back out – but there was not a shred of empathy in the gigantic man's body. Instead, he forced me – a 45 kg teenage girl – to be left stranded on the street. It was at this point that I decided to walk back to The Planto, in the hope that I could maybe find a friend to hang out with there until Sharon finished work at 3 am. But as I arrived back at the front steps I found that they, too, were now in 'Lockout.'

'Shit,' I cursed. 'I'm screwed.'

For the second time in 15 minutes I found myself walking south along the main street. I was unsure what to do or where to go and this was the moment where things took an unsettling turn. Suddenly, a man appeared by my side. He was tall and thin, with dark hair and a thick smile that spread warmly across his face.

'Are you okay?'

'Yeah, I guess,' I shrugged, taking a slight step sideways. 'I got locked out and I can't get into my friend's house. So, not the best.'

'No good at all!' he lamented. 'You should come hang with me, I'm off to see some friends. We are going to have – how do you say? – the *best* night.' His thick accent filled the space between us and I frowned, trying to place it.

We walked slowly along the street, the stranger continuing to talk in excited tones about his evening; something about getting a bus to Byron Bay with friends. Though I'd been drinking earlier, I had well and truly sobered up by this point, something that, in hindsight, was extremely lucky. By midnight on a Friday I was usually shitfaced. Tonight, however, I was fairly clear headed, and this clarity allowed me to hear the urgent inner voice of my intuition.

This isn't right.

'I'm just off to meet some friends,' he smiled. 'Want to come hang out?'

'No, I'm okay,' I said politely. 'But thanks.'

'Are you sure? We are going to have the *absolute* best night. I think you should come and meet my friends, they would love you.'

He continued to smile, but I couldn't help but sense the obvious weirdness of the moment. *You don't know me, and you want me to come with you?* I kept thinking. *What is going on here?*

Every time I heard my intuition, it was countered by the voice of my inner good girl. The one who spoke up, interfering with my judgment whenever I tried to create boundaries. *Don't be rude!* she nudged. *He's being perfectly polite. He's probably just high on weed and being super friendly.*

We continued walking, making small talk. There was something strange about the way in which he kept mentioning how beautiful I was and that I should come and meet his friends. But all of this was happening very quickly; so quickly that I didn't have time to really assess it for what it was.

Before I had time to react, there was a movement to my right; so swift that I never even saw it coming. One moment I was talking with this stranger, and the next, two people had hold of me. Without missing a beat, a mystery hand threaded its way through my right arm, as the male stranger also linked in on the other side.

What's happening? What – ? In disbelief and shock I swivelled my head, looking toward the face of the new person who'd just appeared by my side and confidently taken my arm.

It was a woman.

She was much older, tall with a broad body and lips that curved into a gentle smile. A look of contented ease etched across her face – though she never spoke a word or even looked at me. It was sinister and confusing. There was nothing comforting about the way that she had hold of me. There was nothing normal about the subtle force with which she moved me forward, pulling my body closer toward the end of the street. Yet, she looked as though she could have been someone's loving mother.

All of this happened in seconds – in the space of less than 100 metres from where I'd stepped out from the Plantation Hotel. One moment it was just me and the stranger, the next *she* was there. The woman never uttered a word, never looked at me. But instantly, my intuition told me everything I needed to know.

At that moment I could have frozen. It would have been only too easy to go into a state of shock and allow myself to continue being led down the street to where the final pub sat, and the street split off into darkness. I could have waited and continued questioning myself as we headed toward the large, open soccer fields and dark isolated parks. But my intuition, which had always been so strong as a child, now kicked in louder than ever, screaming and shaking me by the shoulders.

No.

In one swift motion, I pulled my arms free and stepped backwards. I braced myself, waiting for her next move. Would she come at me? Would I have to scream, and rake my hands down her face? Would anyone stop to help? I held my ground, the young male still hovering by my side.

But then, as if she'd been nothing more than a bizarre dream, she vanished. The woman continued on, confidently walking down the path until she reached the traffic lights of West High Street, and then, she rounded the corner and disappeared. At no point in this entire interaction did she ever acknowledged me. She was there, and then she wasn't. She knew what she was doing, and the moment I noticed, she simply cut her losses and gave up.

Unfortunately, I still had someone else who was intent on carrying out the rest of the plan.

As I stared off toward the vanishing woman, I felt the presence of the young man once again zeroing in on me; and this time, he was upping his game. The stranger stepped closer, once again urging me to come and meet his friends. Though his words were light and fluffy, I felt nervous at his insistent tone. It just wasn't right. Fear began to run through my body. Goosebumps prickled my skin, urging me to run but at the same time demanding calmness. *Think,* I chastised. *Think.*

Then, I spotted it. The answer that was going to get me out of here. Right inside the window of the local kebab shop.

My solution was a young man named Kieran.

'Hey!' I leapt forward, rushing toward the 20-year-old-guy and throwing my arms around him. 'How are you?' I gushed. 'Oh my gosh, I haven't seen you in forever!' For a moment he stared back in shock, and I felt the presence of the stranger growing closer.

Come on Kieran, I thought. *Don't blow this.* Though we weren't close, we'd hung out in the same circles a few times and I knew he was trustworthy. I just needed him to go along with the plan. Kieran leaned in, accepting my overly enthusiastic hug with a shy smile and I pressed my lips against his ear, my words rushing out in a hurried stream of anxiety.

'There's a guy following me and I don't know who he is or how to get rid of him. He won't leave. Can you pretend to be my boyfriend? Please?'

He stared at me, his eyes flickering to the stranger who was now standing by my side. It was a big ask, given that I barely ever talked to him when we crossed paths at work. Kieran was a bit of a geek and sort of shy, but he was caring and kind, and right now I desperately needed his help.

He shuffled forward, angling his body toward the stranger.

'Isn't she so beautiful?' gushed the man with the accent, sidling up to me as if he were my boyfriend. 'I was just telling her about my friends and the party we're going to.'

'I don't think so, man,' said Kieran, his voice quiet but very firm. 'I'm her boyfriend, so I'll take her home.'

'Oh.'

The two men suddenly stood in a stand-off, their eyes fixed on each other.

'Are you sure?'

'She's with me,' Kieran repeated.

Realisation began to dawn, the stranger slowly shuffling from side to side. He tried one last time – a half-hearted attempt to convince me – but then he disappeared, slinking off into the night just like his female associate.

How did this all happen so quickly? I wondered. *Who the hell was that woman? Who was he?*

I exhaled shakily, my fingers trembling. 'Thank you. Thank you so much,' I breathed. My legs suddenly felt very wobbly.

'Are you okay to get home?'

'I don't have any keys for Sharon's, but I can sleep in my car. I just need to get back to her house,' I explained.

The Stories We Carry

'I'll walk you.'

'Are you sure?'

'Of course! I'm not going to let you walk alone after that!' Kieran stood, leading the way.

True to his word, he walked beside me for the 20 minute journey back to my friend's house in West Coffs and dropped me off outside, where, exhausted, I climbed into the front seat of my car, locked the doors, pushed down the chair, and tried to curl up into a ball.

It would not be the last time that I found myself in danger over the years to come. Nor would it be the last time that I ever thought about things like human trafficking. Little did I know that one day, I would be the one walking the streets at night, watching out for other girls. One day it would be me who was walking through red-light districts and staring into the faces of young women who had been trapped in the living nightmare of human trafficking.

But all of this was so far in the future; light years beyond anything my 19-year-old mind could imagine... Right now, at 1 am on a Saturday morning, I was simply a girl who felt so very lucky to be alone and safe.

Why am I even here? This is a total waste of time.

Sitting on the cold plastic seat of the medical office, I stared into the ancient face of the doctor and bit my lip.

'Your mother says you've been struggling with depression and suicidal thoughts,' he noted briskly, eyes focused on the screen of a small computer. 'How long have you felt this way?'

I shrugged, half rolling my eyes. 'I don't know. About as long as I can remember?'

'You scored very high in the self-diagnosis test,' he mentioned. 'You're in the chronic depression category.'

Wow, news to me, I thought sarcastically. *I've known that since I was 12. Bit late, Doc.*

'I'd like to start you on a prescription of antidepressants.' He frowned, his face creasing into a thousand deep wrinkles as I stared defiantly at the floor, one leg jiggling up and down nervously.

Antidepressants? Surely I don't need that shit – that stuff is for people with way bigger problems than me. Right?

Unfortunately, my mother didn't agree. In fact, she was the reason I was sitting in the doctor's office right now, talking to a man who clearly didn't care about anything other than filling out a script and sending me on my way.

What's the point? I thought. *This is just who I am now. This feeling is me. It's never going to leave.*

'Here's the script,' he said casually, ripping it off the prescription pad. 'Any questions?'

I thought for a moment, eyes focused on the thin slip of paper he'd just handed over. 'Can I drink while I'm on these?'

The Stories We Carry

He paused, conflicted. I'm sure he could tell that – to a 19-year-old girl – this wasn't something I would take his advice on. He probably knew that many young people don't care about 'safety' advice. But as a doctor, I trusted him. At my core I was still a good girl who played by the rules, and I needed him to tell me the truth. To say sternly, 'No. No, you absolutely cannot. Choose to live, or choose to throw yourself down into a hole that's so deep you may never come out of it.'

The doctor shrugged lazily, a small puff of air escaping his lips. 'Well, usually we say not to. But you can still drink on them if you want.'

There it is, screamed my head. *You're good to go!*

In my eyes the doctor had given me the green light, and with that, I breathed a sigh of relief. I was barely out the front door before I was planning the next night of weekend drinks with my friends.

That day, those words, have forever haunted my mother. They turned her inside out with rage and frustration, leaving her feeling more defeated than ever. Here she was, trying desperately to save her suicidal daughter and get her the help she needed, and instead, the doctor had given me a gold star endorsement to continue on as I had been.

Sometimes I wonder if he knew just how dangerous that advice was. If he'd take it all back, if only he knew what was to come. Or if he was simply too jaded to care.

In the end it didn't matter; he did what he did – and his actions had consequences.

Little did he know I'd be back in his office in just a few short months. But not for another script. This time, I'd be there because I'd overdosed.

Things didn't change straight away, but when the day came, *my God it was magical.*

One moment I was stuck in a void of depression, the next, I was literally high on life. Something as mundane as walking through the shops made me break into a full body smile, my lips stretched wide with a permanent grin. At one point I thought I might actually skip down the aisle of the supermarket. *If this is what being on antidepressants feels like, I never want to stop taking them!* I thought, giddily. *This shit is magic!*

Initially, the changes happening within my brain were everything that modern medicine could hope for. But in the background, more sinister changes were bubbling to the surface. Ones that were downright dangerous.

At first, I struggled to put together the puzzle pieces of what was going on within; why I suddenly felt as though nothing and no one could hurt me. Eventually, though, the words came to me. *This is how it feels to be invincible,* I thought. *I'm untouchable.*

That weekend I went straight to my friend's house and proceeded to throw back shots of Kahlua and milk, followed by glasses of Malibu and lemonade. *Well, the Doc said it was fine,* I told myself. *So why change anything?*

I was out at The Planto with a girl from school when suddenly, a guy I'd been crushing on for months invited me to 'come and hang' at the hotel room that he and his footy mates were staying in. Normally, my response would be to stay far away from a dodgy situation like that. I never went home with strangers, or to the homes of guys I'd been talking with – even if we were dating. Like most young women, I'd become innately aware of the dangers of being female from the time I hit puberty, and long before I even learned how to drive I knew how to hold a set of keys between my fingers – always poised and ready to defend myself. But tonight, my intuition had well and truly left the building. Thanks to my medication I felt invincible, and all the little alarm bells that would usually sound loudly were completely broken.

An hour later, I was making out with this guy on a fold-out lounge when all of a sudden a voice sounded from behind. With a jolt, I swivelled around, my eyes landing on the silhouette of a huge, six-foot-something hulk of a man who'd just walked through the front door.

'Hey, who's *this?*'

The stranger smiled lustfully, his eyes drifting over my rainbow corduroy jeans and spaghetti strap singlet. Instantly, my skin began to crawl.

'Hey, Ben,' he began, taking a step forward with a grin. 'You know what they say... caring is sharing.'

Suddenly I felt very awake, the alcoholic haze lifting from my brain in an instant. *Oh shit. Oh shit. Oh shit. Why did you come here, Jas? What the hell were you thinking?*

My date stiffened, his jaw clenching. I waited for him to speak, all the while staring at the nightmare before me. All the ways it could play out. How very wrong this could go. I was a small animal caught between two potential predators, and the invincibility I'd felt only moments ago now felt so very foolish.

'Fuck off,' breathed Ben, annoyed. 'She's mine.'

The footy player stood still for a moment. Then he released a small, amused snort from the back of his throat. 'Have fun,' he laughed, walking past us to the staircase.

The whole interaction lasted only seconds, but those seconds were ones that stuck with me later. It was the first time that my sense of invincibility was shaken. The moment I realised that maybe, just maybe, I *was* making risky decisions. Maybe my mother was right; drinking on antidepressants was a recipe for disaster, and making out with unknown boys at night was not only naïve – it was dangerous.

The next day, as I drove home, I thanked God that I'd walked out of that resort with nothing more than a head full of questions about whether my new crush would or wouldn't call me. (He didn't.) I was fortunate that my story of that night didn't end the way it does for so many women.

You might be asking: *Didn't you know that you were putting yourself in unsafe environments, Jas? Did you really not understand that so many of these men who were taking advantage of you and treating you in misogynistic ways only wanted one thing?* Well, the answer is complicated. In some ways I truly was that innocent – I expected good things to happen to good people and that when a boy told me he loved me, he meant it. I was, after all, only six months into my first year out of high school and I'd not yet become jaded about the types of men I was meeting while out on the town. So, in all honesty, I didn't always know. There were situations in the months ahead where I was pushed to do things I didn't want to; sometimes even physically restrained until I eventually said yes. (Heads up to any men reading: if you have to coerce, convince, or physically restrain someone to get them to give in and do something you want, *it's not consent.* That is not a 'Yes.') There were situations where young men acted out disgusting, porn-fuelled fantasies on me, without ever asking if I wanted it. But never did I recognise the complex warning signs of emotional abuse – let alone sexual coercion. More to the point, I didn't really care. I just wanted to feel something. *Anything* other than the bleak, unrelenting pain of depression. The kind that had led me to overdose on my medication by August of that year, leaving my poor mother wondering, as she walked into my room that morning, if I were dead or alive.

It was the perfect recipe for disaster. And it was exactly what led me to meet Blake.

Chapter 12

'*H*ave fun you two!'

Farewelling us from the driveway, Mum smiled as Blake and I rumbled down the hill in his car and disappeared out onto the dirt road. It was our first time alone together, and I was filled with nervous energy. Me, on a date with a cute 23-year-old who had his own car and a job? Hello, adult life! (Yes, I know – I set the bar incredibly low back then. As it turned out, I'm not even sure the car was his.)

Blake and I had first met during a night out at a local pub, where we'd been introduced by a mutual friend. Instantly, I was intrigued by his larger than life personality and childlike laugh. With his neat little dreadlocks, broad chest, and piercing blue eyes, he was unlike any guy I'd ever dated, and given how desperate I was to be loved, it wasn't long before I agreed to his offer to take me out. Especially, when he announced he was taking me for a picnic on the banks of the Bellingen River. *Wow, he organised all of this?* I thought. *Most guys I go out with don't even have a licence. I can't believe he planned a romantic picnic!*

As we stretched out on a picnic rug, the sun glinting off the shallow pools of water below, I looked up at Blake and wondered what it was that he saw in me. He seemed so captivated by my innocence, and every time he looked at me with his intense gaze I felt as though he were drinking me in. It was as though he couldn't get enough. His hands were a little too rough when he grabbed me; his lips almost smothering when they pressed against mine. It felt overwhelming – but what did I really have to compare it to? My grand total of two relationships had both happened during high school with guys close in age to me and we rarely went on real dates. Not like this.

It was during the drive home that afternoon, as we wove through the winding hills of the Bellingen Valley, that I felt it; the niggling, warning bells of my intuition. *Why do I feel this way?* I wondered. *He's perfectly nice... why do I feel like I don't really want to see him again?*

In hindsight, I now know that my intuition was spot on. From the time that I was a child it had protected me from so many different things – starting at the age of four, when I noticed something strange about the sound of our front door and instantly threw myself underneath my mother's bed, knowing intuitively that I needed to make myself small. What I didn't know was that at that moment, a drug-affected woman had walked through the door of our home and proceeded to put her hands around my mother's throat, strangling her until she could barely breathe. I never heard her speak; never saw her face. Most kids would have heard the swing of a screen door and assumed it was their mother. But I knew. I knew it wasn't her. That one sound had told me so much, and it kept me safe.

That day, in a Herculean effort, Mum managed to free herself from the strange woman's grip and pushed her out the front door, rescuing the two of us from whatever may have happened next.

My intuition continued to protect me from that moment on, but somewhere along the way, it became dulled. Dampened through trauma and abuse and made blunt by a need to be loved at all costs. Maybe that's why I ignored its call when it came to Blake.

The Stories We Carry

As an adult, I've tried desperately to work out why I went back; what it was that made me chase after him despite that early feeling that he wasn't right for me. It was only when I flipped through my diaries many years later that I saw how it all unfolded. The way in which our 'reunion' occurred after a very traumatic event in my life – the night that I overdosed on my medication.

It was around August of 2004 and I'd once again been let down by a guy that I trusted. I can't remember what happened, only that I was devastated and heartbroken and I felt in that moment that I couldn't go on. It's not necessarily that I wanted to die; I just wanted the pain to stop. That evening I downed several glasses of wine, threw back some extra pills, and curled up in bed as I tried to ignore the fiery pain stabbing through my stomach. The last message I sent before going to sleep was to my friend Damo, who lived in Perth. The two of us had met over MSN Messenger as teens and he was one of the few people who I could be my complete self with, despite never meeting in person.

'I did something stupid,' I wrote. 'I'm sorry.' Frantic messages appeared on my screen, Damo begging me to tell him what had happened and if I was okay. But then I fell asleep.

Thankfully, I did awaken the next morning, though understandably groggy and hungover. That afternoon my traumatised mother took me in to see the doctor who'd first prescribed my antidepressant medication, only to find that his advice was to simply 'up' my dosage. No care plan. No counselling. Just a generic, 'Here, take some more meds!' approach.

It was shortly after this that I found my way back to Blake. I'm guessing that I looked at the young men in my life who'd caused me so much mental pain, and figured that it was time I dated a 'nice guy.' Someone who was older and more mature. Someone like Blake.

From the very start it was obvious that Blake didn't fit the mould of what I was searching for. He didn't have a phone, was always disappearing for days or weeks at a time, and struggled with certain addictions. But after all the trauma I'd been through I was either blind to these red flags, or apathetic. I needed love, and I was determined to get it any way I could.

One afternoon as I stood out the front of my workplace waiting, again, for Blake to show up, I confided in my co-worker about his behaviour. 'I can't believe he didn't come,' I said sadly. 'He promised he'd be here.'

Meg listened quietly, before shooting a knowing glance my way. She was a 'take no bullshit' kind of woman. With at least 15 years of life experience on me, plus a husband and two kids, she saw exactly what kind of guy Blake was and she refused to enable our relationship in any way. So, when Blake turned up days later asking about me at work, she 'conveniently' forgot to tell me. In reality, she was a fierce mama bear trying to protect a young, naïve girl – but all I saw was an annoying, controlling woman.

'I can't believe you didn't tell me he came around!' I exploded, as we stood in the lay-by office together one day.

Meg sighed in frustration, her eyes focused on the register she was cashing up. 'Jas, look, I just don't think you should trust him.'

'It's not your place to tell me that,' I seethed. 'I don't need you to protect me.'

She opened her mouth to speak but suddenly thought better, snapping it shut and shaking her head. Then she walked past me and left through the side door.

The Stories We Carry

The next week while closing up after a shift, I flipped through the staff logbook to leave a note for the next person coming in. Then I saw it.

'Jas, don't get angry at me okay but I feel like I have to say this. I don't trust that guy, Blake. You can do better.'

Ugh. Why does she have to be so negative!

With a quick flick, I snapped the notebook closed. Why was everyone so down on Blake? Why didn't they see what I saw? *Yeah, okay, he stood me up the week before*, I thought. *But what's the big deal? Maybe something important came up.*

Leaving work I headed for my old Celica, threw my bag inside, and drove home wondering when I'd see Blake again. There was just something about him. The adrenaline that raced through me, when I finally ran into him by surprise after days or weeks without contact. The way I felt when we walked hand in hand along the beach, my fingers swallowed up inside his large, calloused palm. The childlike way he laughed when I did impersonations or told crazy stories. How beautiful he made me feel all the time. More than that, the way he *wanted* me. It was almost all-consuming at times but I loved the way he respected my boundaries, never making me feel that I had to go back on the things that were important to me. I mean, sure, he made some comments at times about things he'd like to change about my body – but that wasn't really a big deal, right? I just figured *all* guys wanted women's bodies to look that way. They certainly did in my Cosmo and Cleo magazines.

As I exited the car park and pulled up at a red light outside the Zebra Motel, I thought more about how wrong Meg was. *So what that he didn't turn up the other day?* I thought. *I'll get over it.*

That night, while I was putting the dogs away for the night, my mobile suddenly rang, jingling with the gaudy Beyonce ringtone I'd purchased. I scooped it up, my heart catching in my throat as I recognised the number of Blake's mum's landline. *It's him!*

'Hey baby girl, how's it going?'

'Good! How about you? Did you have work today?' Falling backwards onto my bed, I lay amongst the yellow butterflies of my bedspread and let my eyes flitter over the sky blue rafters above. On the other end of the phone, Blake talked about his day before finally saying the words I'd been dreaming of.

'I've missed you.'

'Me too.'

'I'm hanging at a mate's house tonight. Wanna come over?'

I looked at the time on my phone, noticing it was already after 8 pm. It was later than I'd usually go out, but I didn't want to miss a chance to see Blake. 'Sure!'

'Cool, see ya later little princess.'

Feeling giddy with excitement I rushed through dinner, too excited to eat. But as I finished up some things around the house, I was suddenly swamped with tiredness. All I really wanted to do was to curl up and sleep – not go to a party late on a Tuesday night. For a few minutes I paced around my room, trying to talk myself into it, but eventually I called Blake back.

The Stories We Carry

'Hey, I'm so sorry but I don't think I can come in tonight. I just realised that it's going to be about 9.30 pm by the time I get into town, and I think I'm a bit too tired.' Almost on cue, a slow yawn stretched through my jaw. 'Sorry,' I said lightly. 'But maybe we can hang out tomorrow instead?'

On the other end, Blake was silent.

'Hey, you there?'

'You don't *do* that,' he said coldly. 'You don't make a promise and then go back on it.'

For a split second I thought of laughing. *Ha! He almost got me with that one.* But then the iciness of his tone hit me full force. He was disappointed, I could feel it.

My eyebrows drew together and I sat up, suddenly alert. 'Blake... I'm sorry. I really do want to come, I'm just really tired. I didn't realise how late it was.'

'Well you should have thought of that first. You don't make plans and then go back on them. It's rude.'

Suddenly I felt very small, my stomach filling with a heavy blanket of sadness. It was the same sensation that came over me every time I was in trouble with Dad. 'I'm sorry,' I repeated.

'Yeah... well. I have to go. Talk later.'

Then he hung up on me.

Jas Rawlinson

For a moment I thought about pushing past the exhaustion and honouring the 'promise' I'd made. But in the end I was just too tired.

Instead, I crawled sadly under the covers and tried to sleep. *I'll make it up to him*, I thought. *I can fix this. Next time I won't let him down.*

Chapter 13

'Alright, which one of you did this?'

In the dim lighting of the sedan's back seat, I ran a hand across my nose and sniffed twice. Something had clearly just been shoved inside my left nostril while I was asleep, and I had a good feeling I knew exactly who was at the centre of this prank.

In the front seat, my friends SJ and Dan tried their best to stifle a laugh, while my mates Matty and Howie, who I was squashed between, shot me their best puppy dog eyes. The five of us had just been to a rave somewhere in the middle of nowhere, and since I was pretty much the only person *not* doing drugs, I'd fallen asleep as soon as I'd climbed into the back seat.

Lesson number one – never fall asleep when you're around a bunch of rascals who've been at a rave. I sniffed again, rubbing the sleep out of my eyes and looking around. Then, in the flash of an overhead street lamp I saw a long, fluro-pink tube lying in my lap.

'Are you serious?' I whined. 'Were you sticking glowsticks up my nose while I was asleep?'

Instantly, the car erupted into laughter, everyone swapping high fives as we meandered through the back roads of Grafton toward the highway.

Matty jabbed an elbow into my rib, grinning. 'Sorry, but what else was I meant to do with two good glowsticks? Serves you right for falling asleep at a rave!'

'He does have a point,' added Dan.

'Ugh, shut up,' I slurred, my speech still heavy from sleep and alcohol. I closed my eyes briefly, only to once again feel something poking at the tip of my nose, followed by another round of hysterical laughter.

'Freaking leave me alone! You guys are the worst.'

'Even when you're angry you still won't swear at us,' laughed Dan. Behind him, Matty just smiled, both eyebrows wiggling comically.

'You know you love us.'

'Whatever.'

I turned toward the window, hiding a little smile. As different as we were, I was grateful for this weird and wonderful little gang. Even though I wasn't into drugs and was constantly teased for being 'the innocent one', they still took me under their wings and respected me for who I was. (The glowsticks were a different matter!) There was a guy in our group who was well known for supplying a lot of people in our area and our workplace with drugs, and yet, even he kept them away from me. Not a single one of my friends ever tried to make me join in, and most importantly, they never excluded me from their catch ups because of it. It was unconventional, but it worked, and in so many ways these friendships were one of the best things that happened to me in the year after Dad's death.

The Stories We Carry

Most weekends were spent with Dan, SJ, and Matty, and even though there was always a lot of alcohol involved they always went above and beyond to look after me. And of course, they also gave me a lot of shit. That was just part of being friends in Australia. Sometimes this meant they hid my mattress in odd places around the house, or stole my phone to send random messages – or in Dan's case, he liked to prank call me pretending to be my doctor. Anything went in our group – we were all a bit mad like that!

Though it wasn't the healthiest time of my life, I was grateful for the wild nights because it gave me a distraction, not only from the constant loneliness that enveloped me, but also from the mental hoops that I was jumping through trying to make sense of Blake's erratic behaviour.

It was always so hard to explain what was going on between the two of us. For me, it was clear; I was deeply and utterly infatuated with him and all I wanted was for us to be together. But when it came to Blake, things were always complicated. He was like a light switch, constantly flickering between showering me with compliments and attention ('I've never met anyone like you, Jas!') and then going cold. Often he'd blame his rollercoaster emotions on hypothetical things that might be happening in the future, telling me, 'I just can't make things official with you yet, because I might be moving away soon,' or 'When I move into a new place, then we can be together.' And so, like an eager puppy I sat on my haunches, ready to spring to attention the moment he called.

The only problem was, nothing he talked about ever happened. The job never came and the 'big move' interstate never eventuated. As for the 'super cool' place he was moving into? Well, I never saw it, let alone ever heard of him living there. Instead, he continued to stay at his mother's house. His life consisted of casual jobs, smoking pot, and disappearing to God-knows-where for days or weeks.

The only thing that was consistent throughout our relationship was his ability to play on my emotions; seeing me when he wanted and ignoring me when it suited. He didn't have a mobile phone, so I was dependent on either catching him via his mother's home line, or waiting for a random call from him. His behaviour was up and down, as was his use of various drugs, and despite the toll it took on me emotionally, I couldn't help but be drawn back to him every time. *I can help him,* I'd think to myself. *I just need to be more patient. He said that when he finds out about the job, we can be together – so I just need to show him more love in the meantime. Once he realises that we're meant to be together – once he gets this new opportunity – everything will be perfect.*

I felt that if I could only help him work through the personal issues he was dealing with, then everything would be okay. And so – between occasional dates with other guys – I would always run back the moment he was ready.

There were magical days spent walking the beaches hand in hand, him kissing me deeply and squinting against the sun as he looked at me in a way no one ever had. There were also afternoons where I organised a surprise dinner to cheer him up, or he surprised me by coming to my workplace, leaning across the counter and kissing me dramatically (much to my embarrassment), before jogging off with a wave.

And then there were all the long, empty times in between.

Me, standing alone outside my workplace because he didn't show up as promised.

The Stories We Carry

Him, giving me the cold shoulder while we were out and refusing to talk to me.

My friend Lara, telling me that Blake had secretly told her he couldn't handle going out with a virgin – and that's why he'd disappeared off the face of the earth.

Then there were things that went far beyond any of this; things that were too shameful for me to tell anyone. Like the night I slept over at his mother's house and awoke in the morning to find the buttons of my jeans undone, and his hands on my body. When I asked Blake what he was doing, he replied with a grin, 'Oh, we were just mucking around.'

We?

'But I was asleep,' I said, somewhat alarmed.

He just grinned. As I was quickly discovering, he had lots of ideas of what I 'should' find enjoyable – including things being done to me when I was asleep. It was confusing, especially since I'd been so upfront with Blake about my personal boundaries – and considering he still refused to officially call me his girlfriend, he knew very clearly where I stood.

'Don't worry about it, nothing happened,' he said lightly, before changing the subject. 'Hey, let's go to the beach! Come on, gorgeous.'

This, right here, is how the cycle began. The patterns of abuse were almost textbook, following the same script that many victim-survivors know only too well. The abuser finds a person with a history of trauma and vulnerability, and overwhelms them with love, adoration, and attention. They fill the void that is aching to be filled, building up the person's belief that this relationship or friendship is what they need. And when something goes wrong – when a boundary is crossed, or they hurt their victim in some way – they once again overwhelm their target with love and affection. It's a cycle known as love-bombing, one that allows a perpetrator to accelerate and intensify the bond between themselves and the other person. Sometimes, the person will also dig into their victim's trauma history, searching for things that can be weaponized in order to bring them closer together.

For me, the latter wasn't so much a part of the picture. In all honesty, Blake didn't have to try too hard. But what he *did* do well was to manipulate my emotions with the promise of love and to gaslight me into downplaying events that he believed 'weren't a big deal.'

In quiet moments, when I sat with myself, I knew – really knew – that this wasn't right. That I deserved more. Yet, knowing and accepting the truth are two very different beasts. The knowing gets pushed down by the *want*; the desire for something that will ease your pain. In my case, I couldn't *accept* that I deserved better because I'd never known what that looked like. I'd write honestly in my diary, scrawling reflections about how I deserved 'better than to be with junkies and alcoholics but couldn't stop going back to them.'

The trauma wounds inside of me were so deep that I couldn't stop myself from chasing 'love' in whatever form I could find it – even if it was just a mirage. A promised oasis that looked so wonderful and fulfilling, yet, the closer I got, simply vanished. Young men who pushed my boundaries, telling me they were 'falling in love with me,' only to stand me up or vanish days later. Guys like Blake who kept me on a string – one that I could have broken at any moment, yet never did. Over and over I went back. *I* did that – not them. But the emotional manipulation from each of these men, combined with the mental wounds inflicted by my father, left me in a vicious cycle of chasing, chasing, chasing.

It was as though I had a neon sign over my head, one that read: 'Tell me you love me, then disrespect me and watch how fast I run back to you.'

Every guy around me could sense it – and so could Blake. Everything was happening at micro speed, so slowly that it was impossible to clearly see the calculated patterns. It was a 'drip, drip, drip' effect, like a bathroom tap that hadn't been shut off tightly enough. At first you don't really hear it; you don't notice the accumulation of water pooling in the bathtub. You go about your day, focusing on all the other things that are vying for your attention, and it's only so much later that you see what's happening. When the bath inevitably begins to overflow you run to the tub and pull up the plug, releasing the pressure and sighing with relief.

But if you don't fix the leaky tap, it just builds all over again. Building, and building until, one day, you're drowning. Gasping for air as you flail around, staring at the wreckage of the life you knew and wondering how this could have happened. *Why didn't I see it? Why didn't I notice?*

This is where things were heading with Blake and I. Life was moving forward one drip at a time, and I was running around in ankle-deep water believing everything was just fine.

Chapter 14

'Happy birthday, baby!'

Blake stood before me, holding out a handful of gorgeous pink and yellow roses, each of them bursting with fresh droplets of morning dew. With a huge smile, I leapt into his arms and kissed him deeply. Things had been up and down lately, but I easily forgot them all the moment I laid eyes on the gorgeous blooms in his hands.

I wish he'd bought them himself, instead of stealing them from his neighbour's garden, I thought. Still, I kind of liked that Bad Boy side of him – and who was I to get picky about a bunch of flowers?

Jumping in my car, we headed down toward The Jetty, stopping in at a bottle shop on our way to meet up with SJ, Dan, and a bunch of my school mates. As I sat in the car daydreaming about the afternoon ahead, Blake's voice cut through my head.

'Hey, can I borrow some money?'

Standing outside the car, he leaned forward, both arms hanging through the open window. 'Just for some beers, you know?'

Are you for real? You're asking me for money on my birthday to buy drinks for yourself?

I stared back, pausing for just a moment before quickly hiding my anger.

'I... yeah, I guess.'

With a smile he skipped off, slinging a carton onto his back and then jumping back into the driver's seat with a grin. 'Let's go, birthday girl!' he cried, hitting the pedal and speeding down toward the beach.

Hours went by with laughter, drinks, and jokes, and Blake continued to get louder and rowdier as the sun sank lower toward the ocean. Counting the empty bottles on the bench-side table I felt my heart begin to sink. *How are we going to get home?* I wondered. *There's no way he's going to be under the legal drinking limit.* When I asked Blake, he waved away my concerns, stressing that he was fine to drive. I was tense and on edge the entire drive home, but there was nothing else I could do. I'd gotten myself into this situation and I wasn't going to ask Mum to come rescue me – I knew she disliked Blake, and this would only make it worse. However, as we arrived at my back door, it became obvious that he was in no condition to drive home and that he'd need to stay in our spare room. Mum was furious, her disgust tangible. *What is her problem?* I thought. *So he got a bit excited and drank too much? Big deal. When's she going to get over this and accept that we're together?*

Things continued on and off over the next few months, but once again, Blake was full of excuses as to why he couldn't commit to me. At this point I started dating a guy from my work, convinced that it was time to move on.

On a night in mid-2005 I was out for a few drinks with my boyfriend and some friends, and since I had no one to stay with in town that night, I asked Blake's mother if I could stay in their spare room. This in itself wasn't unusual. We got along really well, the two of us sharing a mutual love for her son and a desire to see him break free from his alcohol and drug issues, so I asked if it was okay to stay the night. This also shows the level of naïvety and innocence I still lived under, because I could have just stayed with my new boyfriend, but I thought it 'safer' to stay somewhere familiar until I got to know him better. On top of this, Blake was often away for large chunks of time, so there was every chance he wouldn't even be there.

As it turned out, he was, but he was quick to reassure me that I could sleep on the sofa. All was good. That is, until I came back later that night after my date and found Blake asleep in the living room; right where I should have been.

'What are you doing here?' I whispered.

'What do you mean?' Blake rolled over, staring at me. 'Oh, this? Yeah, looks like my sister's friend is staying over so I gave her my bed.'

'But you told me earlier that she was out!'

He shrugged, a sly smile on his face.

With nowhere to go, I climbed nervously onto the foldout, keeping my body as close to the edge as possible. As I tried to sleep, Blake leaned over and began to push his body toward mine, kissing the back of my neck. I pushed him away. Again and again, ignoring his advances until finally, he gave up. When his breathing evened out into a deep slumber I drifted off. Everything was okay until the next morning when I, once again, awoke to find that my jeans were undone. 'What did you do?' I barked.

'Can't you remember?' he smirked.

'I was asleep! I told you to leave me alone.'

'Well, you're in my bed, what was I meant to do?'

I sat in stunned silence. He asked the question as innocently as if he were asking me the time of day. It was infuriating.

'I told you I have a boyfriend, why would you do this?'

Suddenly he stared at me, his entire face changing. 'What? You never told me that.'

'I did! I told you that twice. *You knew.*'

'I didn't know.'

It was gaslighting in its purest form, and yet, I felt like I was going insane. That day, I left Blake's mother's house and with tears in my eyes, I swore that I would never go near him again. I was sick to my core and the thought of his leering face made me physically ill. *This time it's for real*, I resolved. *I'm never going back to him.*

For months I kept my distance, ignoring Blake anytime our paths crossed at the pub. It was around this time that I also got off my antidepressants. For me, I decided that I'd had enough. They weren't making a difference (probably because of the alcohol I was consuming) and my doctor didn't seem to care about helping me, so I decided to give them up. Instead, I threw my focus into what I hoped was going to be a fresh start for me – university.

The Stories We Carry

In Coffs Harbour, options for study were fairly limited at that time. Nursing. Marketing. Business. Accounting. That seemed to be about it. As a creative person, none of these ticked any boxes for me, but eventually I settled on a Bachelor of Arts, majoring in Creative Writing and Psychology. It felt like a nice balance between the creative, expressive side of my personality and the part that also longed to understand more about the human brain and why people make the decisions they do. As 2006 rolled around, I jumped head-first into uni life, picking a range of units across journalism, digital media, abnormal psychology, and writing. For the first time in so long I felt excited; like I had a sense of purpose. My friends SJ and Dan were also at the same campus – both of them studying psychology – and often we'd get together to study. Life was ticking along nicely and I was keeping my distance from Blake. But in a small town, it's only a matter of time before you run into people you know, and for me, this was the biggest hurdle when it came to breaking free from the power he had over me.

Sometimes, when I saw him on nights out, he'd shoot a look at me from across the room. Our eyes would lock, and in that moment I'd see a flash of pain. It made me feel so guilty, so torn. With just that one look – or a few words – he'd take me right back to all the memories of how good things could be. How *wanted* he made me feel. The special way that he saw me.

I couldn't bear that feeling; the one that reminded me so painfully of how carefree life felt when he was happy and all was good. I hated it. Hated the feeling of hurting him. Of having to see him and the sadness in his eyes when I was trying to move on with life. *I wish we could just go back to how things were*, I thought to myself. *Maybe I should just forget about all that stuff that happened. Even if we can just get back to being good friends, I won't have to feel so uncomfortable every time I run into him.*

One afternoon, I caved, and before I knew it I was swinging by his mother's house, my head going to war with my heart over what I was doing. My intention was to just hang out and talk. To find out how he was going, to be a good friend and try to encourage him toward something more positive in his life. *Maybe I can invite him along to church?* I thought. *Maybe he'll hear something that helps him to sort his life out?*

It was a naïve and hopeful wish, but that's honestly what I was thinking. Unfortunately, the moment I was there, the moment his eyes locked onto mine, I was back under his spell.

The water was rising once again, and by now, I was just completely ignoring it.

Chapter 15

'What would you do if I proposed right now?'

I stared in shock, my eyebrows darting together as I leaned against the side of the resort pool. Below me, Blake smiled giddily, hands sliding down the side of my hips.

'You idiot,' I smirked, splashing water in his face. 'As if I'd marry you.'

Blake pulled me across the pool, spinning me around and pressing his lips hard against mine. 'Wow, talk about rude,' he laughed. 'Although, I guess I deserved that.'

'Kind of.'

As I lifted my hands to splash another stream of water his way, Blake held them back. 'I know you think I'm joking, but I'm not.' Sensing my hesitation, he continued. 'I'm serious, Jas. It's taken me way too long to realise what I've been missing and I don't want to waste any more time.' He stared at me earnestly, droplets of water dripping from his hair. 'I really do love you.'

A strange little ripple of uncertainty ran through me but I pushed it away, darting out of his grip and kicking water in his face again with a flirty grin. 'Of *course* you do. Every guy loves me,' I teased light-heartedly.

'You are too much, you know that?'

'Yep.'

Things had begun ramping up with Blake since I'd run into him at the pub the night before. He'd been ecstatic to see me, grabbing my hand and twirling me in circles, as we jumped and sang at the top of our lungs to Love Generation. When I'd left at 2 am to head home with SJ and Dan, he'd grabbed my hand and pulled me closer, begging me to stay. 'I adore you, you know that?' he whispered. 'My whole family loves you and I can't believe it's taken me so long to tell you how I feel.' Though his words sank deep into my heart, filling the cracks that had felt like gaping wounds for so much of my life, I still felt a niggling discomfort. I needed more time to think about him – about us – and where things were going. So, instead of leaving with Blake, I stayed with my friends, promising to meet up with him for a morning swim. Now, sitting on the edge of the pool, I wondered if things really were changing for the better. It certainly looked that way from the outside, but instinctively, I wanted to wait and see.

Looking back, I find it difficult to explain how someone who didn't even have a reliable contact number had such a strong pull over me. There were no incessant phone calls or abusive texts. No stalking, or special apps that helped him track where I was. The reality was this: there was a constant mystique around our 'relationship.' The fact that I rarely knew when I'd see him, and that our time together mostly played out through spontaneity, meant that our interactions were always emotionally charged. It was mysterious, secretive, impulsive. He kept me on my toes and the moments we were together were often filled with music and alcohol – two of the most powerful influencers on the brain. When he kissed me on the dance floor, with the lyrics and music of Love Generation or Michael Jackson rushing through my veins, I felt like I was in another world. Almost as if I were sparkling with joy.

A few days later while out with SJ and Dan, I ran into Blake again. With his 'proposal' still fresh in my mind, I ran through the crowd and threw my arms around him. 'Hey *you*,' I winked. In the gyrating, sweaty mess of bodies, I felt his hips swivel, his face turning toward mine. I waited for those narrow blue eyes that I adored to drink me in but the moment I saw them, I felt as though I were looking at a complete stranger. A cloud passed over his face, his gaze hardening into a veneer of contempt. 'What are you doing.' His voice was bitter and terse; more of a statement than a question. 'I'm out with the boys – can't you see?'

'Oh.' Suddenly I felt as though I were in trouble. 'Hey, that's cool,' I said, forcing my voice to stay light and casual. 'But there's no reason we can't have a dance together, yeah?' I slipped my hand into his but he only pushed it away.

'Jas, *I said I'm with the boys.*' He repeated the phrase as though I were a naughty kid who'd done the wrong thing; a child who should know better, but still needed to be reprimanded.

'Blake, what's wrong? I'm just trying to say hi. I don't need you to hang out with me all night,' I reasoned.

'Look,' he sighed, his irritation growing. 'I'm busy. Can't you see? Also, I've got like, a thousand bucks in my pocket right now.' He lifted his nose in the air, staring me down like a stupid, inferior child. 'I could be anywhere. Doing anything.Stop demanding me to hang out with you.'

'But... I... I'm not.' Hot, angry shame coursed through me, my eyes beginning to sting and redden. *Why does he have to be so cruel?* I wondered. *How can he treat me like a queen one day, and then be so mean the next?*

Before I could say another word, Blake turned his back on me and walked away, swaying to the music and laughing heartily with his mates as they chugged down beers. Holding back tears, I turned and made my way back through the drunken crowd in search of my friends. But by now, they were gone; nowhere to be found.

Suddenly, an elbow nudged me gently, a voice calling out from my left. I spun around, my anxiety easing slightly as I looked into the dark brown eyes of my friend Raj, a guy who often hung out with the boys in my friendship circle. 'You all good?' he asked gently.

Quickly, I pasted a fake smile across my face. 'Yeah of course!' I lied. 'How've you been?'

'Yeah, good. Dan and SJ just sent me to find you. They've gone to get some more drinks. Wanna hang here for a bit with me? They should be back soon.'

'Sure.'

I followed Raj to a side table, sitting and talking with him as Blake continued to run around the dance floor like an idiot. We were just starting to get into a deep conversation, with Raj sharing with me about something funny that had happened to him that week, when I saw a flash of movement from behind. Suddenly, Blake appeared beside me, his hand around my waist, his lips curved into a smile. But then he saw Raj, and everything changed.

The Stories We Carry

'What are *you* looking at, *Coco Pop?*'

Instantly my face drained, a burning heat working its way through every pore.

'Blake!' I was so taken aback I could barely speak; I could stare only at Raj, my mouth open in shock. 'What the hell is wrong with you?' I seethed.

Blake, on the other hand, took no notice. 'What are you doing talking to my girl? Huh, *black boy?*'

'Blake, stop it!'

Raj stood, walking around to my side of the table as if nothing had happened. 'Wanna get out of here? We can go find Dan or head somewhere else,' he added quietly.

'Yes. Yes, I do.' I picked up my clutch and jumped down from the bar stool.

Instantly, Blake was behind me.

'Are you seriously going to leave? Aww come on, I'm going to be so *devo* if I have to leave alone.'

I shook my head furiously and walked away, my cheeks feeling as though they were on fire. As we walked through the front doors I turned once and looked back, Blake's eyes staring sadly after me.

I shook my head again, disgusted. Then I left.

There's a place not far from where I grew up called Urunga. Set on the mid-north coast of NSW, between Coffs Harbour and Nambucca Heads, it's a beautiful little town with farmland on one side and stunning, unspoiled beaches on the other. A thin road snakes around the riverbend, following rows of old boat sheds until it brings you to the local pub, a small line of shops, and a long boardwalk that juts straight out to the ocean. There's an overwhelming sense of beauty and peacefulness that envelops the area and as you set foot on the weathered walkway, it feels as though you're in the calmest place on earth. What most tourists don't know, however, is that only a few minutes ahead, the shimmering, still waters transform into a raging current. The wind abruptly slashes around your face, whipping tears into your eyes, and to the left, the river gathers speed, pouring straight into the ocean and dragging everything in its path straight out to sea.

It happens so quickly, you barely even notice until you're right there.

When I think about Blake, this is exactly how I see our relationship. It had taken almost two years to get to this point, and by now, I was caught in a raging torrent that was pulling me faster than I could swim. He was now in overdrive, doing everything he could to prove his love to me and no matter how mortified I was by his recent behaviour, I couldn't see just how bad things were. Like so many victim-survivors, I was blinded and confused by his intense love-bombing and struggled to see the reality of what was happening. On top of that, I was also nervous about confronting him about his behaviour. His unpredictable anger, combined with the way he looked at me when I'd disappointed him, felt too much to handle. It seemed easier to just try and move on. I told myself it must have simply been the alcohol talking. He was trying; he just needed more support.

The Stories We Carry

Was I horrified by his racist, aggressive treatment of Raj? Yes, absolutely. So much so that I still feel a hot flush of shame when I think about it. At the time, however, I didn't understand or know enough about what I was truly going through to escape from the current and choose to swim in a different direction.

Once again, I was repeating the lessons I'd learned during my years with Dad – watching my mother be the mediator. The way she calmed and settled him down. The way she rode out the storms, patiently waiting for the sunshine. Why did I think he was worth it? Because when Blake was good, he was *so good*.

About a month after our awkward night at the pub, he invited me out for dinner. It was significant, because in the 18 months I'd known him, not once had he ever invited me on a real date. Sure, we'd had beach walks, bush hikes, and afternoons spent watching DVDs together – but never a real date. I was under intense stress with Mum being away interstate for surgery, and had been looking after my little brother in her absence, so the promise of a night out was desperately welcoming.

That evening, as I walked through the doors of the Greenhouse Tavern with Blake holding my hand, I felt so grown up. The night was perfect, with laughter and good food and margaritas, and for the first time in almost two years, I realised how simple everything felt. How *easy and carefree* the entire date was. So much so that I forgot the nasty way he'd spoken to me only days prior, telling me to 'stop boring him' by talking about my mum's surgery. Here, in the moment, everything was perfect.

It was only as we exited off the Pacific Highway and made our way through the tree-lined forests of my country suburb, that I felt things change. His voice was light, but it felt forced.

'Do you get a lot of guys looking at you when you're out?'

The question took me by surprise, making me do a double take. 'Um, I dunno,' I laughed, unsure of where he was heading with this odd question. 'I guess.'

'I just...' He let go of my hand, changing gears to slow down for one of the upcoming turns on our narrow, winding road. 'It's just that you're really important to me, Jas. And I know that it's really important to you to wait for the right guy. I guess what I'm saying is, I don't want you giving it away to *just* anyone.' His voice tensed a little, almost as though I'd done something to wound him. 'I'd hate for you to give it away to someone who doesn't really care. The way I do,' he emphasised.

Where is this coming from? I wondered. *Blake and I have known each other for a long time by now. Doesn't he know me? I was dating a guy from work for three months and we never slept together. What makes him think I'm just going to randomly jump into bed with a stranger from the pub?* He knew how much sex meant to me. That I wanted to wait for the right person; whether that meant marriage or not, it had to be the kind of serious relationship that I knew was going to last. Also, given that Blake and I had only just started to become serious after 18 months of him giving me hot/cold vibes, this insinuation felt grossly offensive.

I shrugged it off. 'Guys can pay attention to me, but it doesn't matter,' I stated. 'I'm not that kind of girl.'

'Your first time should be really special. You need a guy who will give you roses, and treat you like a princess. You know that, right?' His jaw tensed, the action catching my eye as we sped toward home.

The Stories We Carry

'Yeah, of course.'

He squeezed my hand tighter, smiling.

When he kissed me goodnight a few minutes later, I walked into my room with more questions than ever.

I thought back to a month or so earlier, when he'd returned from a weekend out of town; the same weekend when he'd suddenly announced that he was in love with me. Something had happened during that trip. What, exactly, I didn't know, but it had something to do with running into his ex-girlfriend. 'She gave me a letter,' he'd said, one side of his lips curving downwards. 'It was full of bullshit. I tried to talk to her but she wouldn't even speak to me.'

At the time I hadn't thought much of it; but to be honest, I was curious. I'd seen where he'd placed it, that day that he pronounced his love for me. I saw the paper sticking out from his bedside table. And in the months to come, I regretted not taking the opportunity to read it.

If only I had, maybe I wouldn't have hung out with Blake that one final time. Maybe I would have walked away, saving myself from the storm that was about to swallow me whole. But we can never know what is coming in life; we can only react. In that time, I was a highly traumatised young woman without the skills to understand or read the warning signs that were waving frantically before her. The rising water was all around me by now, lapping at my neck. And all I could hear was the gentle 'drip, drip, drip' from the rain outside, not realising that I was walking right toward a tidal wave of trouble. One that everyone else except me could see coming a mile away.

Jas Rawlinson

If I have to listen to another word from Zazu, I swear I'm going to lose my shit.

Sitting at the crowded kitchen table, I glared across at my friend's boyfriend and wished, for the millionth time, that I was anywhere other than here. Jeremy was one of those guys who never shut up, and liked to insert *'Fuck'* into every sentence. We'd nicknamed him 'Zazu' after the annoying bird from the Disney classic, 'The Lion King.'

All around, my friends were laughing and having a great time, but all I could think about was how alone I felt. Two years had passed since Dad's death, and in that time, I'd tried my best not to think of him. Only once had I ever visited his gravestone; a quiet, random day in late 2004 when I'd collapsed at the foot of his plot and screamed in agony. 'Are you happy?' I'd sobbed. 'Are you happy that I'm still in so much pain? That every guy I care about hurts me? That nothing in my life ever works out? You must be over the moon that there are so many guys waiting to pick up where you left off when it comes to hurting me.' I'd been full of rage and hatred; so far beyond saving, in that moment. It wasn't long afterwards that I overdosed on my medication.

All this time I'd tried desperately not to think of Dad. For the most part I did a good job, but today, I couldn't hold back the misery any longer. Since I'd awoken that morning I'd felt painfully aware of his absence. I'd never admit it out loud, but deep down, I longed desperately to see him again. I wanted one last chance to talk to him, to know if he'd ever really loved me. Was it his mental illness that made him treat me like a burden? Or did he actually hate me? I had no answers, and answers were what I wanted. It plagued me

The Stories We Carry

all throughout the day; the knowledge that I'd never have a chance to find out. That I'd never have an opportunity to fix things. Even worse, however, was the voice inside my head that told me I was alone with these feelings. *Who's going to understand? Who's going to want to listen to this shit?* I asked myself.

No one, came the reply.

So, even though I hated the thought of spending a night in Zazu's company, I agreed to go out with my friends – if only to escape the pain inside my brain for a few hours. Out of nostalgia I went to the bottle shop and purchased a tall glass bottle of my parents' favourite liquor, even though I usually hated the taste of wine. *You only live once,* I thought.

To this day I'm not sure if it was the trauma of my mental state, the wine, or if the drink I bought at the pub had been spiked, because all I remember is standing at a bar table with Blake, his eyes gazing at me adoringly as he asked me to leave with him. All I wanted was to be comforted; to not be alone as I navigated the pain of no longer having my father in my life. I just wanted it to stop.

I don't remember how Blake got there or what we talked about inside the venue, but to this day I'll never forget what happened afterwards. Most of all, that I trusted him – and in the end, he used that against me in the worst possible way.

'Jas, where are you?'

Standing outside the automatic doors of the Bailey Centre petrol station, I felt my feet sway unsteadily. I laughed, giggling to myself as I took my heels off, clutching my phone in one hand and my shoes in the other. Beside me, Blake reached out a hand.

'I'm oww'side,' I slurred, pulling my phone closer to my ear. 'But don't worry Dan, I'm wif Blake.' I shivered in the cool autumn night air, regretting the ankle-length white skirt and singlet I'd chosen to wear. The outfit seemed like a good idea when I'd picked it out earlier, but now, I was freezing.

'Okay. Just wait there, we'll come and get you.' On the other end of the line I heard a muffled scraping as the phone was passed from Dan to someone else. Then, SJ's voice came through the speaker.

'Jas, wait there, sweetie. We'll come and get you, okay?'

Ugh, why do they care? I wondered. *I've stayed at Blake's mum's house so many times – and anyways, if I have to listen to another minute of Zazu talking, I will honestly lose it.*

Now, standing outside the Bailey Centre, I waved off Dan's concerns. 'Nah,' I giggled. Really, s'all good. Don't worry. I'm wif Blake. S'cool.'

Eventually Dan and SJ gave up, and Blake and I continued, walking along the quiet stretch of highway between the clubs and his house, eventually arriving at the front door. Like I had so many times before, I walked through the screen door, found the warmth of his bed, and lay down to sleep. I was tired, so tired. My eyes drooped, heavier than they'd ever been. On top of that, I felt unusually dizzy. As I lay on the mattress with my long white skirt curled around my ankles, I watched Blake through half-closed lids. Waiting for his arms to wrap protectively around me and to kiss away the pain that was an ever-constant weight on my heart.

The Stories We Carry

Instead, he walked across the room to his chest of drawers and pulled out a small black box. I could see the logo; one I'd glanced at casually in the supermarket while buying tampons. I knew what it was, but I couldn't understand why he was holding it in his hands. *Something here is wrong*, I thought to myself through the fog. *This doesn't make sense.*

My head felt like fairy floss, but somewhere deep inside, a memory pushed forward. One of Blake and I chatting at dinner the week prior. The words he'd spoken as he drove me home.

'I care about you Jas. I don't even keep condoms in my house, because I know how important it is to you to wait. I don't want to be tempted. Your first time has to be special.'

My head swam, but the words kept circling round. Meanwhile, he walked calmly toward me, the small square of plastic still firmly in one hand. He reached down and picked up my arm, placing it on his stomach. But the moment he let go it fell limply by my side.

I was so tired, so exhausted from trauma and a night of drinking that I couldn't move. I felt the alcohol buzzing through me, my eyes begging for sleep, but he wouldn't let me. Again, he lifted my arm, this time sliding down my underwear.

My body lay still, my lips frozen shut. My head suddenly felt very separated from the rest of my body and no matter how much I wanted to, I couldn't move. All the while, four words danced on repeat inside my brain.

This doesn't make sense.

Then, *He wouldn't do this. This isn't happening. This can't be real.*

He spoke four words to me; words that I just can't repeat here, but that I've never forgotten. Those words told me that he was fully conscious of his actions, and that he had absolutely no remorse. He didn't care about me at all at that moment.

The house was eerily quiet; the sky so dark I couldn't see his face. But I heard those cold words. I understood, very clearly, even if my body didn't.

That's when my brain disconnected.

That's when everything went black.

All I remember after this, in the space where my brain and body reconnected, were the tears streaming down my face. The quiet sobs that wracked the cage around my heart and lungs, and the anguish of my voice as I cried for the one person I wanted.

My father.

Instead, there was only Blake. His arms around my chest, his voice steady and comforting. He acted as though he were a loving boyfriend hugging me close after waking from a nightmare – not a cruel, abusive rapist who was *responsible* for the very nightmare.

Eventually, he fell asleep, leaving me in the privacy of my own thoughts as the tears dried on my face. I had no idea what time it was or how long had passed. Only that I felt so alone – so consumed by this feeling of needing my father – that I couldn't even process what had happened beforehand. As I lay there, the sobs once again started. They were growing louder and more hysterical by the moment.

The Stories We Carry

It took some time before I realised that it wasn't me who was screaming; it was someone else.

Quietly, I rolled back the blanket and padded through the house, the sobbing noises intensifying as I reached the living area. There, on the edge of the couch, sat Blake's little sister. Tears streamed down her face, her blonde hair matted, stuck around the edges of her mouth. Two red eyes looked up at me, filled to the brim with shame.

'Rebecca, what's wrong?' I squinted under the harsh lights, curling up beside her and reaching out a hand. I'd met Blake's sister many times over the last two years, and though she was much younger than me, I had a soft spot for her. 'Becca? Hey, let's go outside,' I said softly. 'Come on, come with me.'

Leading the way, I guided her through to the backyard, the two of us sitting on a small brick retaining wall with our feet dangling over the edge.

I spoke again, asking her – more softly this time – what had happened. 'It's just... it sounds stupid, don't worry about it.'

'It's not stupid. What's going on?' I pressed.

'I just really miss my dad,' she sobbed. 'He was such an asshole. He was so awful to me, and I haven't seen him in years, but for some reason I just can't stop loving him.' She broke down as she spoke the last few words, a heavy ball of emotion releasing itself from within. *Oh babe... I get it*, I wanted to say. *Oh, how I get it.* But I couldn't tell her, right now. It wasn't the time, it wasn't the place. I barely even understood what had just been done to me.

'It's not dumb,' I said softly. 'Emotions are a weird thing, aren't they? They don't always make sense, and we can't always turn them off, even when it feels like we should be able to.'

'Yeah,' she sniffed.

I don't remember much of what we talked about after that. The trauma of her story was so overwhelming that I could focus only on giving myself fully to Becca, of holding this space for her, as she cried and sobbed, until she was utterly empty. Then, I helped her back to bed.

There was no space left within my brain to think about the extraordinary irony of this moment. That I was sitting in my abuser's house, comforting his sister about the harms that men had acted out against her at such a young age. Empathising over the love for an absent father who had broken the trust invested in him, over and over again. The shock that her own brother had just done the same thing to me.

I told myself that there would be time later. Right now though, it was all too much.

Chapter 16

As a child, I was addicted to a movie named The Neverending Story. It was a 1980s classic, and one that many adults probably remember well. On weekends I'd curl my body into a small ball on the end of my neighbour's couch, and sit wide-eyed as a story filled with dragons, mystery, and adventure took place. We'd cower as the young boy Atreyu fought a wolf-like monster called Gmork – a creature that wanted to help The Nothing (a force of bleak despair that was overtaking the world) to destroy everyone and everything; and we'd whoop with joy as the main character, Bastian – once a bullied, fragile kid – found his strength, swooping down from the sky on his beloved Luck Dragon Falkor, to chase down the boys who'd once tormented him.

It was a movie about many things; of courage and bravery and the power of books. A story about taking a stand – for both the world and yourself – and not giving in to The Nothing. Or, equally as terrifying, the Swamp of Sadness – a place that had the power to kill you if you allowed your sadness to take hold. Ask any child of the '80s and they'll probably tell you that the one scene they remember most in The Neverending Story is the one in which Atreyu attempts to cross the Swamp of Sadness, only for his beloved horse to become stuck, his hooves and legs sinking into the molasses-like water. Atreyu screams and lashes out, begging for Artax to fight against the sadness; to 'try'. In the end, though, nothing he says makes a difference. Artax can't move – won't move – and so, he eventually perishes beneath the muddy waters of the Swamp of Sadness.

It was a deeply upsetting film for a sensitive young girl like myself to watch and I could never get past that scene without collapsing into a flood of tears, but as the years went on, I realised something else. Something I'd never thought of.

I was Artax.

Since the age of ten I'd felt just like that horse; trapped, and too afraid to step forward and fight for a life that I deserved. For almost a decade I'd lived inside a fantasy world where, if only Dad could disappear, I believed I'd be freed from the Swamp of Sadness. Now, I could see that the swamp had never really left. At times it rippled and dipped, retreating just enough to allow my toes to touch solid ground; giving me space to catch my breath and hold myself above water for a little longer – but it was never gone. All this time I'd thought of my depression as a black dog, but now I saw that it was more like *The Nothing*; an invisible force of despair that never ended.

Now, lying alone in my room, I felt like I understood the film in a way that the ten-year-old version of me couldn't. Blake hadn't created The Nothing, but his abuse was the final nail in the coffin; the thing that might just allow the bleakness to finally take over.

From beneath the covers of my bed, I gazed vacantly toward the sky blue rafters, watching the way the cobwebs swayed like delicate, frayed tissue paper. Somewhere in the distance a cow bellowed and a kookaburra cackled wildly. There was the soft creak of the roof as it expanded from the warmth of the sun, a bark from a neighbour's dog; signs of life that told me it was well and truly time to get up. Underneath my blankets, however, I lay motionless, weighted down by the invisible concrete blocks that pinned me to the mattress. Two across each arm and another one placed over my stomach. The weight of all that I was carrying, all that was weighing me down, felt enormous; it was almost as though I could feel the death of my soul as it leached into the mattress, leaving an imprint of pain and shame in its place. I wondered, did Blake have any idea how I was feeling? Did he care? Or was he still walking around with a smile on his face, the same way he had on the morning after he raped me.

Don't think about it, screamed my head. *Get up. It's time to get up.*

All I wanted to do was forget about everything he'd done, but I was so confused by what had happened that I couldn't stop going over and over and over it. I was like a pedantic mother with a fine-toothed comb, clawing through every inch of her child's hair as she searched for the last remaining knot; the one that she couldn't quite untangle. I analysed it all: the nice breakfast that he'd taken me out for in the morning, hours after his assault. The shame, as I'd asked him what had happened the night before. The sickening smirk he couldn't quite hide, as he took delight in magnifying my confusion. His words. The countless *What do you mean?* and *Nothing happened* comments. The way he belittled and gaslit me, as he switched – with a smile and stroke of my hair – to, 'Awww, can't you remember? You're so cute. Just don't worry about it baby, it's no big deal. We had fun.'

And finally, his dismissal: 'Nothing happened, Jas. Don't worry about it.'

At no point did I ever think seriously about going to the police. Truthfully, I never knew it was an option. As a young woman barely out of my teens, I didn't believe you could be raped by someone you knew, or had dated, and when I tried to tell a girl from school what had happened, she told me just as much. 'You dated him, so you can't claim he raped you, Jas,' she frowned. 'You were hanging out, so you can't blame him.'

My intuition told me that she was wrong – that I had every right to be upset – but I couldn't fight against the stigma and shame within; all the other voices that talked me down, when I tried to get to the core of what had been done to me. The ones that told me, 'You deserved it,' and, 'You heard what Blake said – nothing happened.'

So I stayed silent. I swapped social gatherings for the safety of my home, and spent my mornings struggling to peel myself off my mattress.

Now, lying in bed under the weight of all these thoughts, I stared at the ceiling and wondered how I was going to make it through the day. Eventually, with just enough strength to roll out from under the covers, I shuffled my way out the door and down the hallway. Like a robot completing a checklist, I moved through each action. *Shower. Find ugly blue uniform. Eat. Grab keys. Drive to work. Survive the day. Smile at people and pretend everything is okay.*

Some hours later, I was standing behind my desk, printing some package labels, when a male voice broke through my concentration.

'Hey.'

I jumped, my throat closing over in panic. Then I saw his face – middle aged and normal, with kind and concerned eyes. It wasn't Blake. *Pull yourself together, Jas. It's not him, it's fine.* Mentally, I chastised myself, trying to force my nervous system to calm down. No matter what I did, though, my body just wouldn't listen. There was a tornado rising within, and it was growing stronger by the second.

The man dumped a pile of items onto the counter. 'Can I lay-by these? Not sure if I have an account. But you can use this if you need,' he said casually, flicking an ID card onto the bench.

The Stories We Carry

I nodded politely, averting my gaze and trying my best to force my lips into a thin smile. By now my fingers were trembling and my jaw clenched so hard I thought my teeth might break. The stranger shuffled on the spot, his eyes narrowing in on me.

'Hey, are you okay?'

Briefly, I stole a quick glance upwards, taking in his kind eyes and the worried etchings between each brow.

'I'm...' My speech slowed, my head whirring. Inside, the hurricane spun faster.

Please don't hurt me. Please don't hurt me. Please don't hurt me.

The words begged to be released but I held them back, allowing each one to continue circling inside my throat. Instead, I forced a lie; an excuse about how it had been a 'long day.' I could barely remember the words as they left my lips. I just wanted the man to go. To leave. To never come near me again.

After what felt like an eternity I handed over his receipt and pasted on a clumsy smile, the tornado slowly dissipating as he retreated. Only when he – and the storm – had disappeared, did I see the aftermath of all I had been left with, as a survivor of sexual assault. In one word, it was this: *Loss.*

Loss is what I had been left with.

In the back of the lay-by department, hidden from sight, I grieved silently for the girl who had been lost on that night, several days earlier. I grieved the loss of her innocence and all that Blake had taken in the space of just one night. Not just her trust in him, but in herself and the world. Something as simple as going to work now felt like an enormous mountain that had to be overcome every day. Something as simple as speaking to a male customer, now felt intimidating and terrifying, and all because of his biological sex.

Once upon a time, I only had to worry about being hurt by men in clubs or in dark alleyways. Now, that danger felt like it was everywhere. It made no sense logically, but that's the thing about trauma – it manifests in unique ways; ways designed to keep us safe.

Loud and clear, I could hear my trauma telling me: 'You are not safe. No matter where you go, or what you do…' More than ever, there seemed to be so many things to worry about. But my worries were not just for my own safety, they were also for what might be going on *inside* of me.

Suddenly, I remembered the pregnancy test I'd seen in the back of the layby area; a half-open packet that had been added to the 'stolen goods' bucket. It was a basket where empty packets or unsellable, damaged items were kept so that the team could write up a loss statement, and earlier that day I'd spotted a Clear Blue packet poking out from the top. One of the tests had been stolen, but the other was still there.

Now, I dug it out from the bin, staring once again at the box. *Maybe it would be okay if the other one went missing, too. I mean, it's only going to end up in the trash.*

Heart pounding, I grabbed the plastic-covered stick and shoved it into my pocket, ready and waiting for the moment my shift finished. Then, I rushed to the upstairs bathroom and tore the plain white wand from its protective film.

The Stories We Carry

What will I do if it's positive? I wondered. *Oh God, please don't let it be positive. I don't think I can go through with something like this. I don't want to have to even think about things like abortions. What will Mum say if I decide not to have it? What will people think of me? Will I go to hell?*

Alone on the toilet, I thought of all the times in high school that I'd looked down on women who'd chosen abortions. How simplistically I'd viewed it; that a woman should absolutely, 100%, *always* keep the baby. Now, as I waited for the test to develop, I thought about the cold facts of reality.

I was a 20-year-old girl working in retail. I'd just started university. I was facing a future where, if I was pregnant, Blake would have leverage to force his way back into my life and might pressure me to share that baby with him. I'd be a young, single mother whose opportunities of graduating from university would now be so much harder. How would I even support a kid on my meagre part-time wage? How would I have the energy to finish my studies? How would I feel when I passed Blake or his family in town, and they saw me with a baby?

Nothing was simple anymore.

Holding my breath, I stared down at the stick. Then I blinked. *Is it... is it true?* I looked for a moment longer, focusing on the thin blue line. And then, in one long rush of air, I exhaled.

It was negative.

That day, I felt the smallest brick being taken from my back and placed onto the ground. I realised, in the bathroom of my workplace, just how much a woman's life could change in a second. For better or worse. How one man's actions had put me in a place where I had to question my own values, and most importantly, what I'd truly do in order to be free from him.

There are so many things to consider when you've been through something as soul-destroying as rape or sexual assault. But the thought of telling my family was about the worst. For the first two weeks I tried to keep it to myself, ignoring my mother's concerned questions and the fear that was bubbling just below the surface every time she looked at me. The way that she could sense my secrecy; that inner knowing that every loving parent holds, when they sense something isn't right. I couldn't stand to hurt her, so I went about my days as normally as possible, lying and pretending, while dying on the inside.

Then, one afternoon, everything changed.

'Hey Jas! Blake's on the phone.'

Standing in the hallway, I felt my body root into the ground. My face drained of blood and my brain slowed down. In a panic I rushed in the opposite direction, stepping into the shower. 'I'm in the bathroom!' I yelled back. 'Can't talk right now.'

Minutes later, Mum appeared outside my bedroom door, turning the knob and walking in before I could protest. 'Jas, what's going on?' she prodded. 'Why do you suddenly not want to talk to him?'

'I just don't. Okay?' I turned away, my words flinging sharply outward like barbed weapons. Instantly my eyes began to mist over.

The Stories We Carry

'What happened?' Mum's voice was quickly moving from curiosity to anger; she knew something was wrong, and as the most intuitive person I'd ever met, I knew she wouldn't give up until I relented. In all honesty, I think she already knew.

That moment of having to tell my mother the truth was, in some ways, worse than what I actually experienced. It was like handing a baton of death to another human and knowing exactly what was about to happen, and worst of all that you were responsible.

There are few times I've ever seen my mother so angry and devastated. Even after Dad's suicide, I rarely saw her cry. Sometimes I'd hear a strangled sob coming from the privacy of her bedroom – the intense kind of grief that was kept behind closed doors – but I never saw that rage or hurt spill out before me. Blake's actions on that night unleashed a side of her that I'd never experienced; a side I hope to never again witness. At the time I hated my mother for how she reacted, but in time I realised that she was a heartbroken parent who was trying to process the gravity of the harm done to her child. She was a woman blaming herself for not being able to keep her daughter safe, and that anger spilled outwards in imperfect ways.

When the storm quietened and my mother's voice grew smaller, I saw a change come over her. With shaking hands, she leaned across the space between us and looked at me. "You can make a choice right now,' she said somberly. 'You can decide whether you give him the power, or you take that power back.'

'What do you mean?'

'You can choose to deny him that power. To decide that he hasn't taken anything from you,' she repeated firmly. 'It's your choice.'

Amidst everything that she'd said, this was what I focused on.

Over the next week Blake tried to call a few more times, but I ignored them. It took me two weeks, but eventually, when I realised that the flashbacks and nightmares weren't going anywhere, I knew there was only one thing left to do. I had to confront him.* With trembling fingers I dialled his number, forcing my voice to stay calm and steady. *Be fun*, I told myself. *Pretend everything is okay. Just listen to this dumb story he's telling about his favourite musician and play along. Tell him you want to hang out and then leave it at that.*

Carrying out my plan to confront Blake was one of the hardest things I'd ever done up until that point, but I knew it was important for me, so I held my ground. On a weekday afternoon in autumn, just before my 21st birthday, I called him and arranged to meet outside a public venue where he often spent a lot of time. Then, I sat anxiously in the driver's seat of my car, watching and waiting as he bounded across the road like a happy-go-lucky dog.

'What's up, baby?'

What's up?! How about I rip that stupid smile right off your dumb face and show you what's up? I seethed.

'Get in the car for a sec.' My voice was shaky, my fingers trembling. For a moment he looked back over one shoulder, briefly hesitating. Then, he eased inside.

The moment his hips dipped into the seat of my car, I lost it. All composure was gone, my plans for 'keeping calm' a thing of the

---

* Every person's experience of Domestic Violence is different and it is not always safe to confront an abuser. Your personal safety should be the utmost priority.

past. I yelled. I screeched. I coughed up a garbled stream of words about how sick I'd been for the past few weeks; how nauseous I'd made myself as I struggled with the burden of wondering if I was pregnant or had some kind of STD. How degraded and angry I felt. How devastating it was to have him take my trust and break it in such a horrific way. The words continued streaming out; a torrent of verbal vomit. And all the while, he stared at me in shock. As though I were a stranger, someone he'd never met. *What's happened to her? She's totally lost it.*

He leaned backwards, creating distance between our bodies. 'What's your problem?' he spat. 'It's not like we've never done anything sexual before.'

Is he kidding? Is he actually kidding right now?

I felt the sucker punch of his words colliding with my insides, causing me to inhale sharply. 'Yes, WHEN I WAS SOBER,' I yelled. 'Never like this... and never what you did. You knew what my boundaries were. *You knew.* You've always known!' I choked on a large, salty sob. 'When are you going to grow up, Blake? When are you going to stop acting like a kid with no responsibilities and actually take responsibility for the things you do to people?'

He turned, eyes ablaze. It was a look I'd seen so many times before on my father's face. Cold contempt mixed with the joy of stabbing a verbal knife into your gut and twisting it. *My God*, I realised. *He's Jekyll and Hyde. He's my father. All along, he's been this person. All this time.*

A childish sneer came over his lips and he half-choked on a laugh. 'Never,' he jeered. 'I'm never going to grow up. I'm more than happy smoking cones and playing golf forever.'

I stared for a half second, and then I erupted. 'Get out!' I raised my voice higher than I'd ever dreamed possible, my words travelling outside of the bubble in which we sat. 'Get out and never, ever speak to me again. GET OUT GET OUT GET –'

Whoomp!

The door slammed on my voice, Blake's legs propelling him around the car as he fled back toward the pub with a dismissive shake of his head. I could read everything in that one movement. I knew exactly what his first words would be when he found his mates. *Wow. What a crazy bitch she turned out to be. Ruined my fucking night and everything.*

Knuckles white, hands wrapped around the wheel, I realised for the first time that this feeling was what had kept me in a cycle of running back to him. That look on his face, right there. For 18 months I'd allowed my need to be loved at all costs to rule my decisions, and it stopped me from saying what needed to be said. I ran from the discomfort of my feelings, from the fear of what might happen if I took a stand, and the confusion that overwhelmed me every time I was under the warm glow of his smile. The one that made me question everything. *Was it really that bad or are you just making things worse in your own head? He said he didn't do anything when you were asleep — why are you making a big deal? Maybe you didn't make it clear you had a boyfriend and that's why he tried to touch you. I mean, you did say you'd told him, but maybe it wasn't obvious enough.*

Every time he hurt me, I burned and erased the memories; watching them shrivel into soft, flaky ashes, like the high school notebooks I'd tossed into the fireplace after graduation. *Don't need to remember that anymore.* Every time, Dr Jekyll would be there to blur the truth and cover for the actions of Mr Hyde, making me believe I was going insane, and that it was all in my head. But now, I couldn't forget. No matter how much I wanted to.

As I pulled away from the curb, heading toward town, I remembered a conversation I'd had with April a few days earlier and the anger that had exploded from her lips when I'd finally told her what Blake had done to me. 'But he took me out for breakfast the next morning,' I said. 'He paid so much money for my meal – it was really expensive. How can I turn around and be angry at him and accuse him of assault after that?' On my phone screen, her words appeared in short, angry lines.

'Jas, I don't care if he fucking bought you a $100 dress. *What he did was wrong!*'

I couldn't believe it then, but I believed it now. Most importantly, I knew with finality that nothing would ever make me run back to him. The fog of his emotional abuse had lifted, and just like sunlight beaming through the haze of a cold, frosty morning, I could finally see the glimmer of what lay beyond. A road forward; a path toward something more.

Chapter 17

What helped you move forward after that experience? How did you learn to have healthy relationships?

Over the years, I've been asked variations on these questions many times by podcast hosts and audience members, and every time I think about the two very different answers I have. One is complex, and includes a lot of detail about the lengths I had to go to in order to learn how to create boundaries, to reconnect with my intuition, and to work through my trauma. Another part of me feels that I just got lucky – that I was sent a blessing from God/The Universe that made my journey so much easier. I feel it's important to talk about both, and how they intertwine.

In the days and weeks after that intense confrontation, I did what I had to in order to survive; I literally got out of bed each day, got dressed, and made my way to work or university. One of the kindest things that happened during this time – a moment I've never forgotten – was the morning where my friend SJ asked me to hang out with her boyfriend for the day while she was at work. On the surface it wasn't that odd, as Dan and I had been best friends since the day we'd met – even after the infamous 'Glow Stick Incident' of 2005. He was a gentle soul; two mischievous blue eyes set beneath a mop of light brown hair and a silver eyebrow piercing. With Dan, a guitar was never far from sight and most of our time together involved the two of us playing jokes on each other – usually by making up silly songs, or planning prank calls. Like, for example, the day he called me up pretending to be my doctor. 'Hello, is this Jasmine? Hi, this is Doctor Daniel... I've got your test results with me,' he said, his voice sombre and deep. 'I'm very sorry, but it appears you have crabs. Yes, you definitely have crabs. The sexual kind.'

'Oh fuck off,' I yelled, laughing hysterically as I finally recognised his voice. 'That's going too far!' Dan and I were always messing around, and hanging out wasn't unusual – but after that night with Blake, I knew that SJ's request for me to take him shopping for new shirts wasn't about helping Dan – not at all. She knew exactly what I needed. There were so few guys that I felt safe around, and Dan was the only one who made me feel that there were still good men in the world.

At the time, none of these little moments erased the memory of what I'd been through. They didn't stop the shame from barrelling me over and leaving me staring at the rafters of my bedroom, unable to get up. But these friendships – these moments – were like a bandage; they patched and comforted and held me together. They helped me to walk bruised and wounded through each day. They gave me the strength and the space to breathe, to think, to question. To ask myself, *What do I need to do to truly change my life? How do I make sure I never end up in another situation like that one?*

That night with Blake had changed me forever and I knew that I needed to make drastic changes in my life if I were going to avoid repeating the same destructive patterns with new men. The only problem was, I had no idea *how*. You may as well have asked me to build a house without any tools, or navigate myself to a faraway town without a GPS or a map. Sure, I could make an attempt – but would I be successful? *Unlikely.*

The Stories We Carry

In so many ways, I believe I got incredibly lucky. Barely six weeks had passed since I'd cut Blake from my life, and although I didn't know it, I'd already met the guy who was about to become my future partner. In fact, he'd been sitting in front of me for the last six months. All along, Raj was there – but I'd never been in the right headspace to realise.

Raj was a quiet soul; a deep thinker. Often the boys in our group joked about how he 'must be gay' – mostly because he didn't talk disrespectfully about women or go around looking for casual hook-ups. In reality, he was a lot like me – sensitive, shy, loyal, and respectful. All the things that should make up the fabric of a good human being, but seemed to be overlooked by many of the young men I'd come into contact with. Boys who only valued what they could *take* from a woman. What they could *get* from her.

Raj and I had bumped into each other at least half a dozen times over the past few months, and we'd even had an 'almost, could-have-been-something-more' moment just before I'd been assaulted. It was the same night that Blake had been pushing me away, telling me he was 'with the boys' and 'too busy to talk.' The same night he'd spotted Raj in the pub and started levelling racist insults at him. When Raj had asked if I'd wanted to go for a late-night walk, I'd agreed.

On that cold Saturday evening, we'd spent an entire night sitting amongst the jagged, misshapen rocks of the jetty, our bodies tucked within the grey, concrete boulders as we stared outward to the stars. With an air of quiet confidence and not a shred of ego, he'd leaned across from where he sat and placed one hand on the side of my face, turning it toward him. 'How do you like to be kissed?' he asked cheekily.

The question had taken me by surprise; almost as though I'd been hit in the face with a cold fish. How did I *like* to be treated? Was that something that I was allowed to actually think about? I'd looked into his deep brown eyes, the waves crashing behind us. 'Well, I'm kind of used to guys just being really rough,' I answered. 'But I guess that's not really what I like or want,' I continued.

Raj nodded. 'Every time I go out I see guys pretty much undressing a girl on the dance floor.' He leaned in closer. 'But that's not how it should be.'

'No?'

'No.' Then he leaned over and kissed me in a way I'd never experienced.

All night we'd stayed on those rocks, talking about his family and culture, our favourite movies, and things that no one knew about us. As the sun rose we peeled ourselves from the rocks and ran to the sand, screaming at the horizon as we danced around with frozen toes and goose-pimpled limbs. 'Come on! Come on!' we yelled deliriously. 'Hurry up, Mister Sunshine!!'

Later that morning, when I'd gotten a taxi back to SJ's place and then slept for a few hours, I'd realised that there was something very different about Raj. I found myself wondering what it would be like to be with someone so mature; someone who was at ease with deep conversations and had no sense of entitlement or expectations. Sadly, I never found out. He went overseas shortly afterwards for a holiday, and in that time, Blake shattered my trust. When Raj returned, I was a deeply depressed, wary, and broken young woman.

The Stories We Carry

When I think back to the person I was on my 21st birthday, I find it hard to believe that Raj could see beneath all of that trauma to find the real me, tucked away inside. Somehow, though, he did. Somehow, he thought I was worth fighting for, and in the months to come, I began to slowly find my way back to the real me.

Despite the kiss we had shared months earlier, I don't think Raj or I assumed that anything would ever happen between us. We were simply two humans who discovered we really liked each other's company and wanted to spend time together. It really was as innocent as that. We had movie nights where we laughed hysterically over cult classics like Napoleon Dynamite and then went out dancing to live bands, and afternoons where we walked along beaches and adventured up the coast to little beachside towns like Yamba. He made picnic lunches for us and we explored old, abandoned boat sheds along the Urunga River, and at all times he was kindness personified.

Sometimes he'd hold my hand or sneak a quick kiss, but there was also a part of him that held back. *Why doesn't he just grab me and make a move like other guys?* I'd wonder. It was completely foreign and at times frustrating to have someone treat me so well, yet have enough self-control to hold back and assess our friendship for what it might be turning into. For the last three years I'd become used to having men treat me in the exact ways Raj had talked about at the beach that autumn night. They'd grope and pull at me on the dance floor, guilt-tripping me any time I tried to create boundaries. They were the types of men who thought nothing of walking up to girls and crassly saying, 'Hey, haven't seen you in a while. Just one question. Have your tits gotten bigger?'

Raj wasn't that kind of man, and he never showed an ounce of disrespect. He was everything I wanted in a partner, but I didn't know how to accept such love and kindness, and so I began to self sabotage our relationship. This, to someone who hasn't experienced the trauma of sexual or domestic violence, might sound absolutely insane. If so, it's understandable. *Why wouldn't you just appreciate what you have, and do everything in your power to keep hold of it? Why would you do anything to risk losing that kind of person in your life?* The truth of trauma, however, is that it's a tricky beast; when you've spent most of your life 'waiting for the other shoe to drop,' you get very good at learning to run before the problem appears. In my mind, it was only a matter of time before Raj turned out to be 'too good to be true,' and I wanted to get in first.

As I stood inside the layby department one afternoon, waiting for him to come by and visit, a cold, hateful voice began threading itself through my ears. *As if he would ever like you*, it whispered spitefully. *There's no way he's going to come and visit you at work tonight. He's going to turn out to be just like Blake. He'll make promises and then go back on them. Why are you even letting yourself dream about him liking you?* With every negative thought, my loop of anxiety and self-hatred grew tenfold, intensifying to the point of no return. I dropped so far into The Nothing that when he sent a text to tell me he was on his way, I could no longer bear to see his face. Instead, I slipped out the front door of work, and drove home while continuing to throw silent hatred at myself.

Once again I was lost within the Swamp of Sadness and all I knew was that I needed the pain to stop. So, I reverted to the 16-year-old girl inside of me; the one who'd climbed atop the horse shed at her school. The one who took risks and searched for a feeling that was greater than the numbness within. It was here, tucked inside my car with the rain coating the road in a slick film of droplets, that the idea came to me. A very dangerous idea.

Clutching the steering wheel tightly, I smashed my foot down on the accelerator. Then, I quickly hit the brakes, causing the back end of my car to fishtail out. Tears began pouring down my face, but I couldn't stop. Couldn't hold back the voice inside that kept urging me to go harder; to do something that would really make me *feel* something. As my tyres sped along the dark country road toward our house, I tried again, adrenalin barrelling upwards and into each white-knuckled fingertip.

Skkkrrrrpppppp.

With a jolt, my head bumped the back of the seat, the rain falling steadily against the windshield. But it wasn't enough. Nothing was enough. So this time, I headed toward the opening of a dark tree-lined forest, where the road fell away steeply on one side. Then, I mashed the pedals again. Tears began to fall faster as I skidded and accelerated in the rain, terrified of what I might do next.

When I arrived – unharmed but on edge – at the opening of our country road just minutes later, I pulled over and reached into my backpack for a small paper bag. It was my last chance to feel something before I pasted on a smile for Mum, so I quickly pulled the mini bottle of alcohol from its secret pouch and drank it down. Then I walked in the door and skulled two glasses of wine, following it up with a lashing of Jack Daniels that I poured over a mug of ice-cream.

When I awoke the next morning I found that Raj had left several messages, checking in because he hadn't been able to find me at the end of my shift. Suddenly I felt so stupid, so childish. If I'd had more grace for myself, I would have realised the truth; that after so many years of being hurt by so many men, I just didn't know how to trust.

Somehow, despite my private battles, Raj saw something in me, something I couldn't. To this day I'm eternally grateful, because I honestly don't know where I'd be if not for him.

Over the coming weeks we continued to meet up often, going hiking, having movie dates, or hanging out together with SJ and Dan. One night, after going to see Hilltop Hoods together, we sat in the main street waiting for our 4 am post-drinking 'comfort kebabs,' when suddenly, my anxiety bubbled to the surface. Sitting on Raj's lap atop a plastic cafe chair, I listened as he talked about all the fun things we could do together over the months ahead, but all I could think about was Blake and all his empty promises.

'You don't have to pretend. You know that, right?' I blurted out the words, looking down at my fingertips where I was anxiously shredding the silver foil of my kebab wrapper. 'You can tell me the truth.'

Raj's eyebrows drew together, his usually relaxed face suddenly serious. 'What do you mean?'

'I know you're just saying all this stuff to be nice. I know you're going to get tired of hanging out with me soon.'

He pulled back, swivelling me around to face him. 'Jas, I treat you like a princess – I don't understand what you're so worried about? What do you think I'm going to do to you?'

I stared at him blankly, biting down on all the words begging to be brought to the surface.

The Stories We Carry

'I... That's what I'm used to,' I admitted.

'Being hurt?'

'Yeah.'

'What happened, Jas?' His voice was soft, barely audible over the drunken laughter all around us. But I felt it; the comfort of his palms wrapped around mine. The safety of his arms. And so, inch by inch, I began to let him in on the truth of what I'd been through – just snippets. A comment here or there. A trail of threads that, if he truly cared, maybe he could weave together in time.

The combination of wariness and distrust, mixed with trauma and a deep need to be loved, could easily have led me straight into another toxic relationship. I wasn't yet far enough out of The Jungle to see how much better things could be in the space that existed beyond. So, in many ways, I simply was lucky. Without a doubt, I can say that Raj was a catalyst for the complete 180° turn that I later made in my life – but he wasn't a miracle worker. I say that in the kindest of ways. I was still deeply traumatised and broken, and he alone couldn't fix that. Had it not been for the miracle that was about to happen in my life I'm not sure where I'd be today.

Chapter 18

To this day I can't explain what happened in my life in September of 2006. I can only share the truth, because the truth is this: what happened was unexplainable.

Though Raj and I had been spending time together, I was still trapped inside my depression, and this time there was a serious risk it would take me down. I remember standing in the upstairs room of our house as my brother looked at me quizzically, his face soft and his eyes alert. I remember the way he cautiously asked if I was okay, and the stabbing pains inside my gut as I – drunkenly – told him all was fine. I'd been drinking almost every day for two weeks, and things were not looking good.

Somehow, while sulking in my pit of despair, I discovered that my favourite comedy duo, Lano and Woodley, were scheduled to perform at the Brisbane Powerhouse. Having been raised on a diet of ABC-only television for the majority of my life, I had watched every episode that Frank Woodley and Colin Lane had ever put out, and as a teenager, their slapstick antics and ridiculous one-liners were the soundtrack to my high school days. They were stupid and funny and ridiculous and we loved it. Many times my friends and I would walk around the drama room quoting lines from the show, and singing hilarious lyrics from their CDs.

Looking back, it's odd that I even found out about the show at all. Facebook was only just beginning to become popular amongst my friends and online ads weren't a thing. Somehow, though, I found out about the Brisbane Powerhouse show and knew in an instant that I wanted to be there. Filled with a rush of excitement that I hadn't felt in so long, I scrolled through my phone contacts and tapped out a message to my high school drama buddy, Searle. *Wanna go 2 Lano & Woodley? In BRISBANE? How cool would that be?!*

Not long afterwards, my Nokia beeped. *Hey Jazzy Jazz*, he replied. *I am so in. I have 2 be back for church the next day so we'll have 2 make it a day trip. But let's do it!*

Ugh, church, I thought to myself. *Way to spoil a good road trip*. Still, I wasn't about to say no to a chance to get out of Coffs for a day, so I texted him back to organise the tickets.

Despite spending 12 years in a Christian school and growing up with a strong sense of faith, I'd been drifting further and further from church since I'd turned 18. It just felt so meaningless; so superficial. The people I saw there were always so... *happy*. They walked around with joy-filled smiles and full hearts, a sense of purpose and an unwavering belief in God and his voice. They spoke in weird sentences, talking of 'divine experiences' where 'God spoke to them.' Where 'The Holy Spirit filled them to overflowing.' They wore long jeans or loose fitting dresses that hid their curves, and my God, somehow the women on stage always seemed to have perfect blonde hair and perfect Christian boyfriends or husbands.

I still talked to God, but it always felt one-sided. There were so many long nights where I sobbed alone; black, ebony evenings beneath my covers where I seethed with a fiery rage, asking God why he didn't save us from Dad's abuse. Why he allowed so many bad things to happen to me. Why – despite following all the rules for so long – nothing in my life worked out.

Why, why, why? I never felt that there was an answer, and it always ate me up.

If I'm honest, I couldn't understand what Searle or anyone else found interesting about church, but I wasn't going to turn down an opportunity to escape from The Nothing for a few hours, and so, I went ahead and planned for the trip.

A few weeks later, the two of us jumped in his car and headed up the highway, singing silly songs and joking around to pass the five hour drive. The show itself was exactly what we'd hoped for – two hours of ridiculous, slapstick musical comedy that made us laugh until tears streamed down each cheek, and as we walked out of the Brisbane Powerhouse, I realised it was the first time in so long that I'd actually heard myself laugh.

You're still there, I thought. *You still exist. Even if it's just for a few hours, you're still there.*

As Searle and I settled into the front seats of his car with snacks and CDs ready to go, we groaned at the journey ahead of us. 'If it's 10 pm now, we're not going to be home until...' I glanced at the small light illuminating his dashboard. 'Ugh. 3 am.'

Searle merged his car onto the Story Bridge, the lights from Brisbane City twinkling softly through the guard rails. 'Totally worth it,' he grinned. 'I mean, it's only a 10 hour return trip, yeah?'

'Oh totally. But it's gonna suck to be *you* at church tomorrow.'

He grimaced. 'Let's not think about that right now.'

For the next few hours, we laughed and joked, telling stories and rehashing lines from the show to keep each other awake. But then, eventually, a shrill beep sounded from his phone, interrupting the flow of conversation.

'Woah. Who's messaging *you* at midnight?' I joked.

Hands on the wheel, he tilted his head toward the centre console between us. 'Can you check that for me?'

I reached across, opening the text and reading the name back. 'Oooh, it's from someone called Sarah,' I teased.

'She's just a friend from church.'

I rolled my eyes and half-smiled. 'Sure, sure. Anyway, she says – '

I began reading, but then immediately stopped. Instantly, a small furrow began to dig itself between my brows, my heart quickening as I scrolled through each line.

> **Hey Searle, this is kind of weird, but I felt like God wanted me to send you this message. Because there's someone with you who needs to hear it.**

I began reading, my eyes travelling over the Bible verse and the text she'd attached. Usually, messages like this made me cringe, turning my stomach inside out and transforming my nose into a replica of a scrunched up tissue. But this time, I didn't feel any of that.

The Stories We Carry

I read the message out loud, my heartbeat pounding in my ears as the words travelled between us. Then, I stopped, completely silent and unable to speak. I didn't know this woman and yet the message she'd sent felt as though it had been written just for me. In just a few words, she'd articulated the heart of everything I was experiencing. The darkness that permeated my spirit every moment of the day. The hopelessness. The isolation. The anger. The betrayal. The loneliness.

I felt like someone understood.

'Wow, that was kind of... relevant,' Searle breathed. Deep down, he knew enough about what I was going through to know, just as Sarah said, that her message was for me.

I clenched my fingertips together, winding them around and around each other as I stared out the window. Then I locked the screen and tucked the phone away into the centre console. We said nothing more about it; the two of us travelling in silence as we took turns driving. Trees and mountains sped by, eventually morphing into houses, coastlines, and then, as we passed the sign for Coffs Harbour, the iconic sight of the Big Banana came into view. It was well into the early hours of the morning by the time his tyres crunched up the gravel of our driveway.

'Well, thanks for a great road-trip, Jazzy Jazz,' he yawned. 'Also, if you want to come to church with us tomorrow just let me know.'

'Thanks man. I'll let you know.' *Don't hold your breath*, I thought.

Padding down the hallway to my room, I crept quietly through the door and belly flopped, exhausted, into my bed. But as I drifted off I couldn't stop thinking of the strange message on Searle's phone.

How it felt as though it had been written just for me. I could barely remember the Bible verse by now, but I remembered the feeling. The sensation of being seen; of having someone know the pain I was in, and that something brighter was coming.

Seconds later I fell asleep.

Somewhere, in the depths of unconsciousness – a place where we think so very little happens – The Nothing fell away. After 10 years of following me around every moment of the day, she packed her bags and left. When I opened my eyes four hours later, she was gone. Gone for good.

Something's different.

This was my first thought, as I rolled over in bed and placed my feet on the thin linoleum flooring. Beside me, the sun peeked through my curtains, a razor-thin beam of light striking down the centre where the two pieces of fabric hadn't quite drawn together. It was only 7.30 am; barely four hours from when I'd fallen asleep, and though I was exhausted I felt strangely energised. *Weird*, I thought, as I padded down the hallway toward the kitchen. *Usually I'd be a wreck after only four hours of sleep.*

As I ate breakfast and thought about the day ahead, I realised that, for the first time in weeks, my brain felt fresh and light. Usually the 'loop' began shortly after I woke; the soundtrack to my daily existence that ran day and night, only interrupted by constant stimulation from friends or alcohol. *No one will ever love you. You're so ugly. Your stomach looks disgusting. You're not good enough for someone like Raj, just give up now because he's never going to want you.*

The Stories We Carry

I popped a piece of toast into my mouth, crunching it down and waiting for the loop to start. But all I could hear was the munching of bread crumbs, and the soft bellowing of cows outside. I thought of Raj; wondered if he'd ever ask me out.

I don't really care, came the reply.

Holy shit, something really is different, I thought. Me, being content on my own? The last time I felt that way was... age 12 maybe? All day I walked around, quietly doing mundane things and waiting expectantly for the bleakness to settle over me, to infiltrate my lungs, eyes, and ears with its haze; the feeling of being suffocated by a blanket of cotton wool.

Instead, the lightness stayed.

The next morning, when I awoke, it was still there. That light, breezy, peaceful feeling. The sensation that all was right in the world; all was okay. *I* was okay.

Almost 16 years have passed since that Sunday morning and I still can't explain it. All I know is that my entire life changed because of the bravery of a stranger. A stranger who was willing to listen to her intuition, and send that one life-changing text message to my friend Searle. A message that was meant for me.

It's the one and only time I've ever felt that God has spoken directly to me. Sometimes I wonder to myself, *Why is that?* At the same time, however, I know that this is more than so many others experience. This also leaves me confused – why was I healed, when so many others aren't? Why me, and not my best friend, who has suffered with chronic health conditions her entire life? Why me, and not children who have been trafficked, or sentenced to a lifetime of abuse from evil individuals? How could I be set free from my prison of pain while so many had to fight for decades to manage debilitating mental illnesses? I don't have answers, though I really wish I did.

Sometimes I still wonder if I deserved to be healed, when so many others are far more deserving – but I know that question isn't helpful.

The only thing I can share is this: God healed me on that Sunday in 2006. On that night, in what can only be described as a miracle, I was lifted out of the Swamp of Sadness. Though I'm not immune to depression or despair, any experiences I've had with the Black Dog in the last 16 years have only ever been circumstantial; a response to a crisis, or something truly challenging. Never again have I been followed around by a 24/7, endless feeling of bleakness. Never again has The Nothing swamped me, refusing to leave my body for even a day. There are so many things in life that just cannot be explained. Sometimes, all we have are our stories; memories that help us remember that at one time, on one morning, a miracle really did happen.

Despite so much trauma and suffering in the world, there is still magic and light and hope.

Chapter 19

When The Nothing disappeared, I finally found myself. For the first time in my entire life I felt happy and content, and it was only a week or two later that Raj finally asked me out. There was something beautiful about that, I thought. Starting a relationship when I was already complete, instead of looking for someone to fix me, gave us the best foundation.

Over the next few months, I experienced everything I'd always hoped for in a partnership. Raj and I often took road trips to distant locations and spent our weekends exploring lush forests or climbing headlands. Whatever we did, it always felt natural and easy. I could be myself, *completely*. And in return, I knew that I was completely accepted.

However, it was *only* that way because I was constantly working to unlearn the triggers and behaviours that had landed me in danger so many times before. Though I had been freed from my depression and self-loathing and felt ready to be in a stable, healthy relationship, I still had a lot of work to do. I think it's important to be real about this, because the mental labour that needed to be completed to pave the way to a brighter future wasn't easy. The miracle that I experienced was just that – a miracle. But it didn't magically download a file into my brain that taught me how to create boundaries, listen to my intuition, and stop self-sabotaging. Those were all things that I had to learn for myself.

There were parts of my soul and brain that remained in conflict, after the assault. The larger part of me wanted to feel safe and at ease, but my body and nervous system didn't know how. I was constantly on edge, alert for the potential threat that was going to attack me. Not only that, but the fear of being physically or mentally harmed made me fearful of speaking up and asserting what I wanted. *What if I tell Raj I'm not ready to be intimate, and he runs away? What if I speak up and lose him?* These were the questions that I wrestled with daily. After all, how many times had I told guys in the past that I didn't like what they were doing to me, only to be told to 'just let it happen' or physically restrained until I acquiesced? How many years had I walked on eggshells around my dad, unable to say how I really felt?

In my experience, speaking up didn't get me anywhere.

As a survivor of sexual assault and family violence, there were so many layers of damage to acknowledge and work through while trying to teach myself the basics of 'Healthy Relationships 101', and my first big test came during a house party with Raj and some friends in November of 2006. We'd been sitting around the table with SJ and Dan, drinking and laughing away the night, when I said my goodnights and made my way to the spare room. Raj and I had been dating for two months by now, and though my logical brain knew that I could trust him, I still struggled. From the very start, I'd talked openly with him about Blake's abuse, and he knew – and accepted, without any hesitation at all – that I wasn't interested in having sex any time in the near future. Never once did he ever try to push or coerce me into anything; and yet, there was still a part of me that was terrified of being hurt.

As I lay on the mattress, my head buzzing from alcohol, Raj leaned over to kiss me – just as he had so many other times. But as the seconds went on, a lump began to form in my stomach, pushing its way up toward my throat. My skin crawled, a thousand invisible warning bells going off within my head. *This is ridiculous*, I thought. *I'm safe inside Dan and SJ's house. I'm with someone who has never hurt me; someone who respects my boundaries. So why do I feel this way?* No matter how I tried to rationalize it, the mounting panic just wouldn't leave, and so, with fear coursing through my veins, I pulled away. Raj drew me close again, and once more I felt the crawling sensation underneath my skin. *NO*, it screamed. *Get out of here now!*

Bringing my knee up between us, I yanked away harder, this time turning my back on Raj. If I could have built a wall between us, I would have, but right now this was all I had the strength for. *Stop!* I wanted to say. *Don't touch me. Get away from me. Get away from me!* But I couldn't force the words from my throat.

'What's wrong, Jas?' asked Raj, quietly.

'Nothing.'

'Hey, it doesn't seem like nothing. What's up?'

I wracked my brain, trying to find words that I could thread into sentences; words that explained the jumble of fear and confusion. Finally, it hit me. I felt the same way that I had many months earlier in Blake's room; the moment where he'd climbed on top of me and I'd become frozen.

'I'm scared,' I said in a tiny voice. 'Scared that you're going to hurt me.'

Though I couldn't see Raj's face, I felt him flinch. It was as though my very words had left a mark; like he'd stepped on a sharp patch of bindis, their thorny spikes digging into soft flesh. 'You think I'm going to hurt you?' His voice was wounded, a mixture of sadness and slight indignation. Never had he ever raised his voice or shown anything other than kindness, but nothing he said changed the feeling inside.

In the darkness, I strained to see the faint silhouette of his face as it pulled away from mine. 'Have I ever done anything to hurt you Jas?'

'No,' I said simply. 'I know you wouldn't. It's just that I'm scared that..." *Ugh, why was this so hard to explain?*

Beside me, Raj waited patiently.

'The last time I was with someone… one of the last times I kissed someone when I'd been drinking… I got hurt,' I explained. 'That was when Blake hurt me.'

In the silence, I lay with my pain, wondering if it would be mine to carry alone forever or if anyone would ever understand. Was it okay to feel this way? Did this make any sense to Raj? I didn't know, but I also had a sense that if I didn't speak up, I'd never move beyond dangerous, unhealthy relationships.

I felt the exhale of Raj's lungs; the instant understanding that passed between us as the tension disappeared. Then I felt the warmth of his arms, gently cradling me against his chest. 'Jas… I'm so sorry. I get it.' His voice was calm and understanding, free of any resentment or intimidation. 'It's okay. We don't have to do anything. *Anything,*' he emphasised.

Relief washed over me, allowing me to finally relax and drift off to sleep. It was the first time I had ever been in a real, adult

The Stories We Carry

relationship and asserted myself. The first time I'd really felt safe to do so. There was still a long way to go, but here, tonight, it felt like I'd made a start.

One of the things that I feared most, when I walked away from Blake, was how I was going to find the strength to continue living in a small town where I constantly bumped into him. I'd run into him a handful of times after that awful confrontation outside the pub – once at my university (a place that he shouldn't have ever been), and also at the bar that Raj and I sometimes went for nights out – and each time I saw his face I wondered, *How will I ever feel safe?* By now he knew that I was with Raj, and yet, whenever we crossed paths he'd flash a smile my way, all the while sneering at Raj and mumbling racist insults. He behaved as if everything were fine; like we were old friends, and nothing had ever happened. It was insane.

This happened for some months, but then, to my great relief, he simply disappeared. It was almost miraculous in a way, because once Raj and I got together officially, I stopped running into him. Not at the pub. Not at the beach. It was as though he'd vanished.

Over the next three years I saw him only twice. The first occurred inside my new workplace, and resulted in me locking myself inside a narrow walk-in cupboard (where we kept all of the mobile phones) and having my first ever panic attack. The second occurrence happened some years later, when a friend accidentally introduced us at a bar when Blake walked up to him.

'Oh, hi *Jas*,' he spat. Then he turned to our mutual friend, all the while keeping his eyes trained on me. 'Yeah, Jas doesn't talk to me anymore. She never talks to me,' he mumbled.

'*Awkward*' didn't even come close to describing that moment, but I held my head high before walking away without a word.

Though it was an awful and anxiety-inducing situation, I was so incredibly grateful that I never saw him again after that day. To date, 13 years have passed and I've never again had to feel the prickling fear of being under his gaze.

At the age of 22, life felt comfortable and with my nervous system finally at ease I was able to focus on things that mattered most – building a life with Raj, running my freelance photography business, and working my way through my Psychology and Creative Writing degree. I had no idea yet what I wanted to do with my studies, but I loved learning. I was particularly fascinated by social injustice issues, as well as the way in which creativity and art could be used to convey difficult emotions. Over the period of my degree, I threw myself into a multitude of different units – from journalism and digital art, to music, Indigenous studies, and abnormal psychology – but it wasn't until the end of my degree that I discovered my true love for memoir and autobiography. One of our final assignments was to write about a difficult period of our lives and how we got through it, and it was the first time that I ever told anyone outside my immediate friendship circle about Dad's suicide and Blake's assault. I titled it, 'Learning the World in 2 Years: Lessons in grief, life, and change.'

It was the most vulnerable I'd ever been. At times, I felt terrified that I'd overshared. But it was also incredibly cathartic and the mark I received from my teacher showed me that there was power in my words. It showed me that vulnerability was where the gold lay.

'*How should we respond in times of loss?*' I'd asked, in the final paragraph of my story. '*Should we cry? Withdraw? Dye our hair a*

The Stories We Carry

ridiculous colour and start wearing clothes that look like underwear on the outside? Does it really matter? Newspapers, health magazines and TV programs are forever telling us the best ways to handle our emotions, but how many of us think of these 'rules' when our lives fall apart? I certainly didn't,' I revealed.

'Change is an incredible force when paired with loss and grief; it builds and can all too easily disassemble us completely. No matter how devastating life can be though, I have learnt that it is never too late to start again. It matters not so much how we find our way, but that we do.'

Recently, I re-read that memoir and had a bit of a laugh. Crazy, colourful hair? Well, I definitely took that on! But I also marvelled on how far I'd come and the wisdom that I had at such a young age. Though so much time has passed I still feel the same way. I still believe that it's never too late to start again. The most important thing is not that we face our trauma 'perfectly', but that we *do* face it. People may not always understand why we make the decisions we do in the face of loss or grief, but all that matters is that we keep going, one step at a time, and that we give ourselves grace for the life lessons and mistakes that happen along the way. Because in the end, that's how we find our way from hopelessness to hope. One imperfect step at a time.

Chapter 20

'It's time.'

I knew, deep within my soul, that there was an expiration date on my time in Coffs Harbour and that time had come. Though both Raj and I loved the quiet lifestyle of the Mid-North Coast, there was a greater part of me that longed for more. Now that my nervous system was no longer looking for metaphorical bears at every turn, I was thinking more about what I truly wanted out of life, and the truth was, my options as a creative person who dreamed of deeply touching people's lives, were very limited in a place like Coffs Harbour.

Throughout 2009, as I finished my final weeks at uni (graduating with a high grade-point average that was testament to the work I'd put in) Raj and I made plans to swap our current lifestyle for the beautiful beaches of Coolangatta and Tweed Heads. We felt that it was close enough to the 'smaller town' vibes that we were used to, but that this new location would give us greater opportunities.

Unfortunately, however, the dreams we had didn't come to fruition. Raj had begun to take over his family business and his father felt strongly about him carrying on their legacy. Without disrespecting his family, I will say only this: in three years, I was only ever invited to spend time with his parents once, and though Raj spoke so highly of me, it was clear that I was never going to be accepted as a future daughter-in-law. His dad, in particular, had a very specific template for the life he wanted his son to lead and this unfortunately didn't include an Australian girl – no matter how much Raj and I suited each other.

In the end, we decided that I would move to the Gold Coast as planned and Raj would follow a few months later once he'd sorted things out at work and home. With the help of Rachael's mum, I found a room to rent just over the border of Queensland, and shortly after Australia Day in 2010, I packed my car and tearfully said my goodbyes.

Leaving home and the certainty of a comfortable relationship wasn't easy. In fact, it was one of the hardest decisions I ever made at that time, but I knew that it had to happen. I'd grown so much in the last three years and I felt that the clock was ticking; I needed to get out of Coffs and try my best to figure out how to fulfil the sensitive, creative side of myself that longed to do something that mattered.

Though I trusted my intuition, there were people who didn't — and they judged me for it. There were questions of, 'Are you really making the right choice?' and 'Is it a good idea to leave someone like Raj behind?' Insinuations were made that it 'wasn't right' to give my partner an 'ultimatum' – to make him choose between his family's dreams or a life with me. But I chose not to listen. I'd lived so many lives in one lifetime, and I couldn't bear the thought of putting my dreams on hold for another moment.

I don't want to tread water anymore, I thought. *I don't want to float in circles. I want to swim in the direction I choose, damn it! I want to glide through the water and feel the searing pain of my muscles as I push them further than ever before. I want to live!*

The Stories We Carry

Every moment I stayed in my dead-end retail job I felt as though I was dying. I couldn't do it anymore.

And so it was, that I took what was to become the first step toward a life that was bigger than any I could have ever imagined. It was time.

A jagged jigsaw of rectangles and squares jutted upwards from the horizon, their windows and rooftops just barely visible from the crystal clear wave on which I floated. Raising my palm like a shield, I squinted against the glare and tried to make out the individual shapes of each small building, running my gaze along the faint outline of Surfers Paradise. Then I swivelled, my feet gliding lazily through the warm, teal-blue water as I looked toward the cliffs of Greenmount Beach.

There it is, I smiled.

Though so many years had passed since my mother had stolen us away for a week of relief from Dad's abuse, I'd never forgotten the sense of freedom and peace that enveloped me every time I set foot on Coolangatta beach. Once upon a time – when my father was still my hero – we'd spent six months living in this beautiful patch of paradise. I'd spent days leaping through waves with Dad's hand wrapped protectively around mine and late afternoons on a basketball court in the backstreets of West Tweed, as he taught me to ride my bike. Each day we'd cycle home to our little tree-top house by the canals, stopping by our neighbour's home to choose a new VHS movie from their pirated collection, before greeting our polka-dot dog, Bindi.

This place — these little beachy towns – had always felt like home to me, even when they became my escape.

Diving deep, I pressed my hands to the bottom of the ocean and then shot back up and through the surface, feeling the sun stream across my face as the water parted. *This is so magical*, I thought to myself. *If only Raj were here.*

Instantly, a pang of guilt rose within my chest. I still hadn't returned his call from the day before, and if I was honest, part of me didn't want to. The truth was, I was struggling with this whole long-distance-relationship-thing. In the beginning I didn't think much of it. I told myself that our love was strong enough to survive anything, including the 12 weeks it was going to take for him to pack up his life and move to the Gold Coast to join me. But as I was fast discovering, freedom and independence were turning me into a different person. I wanted to grow and experience new opportunities. I wanted to make the most of every moment.

Raj, though? Well, it felt like he'd be content to stay in Coffs forever.

So much had happened in the past six weeks. In that time I'd moved house twice – the first time, because the 'room' I'd been given wasn't the beautiful space I'd been promised; it was a concrete box with an automatic door, which is a fancy way of saying that I was paying to live in a garage. At first, I tried to make the best of it – after all, it was only meant to be temporary – but I well and truly lost my patience the day that I came home to find that the owner had thrown my bed up against one wall, and decided to *park her car in my room* because she was holding a party! ('Oh sorry, I didn't think you'd be home for a few days,' she shrugged.)

The Stories We Carry

Now, I was living in the granny flat of my best friend's parents' house and working in a camera and electronics retail store, and while definitely wasn't living the dream, I knew that if I went back to Coffs, I'd have absolutely zero chance of finding a career I loved. I was willing to stick it out; to grit my teeth through the discomfort until I made some progress. To sacrifice the comforts of family and a stable income in a soul-destroying job, while I searched for something better. *I know there's something bigger I'm meant to be doing with my life*, I thought. *I just have to find it.*

The problem was, Raj didn't seem to share the same yearning and I couldn't ignore the niggling feeling that maybe, just maybe, we were growing apart. The two of us were on separate paths now, still walking parallel but finding it harder to see each other through the trees. We were being torn apart by hills and branches and rock walls; different desires, different motivations, different cultures. I felt it. Deep down, I knew that it wasn't working.

With a head full of questions I walked toward the car park, wondering all the while how I could feel this way about someone who was so perfect. *How can I be willing to let go of someone who helped save my life, in pursuit of something so uncertain?* I questioned. *Bloody hell, I don't even have a fulltime job up here! I'm basically throwing away one dead-end town for another. And for what? What?*

I turned and looked over my shoulder one last time, my eyes gazing across the perfect blue ripples to the outline of Surfers Paradise. The clouds had cleared while I'd been out swimming and the city was now visible, its buildings and unmistakable landmarks now more defined against the dark blue canvas of the sky.

Again, I asked myself: *How can I do this? How can I leave Raj behind?*

Jas Rawlinson

Because you must, whispered my intuition. *It's time.*

But I'm going to break his heart – I pressed – *and for what? Am I being courageous here, or just stupid?*

My intuition continued. *Sometimes, all you see are faint outlines; just the smallest of shimmers*, it answered. *But one day the clouds will clear, and when they do, you'll see what was waiting for you all along. The path will be clear, and you'll wonder how you ever doubted that it was there. This, Jas, is where you're meant to be.*

For the first few months we tried to make things work long-distance, but eventually, I realised with a sense of sadness that the obstacles we'd faced from the start of our relationship – mostly to do with his family's expectations – were still as present as they had been three years earlier. It wasn't that I stopped loving Raj; I just knew that I had to keep moving forward. I had to keep chasing after my dreams, with or without him.

While it would be easy to blame other people for the way in which our relationship ended, I feel it's important to take responsibility for my part. I was brash, impatient, and cowardly. I was terrified of facing the truth of my feelings and I didn't give Raj the overwhelming respect and love that he deserved when it came to calling things off. Do you know what I did? I sent a text message. Yes – *a fucking text message!* One that explained that I just didn't feel as though I could do the long-distance thing, and that maybe we were better off having some space until he was ready to join me. Raj deserved so much more than four to five lines of text; he deserved more than the lies that I told over the next few months, as I hid the truth about my declining hope for us. If I could say

The Stories We Carry

anything to him it would be this: *I'm sorry for the lack of care I put into the last few months of our relationship. You are a rare type of gem, one that I was so lucky to find, and I didn't hold the space for you that you so deserved.*

For the first time in over three years I was truly on my own and while the thought of being single was initially exciting, the thrill soon wore off. The hard truth? I was alone in a new town and working in a retail job where, as I later discovered, I'd been selected primarily as 'girlfriend material' for my male co-worker. Add to that a hearty dose of sexism and small-town gossip, and you can likely understand my overwhelming sense of purposelessness. It was nothing for a man to walk in and comment, 'You're far too pretty to be working as a saleswoman,' or, 'I'm not going to be served by a woman – what would she know?' Never mind that I was a professional photographer, with the highest warranty sales out of our entire department, and that I knew the exact specs on every single camera on display and which one was best suited for each customer. In the minds of some of these men, I was merely a girl; and that wasn't enough.

Each day as I drove along the Tweed Heads River towards home, I questioned my decisions. But each day, I persisted. I pressed forward.

Part of the reason I was able to keep going was because of the love and friendship of two beautiful humans – Alice and Matty. Yes, the same Matty who had shoved glowsticks up my nose when I was 19! Though many years had passed and we'd all grown and matured (mostly), we'd never lost touch, and now, by complete coincidence, we'd found ourselves living side by side in the same block of rental apartments. Magic! While Matty and Alice were on one side of the top level, her brother and I were on the other.

One afternoon, as I unloaded my small suitcase of possessions into what was now my new home, I walked up to the cherry hardwood wall that separated the two units and knocked.

'Yo, punk, what's up?' I called out.

From the other side of the wall, I heard Matty's voice. 'Yo, Chubbz!' he called back. 'Having drinks. Come over.'

With a smile on my face, I ran back down the concrete steps and up the other side to his front door. *Never thought this would happen*, I mused, as we sat in the living room drinking and laughing. The fact that I was now living next door to the kid who had spent years teasing me, making my name into freestyle raps, and even comforting me in a kebab shop at 4 am, was just too weird for words.

No matter how hard each day was, I now had two of my best friends next door and I could always walk up those steps, knock on the door, and know that there would be a place for me to forget about whatever was troubling me. Some days Alice and I sat on the small verandah, staring out toward the beach as Matty mixed cocktails for us, his mischievous grin sparking us into fits of laughter as he delivered impromptu raps made up on the spot. On other nights, we played round after round of Kings – a drinking game that usually ended with us skipping a few blocks down the road for a cheeky late-night pie. Another time, we all bunkered in together at their unit when a siege took place downstairs – an eight hour standoff that ended with police, detectives, and other first-responders facing off with an ice addict who had punched out every window in his mother's house, and was now waving a samurai sword around.

(Yes – that's a true story. You can look it up if you want to!)

The Stories We Carry

Despite the fun and laughter, the area we lived in was not the *fanciest* environment (if you get my drift) and my nervous system was often in fight or flight mode due to the violence in our street. Though I loved the freedom to go wherever I liked and do whatever I wanted at any moment, it became clear that my health was suffering. My hands shook constantly from anxiety, I was skinny and gaunt, and the sense of purposelessness within me felt soul-destroying. And so, just after Christmas – almost a year on from leaving Raj – I made a decision to quit my retail job. I literally could not bear another moment of selling USB sticks to bogans, and spending my days grinding my teeth while politely answering questions like, 'So what's an iPod? Is it the same as an iPhone?'

'I want to do something that *matters*,' I lamented one afternoon while venting to my co-worker. 'None of this shit matters. Selling someone a TV? Or a USB? Or a digital photo frame? It's all so meaningless. I'm not making a difference to *any* of these people.'

He nodded, listening quietly. But even still, I could tell that he didn't really get it. No one did. There were plenty of people in that store who were in their 40s or older, with no aspirations for anything other than selling retail goods. It worked for them, and they were perfectly happy to trade personal fulfillment for a paycheck. But me? I just couldn't.

Why do I feel like I'm dying every time I'm here? I wondered. *Why can't I just grin and bear it like everyone else?*

I knew without any doubt that I had to leave. I had to make the switch and pray that God would catch me as I leapt. My hope was that by forcing the door closed on this part of my life, a new opportunity would arise.

Jas Rawlinson

It was scary and I had no safety net to catch me, but I made the decision to trust my intuition. To once again chase after the life that I dreamt of; one where I would make a true difference in the lives of those who felt hopeless, trapped, and weighed down by their traumas.

Many years later I'd come to see that this moment, this one decision, was exactly what the Universe was waiting on me to make.

Chapter 21

'*E*xcuse me, does anyone have any chocolate?'

His voice was deep and classically Californian, his eyes unmistakable; two piercing blue irises that glimmered beneath a mop of almost shoulder-length, sun-bleached hair.

Holy shit. Is it really him?

I craned my head around a table of young writers in front of me, glancing toward the front of the media tent where the voice had come from. Taking in his tall, lean, tanned physique, and the small wry smile that etched a single parenthesis on one side of his lips.

It IS him.

It was Jon Foreman, lead singer of Switchfoot. I could barely believe I was seeing him in the flesh after listening to his music for so many years as a teenager. Beside me, one of the crew walked casually across the tent floor to chat with Jon about the interviews that were planned for that day, before he and the rest of the band took to the stage. As Jon turned to leave, he sidled up to one the desks next to mine. 'By the way, don't suppose you can spare a few of these?' he joked, sneaking one hand into a bowl of colourful Easter eggs.

I grinned, watching as he and his band mates stashed handfuls of tiny chocolates into their pockets, sly child-like smiles tugging at their lips. *Is this actually my life?* I marvelled. *Do I really get to spend this whole weekend surrounded by inspiring musicians and speakers, while getting to organise my own interviews and photography sessions?* I looked down at the all-access pass lanyard hanging from my neck, suddenly feeling like the luckiest girl alive. On any other weekend, I'd probably be sitting on the beach or having drinks with friends, but tonight, I was living my wildest dreams as a photojournalist at one of Queensland's biggest annual art, music, and philanthropy events: *Easterfest.* My job over the next three days would be to look for the biggest stories going on around the festival, and to capture it all through the power of words and photography. I'd be interviewing and snapping photos of international bands, and writing feature articles on everyday people and charity owners, each of whom were using their voices to create social impact in some way. The opportunity had come by complete chance through a friend's sister, and I'd jumped at the chance to volunteer for the long weekend. I intuitively felt that it was what I needed, in order to break free from the monotony and purposelessness I'd been feeling lately. Even though it led to me being fired from my new job (let's just say that my boss wasn't keen to give me a long weekend off), I felt I'd made the right choice. I sensed that somehow, this opportunity would open a door to something greater.

Now, seated at my desk at the back of the media tent, I scanned through the festival schedule, skimming each event and looking for something that really grabbed my attention. 'These look interesting,' I noted, turning toward our media supervisor. 'I'll check them out at 11 am.' As she nodded, I shoved a few Easter eggs in my pocket, slung my camera gear over one shoulder, and then made my way out into the 30,000 strong crowd of men, women, and children. I'd decided that my first stop would be at a small community tent hosted by Ian 'Watto' Watson, an Australian man who had created a space called Shed (or, Shed Happens) – a place where boys, brothers, uncles, fathers, and grandfathers of all ages could come together to chat, share stories, and talk about life. The small summary from the festival programme had intrigued me and I wanted to know more.

Part of me wondered if I was the right person to do this interview; if maybe I should have left it for one of the male journalists. But even so, I continued on, easing my way inside the makeshift shed and waving a shy hello. From across the room a middle-aged man with salt-and-pepper hair smiled; his eyes lit by genuine warmth and kindness. 'Hey, I'm Watto, how's it going?' he grinned.

'Hi, I'm Jas, I'm here to do a story on Shed Happens.' I lifted my lanyard by way of introduction and gave it a little shake.

'Oh that's great! Come on in Jas – I've just got to set a few things up and then I'm all yours. I can be free in around ten minutes if you like?'

'Sounds great.'

Gesturing to one of the many hay-bales, he invited me to take a seat, before continuing to greet some of the men who had already begun to arrive. Sitting down on the bundle of dried straw, I began to take note of the men filing into the shed, all the while marvelling at the diversity all around me. There were teens and single men in their 40s, fathers with and without children, and older men who looked a little lost. As each one took a seat, I suddenly realised that it wasn't their diversity that shocked me most – it was something else entirely.

It seemed so odd, in our culture, to see a group of men hanging out without a single beer in sight. Almost as though something were wrong. So many Australian men had been trained from an early age to swap vulnerability and deep connection for surface level chat and a chance to 'sink the piss.' I'd seen enough of it through my own eyes; hazy nights spent at the home of an ex-boyfriend and his roommates, where they joked about porn, got blind on rum and coke, wrestled, and thought it hilarious to take photos with us girls as they slyly slid open the zippers of their jeans and exposed themselves. Nights of listening to my ex-boyfriend play the same song on a loop, chastising me and my friend for wanting him to turn it off. Over and over we'd listened to that song – *Spank me, choke me, pull my hair! Spank me, choke me, pull my hair!* – and not a single one of my male friends had told him to turn it off. They weren't bad people. They just didn't seem to know how to connect without alcohol and a running soundtrack of misogyny.

Now, I opened my eyes and looked at the men around me – young and old – who craved authentic connection. It felt like a wild rebellion, a refusal to go along with the rules they'd been taught. In reality, they were men coming back to the core of who they truly were: human beings searching for their tribe.

Watto returned, taking a seat beside me as I hit the start button on my phone's voice recorder. 'So, what inspired you to start this space for men?' I asked. 'This is my first time hearing about it, and I can see you've created something really special here. I'd love if you could share with me about how it all got started.'

He nodded, his tanned skin wrinkling around the edges of his mouth as he opened up with deep compassion. 'At the heart of it, Shed Happens is really just about connection,' he shared. 'It's about helping men to open up about what's going on in their lives. To connect and chat with other guys in an environment that feels safe and comfortable. Every man needs a place he can feel at home, where he can share stories with mates and be himself, but from such a young age many men are taught not to – that it's not masculine to express themselves,' he emphasised. 'There's this misconception that they don't need to share what they're feeling – and this only leads to more issues down the track. 'Violence, depression, relationship problems… all of those sorts of things, you know?'

Chills prickled my skin. Oh I knew. *Oh how I knew*. More than Watto could have imagined.

'So, every year we bring Shed Happens to Easterfest so we can give boys and men a place to chat,' he explained. 'It's also here for those guys who want to learn about God, but aren't interested in a religious environment. Because there are a lot of men who are interested in having somewhere to express their faith, but don't want to go to a church. I've been running Shed for over eight years now – I've spoken to thousands of men – and what they love most is that it's 'blokey.' You know? They have a place just for them, where they can share stories and talk one-to-one. I see so many breakthroughs every time these men get together, and that's what's most amazing. The *breakthroughs*.'

I nodded, listening intently, thinking again of my own dad. There had been a time where he did begin to connect with strong male role models in our church and that had been the time where he was at his best. He had accountability. Mateship. Conversations that went beyond the surface. But over time he'd become uncomfortable there – mistakes had been made by the minister – and Dad never returned. As a result, he lost his male network of friends. If only there had been a place like this for him to go, maybe he would have found a new community.

'We've had all these stereotypes for so long,' Watto continued. 'All these beliefs that to be a *real* man, you have to be good at sport, you have to be wealthy, and you need to keep your emotions in check. But that's crap.' His eyes narrowed slightly, overcome by the emotion of his words. 'And that's what we're here to do – break down those stereotypes. For good. I really believe we will. I *know* we will,' he emphasised, voice laden with conviction. 'We're going to turn this whole thing of men and broken relationships around.'

As I finished up the interview and made my way out of the tent, I stole a glance back toward the men who now sat riveted, listening to Watto as they shared stories. Again, a thought bubbled into my mind, refusing to be silenced. *What if Dad had had an opportunity to go to something like this? Would he still be here right now?*

It hurt me to know that I'd never have the answer to this question. But with men like Watto in the world, I couldn't help but feel that maybe, on this very day, a man would find the courage to break away from his own demons.

And in the process, maybe a little girl and her mum would be spared the pain that my family had lived through.

Click! Click, click, click!

Squinting from my VIP position, side of stage, I triggered the button on my Canon 7D and held it down quickly, firing off a round of high-speed shutter shots. Switchfoot had just entered from the wings, and as one of the most anticipated events of the night, I didn't want to miss a moment. The four of them rushed forward, slipping in behind their instruments and raising their hands to a deafening roar, and I felt my heart thunder in anticipation. High above, storm clouds gathered, plump and voluminous and ready to burst.

Then, suddenly, Jon's voice rang out through the golden, late-afternoon glow, and in complete synchronicity, fresh droplets of rain torpedoed down to meet the bare dirt beneath thousands of tired feet, transforming it into a slush of mud.

It was electric. Magnetic. Fierce. And I was loving every minute.

As the band launched into 'Dare You to Move' I followed them with my lens, enshrining the night forever with my camera. I was so engrossed that I didn't notice what was happening only 100 metres to my right. I didn't hear the giant crack, and the splitting of fabric as the deluge of rain tore a hole right through the mainstage 'Big Top' tent. I didn't hear screams or sounds of panic. I was focused solely on the thousands of people dancing happily, their bodies covered in mud, and capturing the joy of the moment.

It was only when the last song played out and the crowd began to disperse that I noticed the chaos. Watching the steady stream of people rushing in all directions, I ran blindly into the rain, squinting against the downpour. Water lapped at our ankles as families linked arms and pulled their children close, scurrying to escape.

'Jas!' yelled a voice. 'The campground is flooding! Come with us.'

I blinked rapidly, pushing my hair from my eyes and searching for the person calling my name. It was Brett, one of the guys in our group.

'We've got to get back there and get our stuff up high,' he called.

Jas Rawlinson

Unsure what we were going to do, or where we'd sleep, we hurried toward the grounds as our hearts thundered wildly. We were barely out of the mainstage area before we ran into Tom, another of our crew. He was standing off to one side, with a young family of three hunkered in close. 'This is Rob and Sandy,' he explained, pointing to the husband and wife. 'They've offered for us to stay at their house, about ten minutes up the road. I was just about to text you, but if you go and grab your stuff from the tent and meet me by the front fence, we can get a lift to their place and camp out there for the night. Just grab what you need, and put everything else up high.'

Brett and I didn't have time to argue, or to question who the couple were. We just needed to get away from the floods, and so, we ran. As I later found out, Rob and Sandy had been making their way through the mud when they'd been separated from their young daughter, her small figure lost amongst 15,000 panicked bodies. But then, Brett had spotted her, helping to reunite the little girl with her parents. As thanks, they'd offered to take us in for the night. It was another moment that showed me just how special this festival was, and the generosity and humanity that was at the centre of Easterfest.

Within 30 minutes, Rob and Sandy returned to pick us up, delivering us to safety before returning for the rest of our group. We were sopping wet and dishevelled – more closely resembling a pack of drowned rats than a bunch of twenty-something year-olds – and yet, we were treated like family. I couldn't believe that two strangers could welcome us into their home with such ease; it was truly something.

Over the next 24 hours, we found out the true extent of the storm. News reports revealed that 50 millimetres of rain fell within the first 30 minutes, and there were estimates that over 40 centimetres of water had inundated parts of Queens Park. Over the next two days,

The Stories We Carry

performances and musicians were moved to the city and campers were relocated to evacuation centres. Miraculously, the items that we left behind in the campground were okay – which was more than I could say for the belongings of many others. I'd never been in the centre of a storm like that and it was truly eye-opening.

When I look back, I think about this weekend with a mixture of awe and nostalgia. Despite the chaos, the storm brought out the best in us. It brought out the best in *humanity*; and though I've seen many wild storms since then, it's the only one that has truly stuck with me.

Chapter 22

After the excitement of Easterfest, coming home to my 'normal' life was a rude awakening. I was still jobless, still uncertain of my future, and still searching for my big break – and on top of it all, my housemate was moving. Despite my grand plans for my time in the Gold Coast, I soon realised that I had few reasons left to stay in the Sunshine State any longer, and after some deep soul searching, I was forced to face reality: I couldn't afford to keep living in Queensland.

Feeling like a puppy with its tail between its legs, I packed my car, cleaned out the apartment that I'd called home for the last 12 months, and made the three-hour trip across the border to my mother's home in the hills. Throughout the whole drive, I tried my best to keep positive and remind myself of how blessed I was to have a parent who was willing to financially support me while I found work, but as a twenty-five-year-old woman who'd had a taste of freedom and independence, it felt like failure. What had I achieved over the last year, other than a string of random stints in hospitality and retail and some failed attempts at romance? Not much.

Coming back home took some adjustment. Whilst I loved seeing my old friends again, it felt – for the most part – boring. I also felt a little weird, being back in the same town as Raj. Over the past year we'd kept in contact fairly regularly, and for the first few weeks after I returned, I began to wonder if maybe I had been wrong to leave him. Did I throw away the best thing that happened to me?

Was now our chance to get back on track? If I'm honest, there was a small flicker of hope within my heart – even if I didn't mention it directly to him – but shortly after I returned, I realised that Raj had found the girl who was meant for him. The door that had been open just a crack was now closed completely.

Desperate to find a way to make the most of this limbo I was in, I began to throw myself into things I'd neglected, like gratitude journaling. Every day, no matter what was happening, I wrote three things I was grateful for.

I'm grateful to have a loving family.

I'm grateful for a roof over my head.

I'm grateful to finally be able to sleep peacefully, without the sounds of domestic violence attacks next door, or police raids under my apartment.

I'm grateful for an abled body, and that the chronic pain I've been battling is finally gone.

I'm grateful for a beautiful day today and perfect beach weather.

They were simple notes. Yet, very quickly I noticed a change in my moods. Purposelessness and depression began to lift just enough to allow me to breathe and the endless hamster wheel inside my mind began to still – even if just for a few moments.

As the weeks went by, I was amazed by what began to manifest in my life. New and healthy friendships suddenly came my way, and opportunities for work arose, including a job at my local university. This was a huge step forward in my career, because prior to this,

The Stories We Carry

I'd been stuck in retail positions with no ability to transition into something else – even though I had a university degree. For a whole year I'd been wanting to move into administration, yet no one would give me a chance because I 'didn't have any experience.' *Yeah, great. How do I get experience without someone giving me a chance to gain experience?* I wanted to scream. I'd tried every avenue, even asking an employment agency (who were being paid to help me find paid work) if I could do a short internship at an administration-based company to get my foot in the door. At this, the male manager laughed in my face, snorting, 'Why on earth would you offer to do that!?' It felt as though no one saw my determination; no one was willing to give me a hand up.

Now, however, things had finally shifted. After six months of unemployment, I was now the student liaison officer for the entire psychology department – a role that felt overwhelming and far beyond my capability but one that I wasn't willing to let slip by. Over the coming months, my contract was renewed three times. I went from student liaison officer to PA for the head of campus. Never once did I feel like I belonged there; self-doubt and imposter syndrome were ever present, and my nervous system was constantly firing off bullets of anxiety, but I stuck with it because I knew that I sure as hell never wanted to go back to selling USB sticks in a dead-end seaside town!

During this time I started talking a lot with a guy named Chris, who was someone I'd met just before leaving the Gold Coast at the start of the year. We'd been introduced by a mutual friend while I was – somewhat reluctantly – attending a youth camp from a local church in early 2011, and I found myself drawn to his easy-going nature and our shared love of cult-classics like The Mighty Boosh. As I'd later discover, he'd fallen for me the minute he'd seen me walk up the driveway of the church camp in a long green dress, with a blue bangle around one arm. Me, on the other hand? Well, unfortunately I was too deep in my head that weekend about my job situation (or lack thereof) and I didn't really pay much attention to him. (Sorry, Chris!)

Although we lived in separate states – and I was currently dating someone in my hometown – we often chatted over social media, sharing about our lives or joking over dumb rap songs we'd made up. It was all very innocent, yet even so, I couldn't help but wonder what it would be like to date someone like Chris. Like me, he was driven, and we also shared a lot of the same values and passions. He cared about things like ending human trafficking. He was moved by injustice against others. And I also knew from the very start that he was the kind of person who respected women completely; the type of man who would never emotionally manipulate or abuse me.

This was important, because only recently, I'd ended a short-term relationship with someone who hadn't treated me well. To be fair, he wasn't a bad person – he was a human who was trying to navigate some major life changes, and struggling to understand his emotions through the process – but even so, his behaviour was toxic. Things had spiralled rapidly toward the end, culminating in him going behind my back to all his friends – some of whom had known me since I was a kid – and gaslighting me into believing that all of them hated me and thought I was an awful person. At the same time, he put me in a position where I found myself abandoned, standing on the shoreline of a frosty, cold beach hundreds of kilometres from home with nothing but the shorts and t-shirt I had on, and only 10% battery on my phone. Whilst I won't go into the details, this meant that I was stranded alone in an unfamiliar city with nowhere to stay. I was lucky that I managed to get hold of an old work colleague from years prior, who took me in for the night and made sure I had a roof over my head.

The Stories We Carry

As scary and upsetting as it was to be forced into a situation like this (essentially, because my ex had suddenly told me that everyone hated me, and his friends didn't want me around), it was the emotional abuse that really stuck with me. That weekend caused me so much emotional pain and confusion, and it took a long time before I stopped second-guessing everything I did, said, or thought.

I'm not sure that I talked to Chris about much of this; mostly, I was focused on finding a sense of direction and purpose. Yet, in the aftermath of this unhealthy relationship, I found that we began to talk a lot more regularly. Some nights I lay in my room, texting over Facebook as I shared with him about my dreams and hopes. The way that I felt when I was travelling with a camera in my hands, or writing articles, and the wild, spontaneous ideas that came to me. Somehow, I felt safe to share with him — even if it was mostly online, or through the occasional phone call.

As much as I loved the familiarity of my hometown, I knew that Coffs Harbour just didn't have the opportunities I was looking for. No matter how hard I tried, the yearning within me — the one that longed for a meaningful life — just never left, and though I tried to satiate it with travel and weekend trips away, I found that it just couldn't be tamed. Like a beast, it grew larger and hungrier, clawing at me until I could no longer ignore it. Thankfully, however, change was coming.

After spending six months sifting through, and applying for, hundreds of jobs all over Australia, I received an invitation to interview for two different positions in Brisbane. One was for an administration role, the other for a children's photography studio. They were two ends of a very different stick, but I was desperate to get out of Coffs, so I quickly replied to both and set up a time for the following week. Within a few days I was on the road and heading for Queensland, where I planned to catch up with some friends and fit in my job interviews at the same time. As I did, a sudden, spontaneous thought popped into my mind. *Why not see what Chris is up to?* I thought. *Can't hurt.*

Long story short, that week in Brisbane changed everything for me. Not only did I land one of the jobs I applied for, but within less than 24 hours of meeting up with Chris, the two of us realised that there was something special between us; something worth exploring. It was unexpected and surprising, and in a way, it reminded me of the night five years earlier, when Raj and I had sat side by side watching a movie, with no expectations, only to turn to each other at the end of the film and know, deep within our hearts, that we were no longer friends – we belonged together.

Just like my relationship with Raj, it came at a time where I was finally ready to step into the next phase of my life. It was fun, natural, and drama-free; everything a relationship was meant to be. Within four weeks I was living permanently in Brisbane and working full time. Everything came together with such ease and I couldn't help but feel that I was exactly where I was meant to be. Finally, my life felt as though it was just beginning.

Chapter 23

Life was great. Chris and I quickly slipped into a routine of date nights, brunch outings with friends, and trips back and forth to visit my mum in Coffs, and though I didn't yet have my dream job, I felt that I was moving in the right direction. Best of all, I had access to a lot of opportunities that just weren't available at that time in my hometown, and before I knew it, I was contributing to several different art and culture blogs.

Soon, every spare minute, outside of work and date nights with Chris, was invested into my writing. As part of this, I also ventured further into volunteer work and advocacy – specifically around issues like child abuse, violence against women, and human trafficking. It was through this process of – as I like to say – 'experimentation without expectation' that I began to find my voice as a writer. Intuitively, I knew there was something inside me that shifted when I wrote about meaty topics as opposed to band reviews. The latter were fun, but I always struggled to find the right words, and as a singer – not a musician – I was always searching for the right technical terms to describe guitarists, bassists, and drummers. It always felt harder than when I wrote about social or cultural topics.

At the same time, I realised that people seemed to be moved by my words and the way I transformed difficult topics and conversations into stories that people couldn't help but read. One of the biggest pieces I wrote during this time was an essay on Jenna Jameson, one of the world's most famous porn performers. It was a deep exploration into her life, the traumas and circumstances that had led her into the trade before she'd even turned 18, and her own words about how the industry had impacted her.

I felt that it would help to open up a more nuanced and meaningful conversation about reality versus expectation for many within the porn industry, but not everyone who read it was thrilled. There were people in my circle – mostly male – who didn't enjoy hearing about the factors that drove women into the sex trade, whether that be through prostitution, the porn industry, or human trafficking. They didn't care about the human being behind the online persona, or the high rates of violence against many people (mostly women and girls) within the sex industry. Some of them even laughed when I expressed distress for women who had been killed by clients, or who had died from the burden of mental health challenges or addictions. It was a buzz kill. An inconvenient dampener on the sexual gratification they felt they were owed by women they'd never even spoken to.

It was around this time that some strange things began to happen to me. Almost, it seemed, as though they were occurring in direct response to the work I was doing with sex industry survivors and charities, and the way in which I was raising my voice. On several occasions I was watched and followed, and each time, it left me shaken.

One night, as I made my way to a dental appointment, I found myself in the middle of what soon became a very frightening situation. I'd been standing on the corner of Ipswich Road in Annerley, dressed in an oversized hoodie that swamped my tiny frame, when I'd become lost. Night fell quickly and the buildings became shrouded in darkness. As I began retracing my steps back up the small street I'd wandered down, I suddenly noticed a man standing to my left. A leather jacket cloaked his broad shoulders, and a hat, almost like a police cap, sat atop his head. In an instant I felt it; a little spark of warning from my intuition. One that screamed at me to get away, and quickly.

As casually as possible I crossed to the opposite side of the narrow alley and began walking up the other side. I glanced quickly over one shoulder, my heart quickening as I noticed that he too, was now switching directions. He'd abandoned his route down the street, deciding instead to follow me back up. By now, the two of us were standing just metres away from each other. He shifted uneasily from one foot to the other, throwing nervous sideways glances my way, and then looking off in another direction. I read his body language, the awkward tap dance we were both doing as we stood on the edge of a busy road eying each other.

Who's going to move first? Me or you...?

My heart roared in my ears, my mouth instantly dry. I backed further into the small alcove of a closed shop, and punched in the number for the dentist. As the receptionist answered, I quickly filled her in on what was happening. 'I'm stuck,' I said quietly. 'I'm at the top of the street but there's a man following me and I'm scared to leave this spot.'

'Stay where you are,' she urged. 'I'll send someone up to get you.'

At that exact moment, I looked across the laneway and directly into the eyes of the stranger. No longer nervous, he was now enraged, his gaze cold and narrowed. He raised one hand, flicking it in my direction. 'Fuck it,' he growled. 'Fuck you.'

And then he was gone.

I began shaking all over, feeling the hatred of his stare and the iciness of each word. Within seconds the receptionist appeared and escorted me safely to the dental practice, but I was thoroughly shaken.

The craziest part of this experience, however, was that it wasn't isolated. Only a few months beforehand I'd gone to see a friend's band, when – once again – I found myself being watched. It was right on dusk, and as I made my way down a street on the outskirts of Surfers Paradise, I noticed a man standing outside a block of units, his eyes just visible in the dim lighting of the early evening. His body was angled, concealed slightly behind a small wall of letterboxes, and as I approached my car, I heard a soft whistle slice eerily through the air. And in an instant, my entire nervous system was on edge and ready to go.

Why? Because I realised that the whistle wasn't for me. It was for someone else.

As the sound pierced through the night sky, a movement caught my eye. Just above the man, a screen door slid open, and a second male – this one much larger in stature – walked out onto his verandah. Both men were in the same apartment block, in units directly above/below each other, and now, they were both laser focused on me. It was intense. It was predatory. And I knew it wasn't good.

I moved faster, holding my breath and feeling the cold steel of my car key as it pressed between my fingers, ready to strike. I all but threw myself into the car, hitting the central lock button and speeding out of the street as quickly as possible as I exhaled loudly.

Initially, I'd dismissed these two incidents, telling myself that 'this is just the way the world is.' But after sharing with a few friends about the incident, one of my mates – an army veteran – said something that left me rattled.

'Jas, you're speaking out about things that some people don't like,' he stated. 'And you're calling out some pretty public and big corporations. I'm just saying, you should be careful.'

He was right. I'd been working alongside a group of women from a NFP named Collective Shout, a grassroots organisation committed to ending the sexualisation of women and girls in the media – and it meant that I was helping to lead campaigns against companies who were profiting from treating women as sex objects, or promoting men's trips to 'red-light districts' where they could take advantage of 'cheap girls' – many of whom were there as a result of either trafficking or financial vulnerabilities.

'I don't know about that,' I said to my friend, waving off his concern. 'Sounds a bit woo-woo to me.'

'You should be careful,' he repeated.

I changed the subject, trying not to let him see how rattled I was. RJ was the least spiritual person I knew. He was straight shooting, and if this was his honest opinion, then… well… it made it harder for me to ignore.

Despite the strange things that had been happening – whether coincidental or not – I found that I just couldn't make myself look away. Every day I was confronted with atrocities that, once seen, couldn't be unseen, and nothing was going to change that. From global companies who sexualised and exploited women's bodies for profit, to children being sold into the global sex trade, and toxic things people had become numb to – like strip clubs who intentionally marketed themselves outside all-boys' schools – I couldn't turn away.

I wasn't going to shut up, no matter how much some wanted me to. I wasn't going to hide.

Instead, I was going to take things much further.

Inside a large glass box, dozens of women sat haphazardly around small tables cramped with tubes and palettes of makeup. I watched on, my eyes peering through the curtainless windows as each woman went through her routine for the night. A line of contour here, a scattering of blush there. A yellow dress draped atop a pink plastic chair, and row after row of thick black fringes. It was like a zoo; a glass cage filled with female bodies, each of them there for the viewing of any stranger who happened to pass. Technically, it was a 'beauty room.' A space where they could be watched – without a shred of privacy – by the hundreds of male 'sex tourists' who surrounded me. But in reality, I knew what these women truly were, to the men who viewed them. *Entertainment… a body without a soul.*

It was a Saturday night and I was standing inside one of the most infamous red-light districts in South East Asia, a place proudly marketed as 'the world's largest adult playground.' It was a three-level, U-shaped plaza, filled with hordes of women and girls, some of whom were as young as 13, presented solely for the sexual gratification of men. I shuddered and turned my eyes toward the closed doors of a club just beyond where I stood; a place where, only weeks earlier, 22 girls had been rescued from exploitation by an anti-human trafficking organisation. Nineteen of those girls were underage.

The Stories We Carry

Yet, the vast majority of people would never know this… in fact, it seemed as though no one cared. All around me, dozens of other bars continued on as normal, their walls thumping with loud pop and electronic music, as young women – even some with swollen pregnant bellies – stood by the doorway with numbers pinned to their bras or crop tops. All afternoon and night, these places carried on as normal, serving women and girls to the highest bidder – sometimes for as little as a packet of fries. All along the footpaths, and on every level of the plaza, men sat around laughing and grinning; some with a beer in one hand and a teen in the other.

In my head, I remembered the words of one of the anti-trafficking workers who I'd spoken to earlier that day. *Some of the girls we've met, particularly in smaller karaoke bars, have been sold for as little as $2.*

I wanted to vomit.

How many other girls are suffering right now, waiting for someone to offer them a hand to escape to a safer life? I wondered. *How many girls are hiding their fear behind fake smiles, counting the seconds until this client leaves, and the next arrives?*

I'd only been in Thailand for a few days, and my entire worldview had shifted so vastly in that time. I'd known when I'd boarded the plane with a small group of strangers, the ten of us heading to South East Asia to learn more about human trafficking with a well-known organisation, that I'd be forced way outside my comfort zone. I'd been prepared to have my heart cracked open as I spent time in red-light districts and rescue homes where girls had been set free and given the tools to thrive. But this place, *My God*. This place was like nothing I'd ever experienced.

All around us, women seemed to be suffering. Mothers sat on filthy streets with their children between their legs as they begged for money. Pregnant girls and 'Lady Boys' stood in sky-high heels, trying to convince men to step inside the pubs with them – where in many cases, they'd then be disrespected, degraded, and exploited – sometimes, for the cost of a small meal. And now, as I was seeing, women were even crammed into glass 'viewing' rooms as they did their makeup. It was a visual assault in every single way but what affected me the most was the overwhelming burden of heaviness and depression in the air. The toxic atmosphere was so thick that it was tangible.

Beside me, my team mate Jana – a tall woman with short blonde hair – tilted her gaze towards a bar just ahead of us. 'Look over there,' she said, gesturing to a small group of women in bikinis. They sat slumped on either side of a doorway, their tiny bodies perched atop stools that were half their size. As we approached, the girls barely moved, but as a group of guys came alongside us they suddenly straightened up, forced a grin, and began giggling and performing. The moment we passed, their eyes once again glazed over, smiles fading as they hunched into a slumped position. This was a scene repeated over and over as we passed each bar. Each time, their body language screamed the same sentence: 'I don't want to be here. I don't want this.'

I looked around at all the men in the building and wondered if they saw it too. *Can't they see what's going on inside these young women's eyes? Do they not see the same things we do? Or do they just not care?*

As we made our way outside the plaza, I felt the gentle brushing of a hand against my arm. It was so soft, I wasn't sure it was real, but then I turned and lifted my gaze, staring straight into the dark brown eyes of a young woman. Dressed in a white polo top and a pleated mini-skirt, she stood outside a bar, a security guard positioned just behind her small frame.

What –?

I was momentarily stunned, confused by the way that she had grabbed my forearm. It wasn't the grasping, flirtatious gesture I'd seen from many of the young women in this building; the ones who tried to convince you to come inside. It wasn't forceful or coercive. Yet, I could feel in her grip that something wasn't right.

Again, I looked into her face, and instantly I saw it. From her tight smile, to the wide expanse of her eyes, it was clear. I knew that look. It was thinly veiled fear.

For a few seconds we stood there, both surrounded by the awful thumping of electronic music and drunken laughter as she held my arm. I looked deeply into her eyes, meeting the small smile she offered with one of my own.

There are few times I've ever felt as helpless as I did in that moment… because there was nothing I could do. There was nothing I could say. There was just the touch of our hands; the small smiles between us as I tried to let her know, *I see you. I hear you.*

And then, I had to leave.

As our group walked in a tight huddle along dark streets toward the humble building we were staying in, I couldn't stop thinking of her. On the rooftop, we stood with our team leader, each of us too overwhelmed by the darkness of the place we'd just passed through to even speak.

To this day I've never forgotten that young woman. Although there's no way of knowing what her story was, or why she reached out to me that night, I know that everything I have done since this day has been in honour of women like her. Those who feel unseen, trapped, and unable to escape.

Whatever I saw in the next few days, no matter what I heard or witnessed, I made a serious commitment: *Don't look away,* I told myself. *Lean into the pain. Remember, nothing changes unless we choose to confront that which we wish to change.*

Thailand was a visual and auditory assault; a melting pot of beauty, culture, resourcefulness, spirituality, poverty, and corruption. There was so much to take in – so much I wanted to see – but I knew that I was there for only one reason; to discover more about the reality of life for women and children in South East Asia, many of whom were trapped in the sex trade with a lack of other viable options. This included those who had been groomed or trafficked, as well as those who had knowingly entered the industry.

So often, when people think of human trafficking, they picture a young girl sitting in a dirty basement, her limbs chained to a wall or tethered to the floor. This is just one of many visual assumptions and stereotypes that people often lean toward and one of many that fails to address the complexity of exploitation. In reality, exploitation occurs in every culture and country across the globe, and those who are trapped inside the sex trade are not always held under physical lock and key. They are not physically 'chained to the wall,' as we often see in popular movies. Instead, the chains that often hold them in place are mental and emotional; their bonds born of financial inequality, cultural expectations, and internalised shame. This is especially true in many South East Asian communities, where young women experience intense pressure to provide for their families – not only their parents, but also male siblings. Girls learn early that they are expected to care for others and that they must do whatever it takes to ensure their mother, father, and siblings are financially safe. As a result, many young women find themselves being groomed into – or 'choosing' – to take jobs in karaoke bars and clubs (illegal brothels). Here, in Thailand, poverty certainly had a lot to answer for when it came to the sheer number of women and children who existed within the sex trade. As I soon discovered, many girls came from Hill Tribe villages, where passports and photo identification didn't exist – another factor that made it all too easy for exploitation and trafficking to occur. With no ID – let alone a university degree or certification – the ability to earn a well-paying income or enter meaningful work was significantly harder.

Add to this the stigmatisation around women's sexuality and you can begin to understand why so many feel powerless to leave the sex trade; regardless of whether they entered knowingly, or were coerced or trafficked. As many girls shared: *I've lost the respect of my family, so who will want me now?*

There were many stories that I learned of, throughout my time in SE Asia, that were hard to shake – but there is one in particular that I've never forgotten. At the time, we were in a more remote part of Thailand where a number of prevention and rehabilitation homes had been created for survivors (or those who were at high risk of being exploited), and I met with dozens of teenage girls who had once been in the industry. There was a young woman who had been studying and working towards one day opening her own hair salon and while in the area I had booked in with her for a wash and style. With a round face and a thick button-nose, she was quiet and shy, often smiling softly as other girls in the salon laughed and joked with us. I'd been warned prior to my booking that she wouldn't be able to provide the massage part of the treatment and to please ensure I didn't take any photographs. As I later discovered, this young woman had encountered horrendous mental abuse while in the sex trade and was often laughed at and tormented by the Mamasan (the female manager of the brothel/club) about how 'fat' and 'ugly' she was. Her days were spent being degraded by men, and then laughed at by the managers and bar girls, who would point her way while oinking like a pig.

I looked into the gentle eyes of this lovely, timid woman and wanted to cry. The *cruelty*. The *trauma*. Was it any wonder so many girls felt trapped and unable to leave? What did they have to go to? What self-worth or confidence did they have?

There were many stories like this; thousands of young girls with different names but near-identical experiences. What astounded me most, however, was not only their ability to survive, but to find a way to begin thriving.

How are these girls not rocking in a corner, unable to function or speak? I wondered. Only recently I'd learned of two 13-year-old girls who had been tricked into leaving their village for a job in a restaurant, only to be kidnapped and raped so violently that they were returned, rather than sold. That story, in particular, broke me. I couldn't get my head around how so many of these women – many of whom were only 15 and had already been out of the sex industry for several years – had been able to find peace, joy, and renewed confidence. I watched them giggling and joking as they rode bicycles with our group through a park, making fun of us as we attempted to speak basic phrases in Thai. I watched the way that they played – just like little girls should – and the courage that they showed as they took charge of their lives. Had

The Stories We Carry

their lived experiences been wiped away? No. Did they still live with anxiety or other mental health challenges due to the abuse they had experienced? Yes. But at the same time, they were so full of *hope*; that's what astounded me most. They had chosen not to allow their trauma to become a life sentence.

Over the fortnight that I was there, I was blown away by how much I witnessed and experienced. I scrubbed, painted, and renovated a two-story building for a young woman who was opening her own hair salon. I dug trenches and played soccer with kids at a local prevention home, where I also met a young woman I'd been sponsoring for many years. Most importantly, I had the opportunity to learn from these young girls, as they shared their culture, taught us how to cook traditional Thai recipes, and demonstrated every day just how strong the human spirit really is.

Hope and gratitude, in particular, seemed to be a staple within Thailand and it astounded and moved me profoundly. One afternoon, I walked to a small stall in a country market, and saw a Thai woman literally dance with joy as she collected money for the goods she'd just sold. 'Lucky money, lucky money!' she grinned, fingers clutched around the colourful notes as she waved them in the air, touching them to each of the items that hung on the shelves. Things that we took for granted were appreciated and honoured; minute moments in time that were acknowledged for their beauty and magic. Just like sunshine after a storm, the people of this country had learned that light could always exist within darkness. They understood that nothing in life was to be taken for granted and it was never too late to try again.

'Hey, has anyone seen Changers?'

On a small, darkened street, I turned and squinted against the blackness. All around me, my teammates shrugged and glanced around, each of us growing increasingly nervous. One of us was missing; a young woman by the name of Stacey – or 'Changers', as we affectionately called her. As the most mischievous girl in our group she was hard to miss; which is why we were now worried. Changers was clearly not with us.

'Shit, you don't think she got left behind, do you?' asked Jen, her blonde hair sticking to the edge of her neck from the humid night air.

'I don't know. She was with us at the last place, yeah?' replied Jana.

'I saw her in the markets for a while… but then I went into a different stall,' added another.

'Shit. She got left behind, didn't she?'

I stared out into the darkness, feeling worried. It was around 7 pm, and we'd just returned to our accommodation after a final night of exploring the local markets. None of us had any way to contact our missing teammate, and worst of all, I was pretty sure she didn't even know the address of where we were staying.

Just as we began to descend into panic, the bright lights of a Tuk Tuk came rumbling toward us, pulling to a stop just outside the front door of the four-level, slightly run-down complex we were staying in. Then, with a smile and wave, out stepped Changers.

'What the hell, Stacey?'

The Stories We Carry

'Where've you been!?'

'How did you get home?'

We all gathered around, waiting for her to speak or explode into anger at having been left behind in a small rural town. After all, I certainly would have, if my team didn't realise I was missing!

Instead, Changers shrugged casually, smiling back at her driver who was now speeding off into the night.

'How did you know where to go?' I asked.

'Oh that's easy,' she smiled. 'I just walked up to a Tuk Tuk driver and asked if he knew where I lived, and he said, "Yep!" and brought me here.'

We stared, mouths agape. 'Are you serious?! *Here*, in the north of Thailand? You just asked a random stranger if he knew where you lived?'

She shrugged, unfazed. 'Well, yeah. He knew most of us were white, and there was only one place a large group of white tourists would be staying!' she laughed.

'Oh my God, only you, Changers!'

We stood around shaking our heads, bursting into laughter as the ten of us walked inside.

Little moments of joy like these were so important, amidst what was a very heavy trip. Only two weeks ago we had all been strangers, yet in the space of 14 days, we'd formed a bond that was hard to articulate. Each of us had grown to know each other's truest fears and desires; the things that moved and shaped us. Secrets – some embarrassing, others hilarious – that we'd never told anyone. And above all, we understood the importance of coming together as a collective to make change.

There are a lot of differing opinions about human trafficking awareness trips (such as the one in which we took part); judgements about whether these trips are helpful to the girls involved, or just an opportunity for white people to virtue signal about how woke or educated they are. For me, I know what I saw and experienced during our time overseas and how genuine each person was in their passion to help stop sexual exploitation. I know of the personal and financial cost that we invested to be there. It wasn't a fun, relaxing holiday by the ocean, with coconuts and cocktails in hand. It was a fortnight of exposing ourselves to some of the most evil things that occur within our world, so that we could take what we'd learned and return home with the knowledge to create change. It was a time of sacrificing our own comfort, in order to hear and remember the stories of those who'd experienced unthinkable pain. It was an opportunity to empower others to join with us in the fight to provide a better future for women and girls. It was all of that and so much more.

Little did I know that – for me – it was also the start of what was to become 18 months of personal investigation into many of these horrors within my very own city.

Chapter 24

Coming home from Thailand felt almost as shocking as arriving there. So much had shifted for me mentally in the space of 14 days and things that once irked or aggravated me – like bad drivers, or having to wait longer than usual for my doctor – now seemed like very minor first-world problems. Particularly, when compared to the horror of what so many little girls and boys were dealing with in other parts of the globe.

In some ways, I felt that I could – at least on a *very* small scale – relate to the disconnect that many soldiers feel when they return from war. The things that people complained about here – such as their coffee being too cold, or a person not picking up their dog's stinky poo at the park – all seemed very mundane. I just couldn't relate.

It sounded silly, but I truly had been changed in the space of just a few weeks, and nothing really cemented this more than returning to my duller-than-dull reception job. While I was grateful to have a comfortable job and a steady income – something that so many don't – I couldn't shake off the feeling that I was wasting my true talents. As someone in a position of privilege, I wanted to *use* that privilege for more. I knew that I had a knack for speaking out about difficult subjects in a way that moved people to take action – I'd seen it time and time again, as I wrote blogs, created content for charities, or ran fundraisers to help rescue more victims of trafficking. And spending my days sitting at a reception desk, while diverting phone calls, or typing numbers into spreadsheets until my brain bled from boredom was not the life I wanted to live. *There has to be more than this*, I thought. *There has to be something meaningful I can do in the world; something that will truly help others.*

As the weeks rolled on following my return home, I began writing more and more about the issue of human trafficking for my blog 'Thoughts From Jas,' and it was soon afterwards that I got a new idea: to begin exploring what was happening right here in Australia. I'd recently picked up a book titled 'Not In My Town' (by Charles Powell and Dillon Burrows), and had been deeply shocked as to the widespread nature of human trafficking and how it often hid 'in plain sight' amidst affluent cities. One of the stories that most stood out to me was that of Chong Kim, a Korean-American woman who had been trafficked within America as a teenager, and sold to hundreds of men from all over the world. With brutal honesty she'd described how her exploitation was carried out in broad daylight, with victims such as herself transported in warehouse trucks to small motels where illegal immigrants were hired to sit at a desk, and tell legitimate travellers that there was 'no vacancy.' There were no real couples or tourists staying in these venues – they existed solely for the sale of young women's bodies.

Chong's story had made me think more deeply about Australia as a destination country and more so, my own neighbourhood. *How many girls or women are being exploited here?* I wondered. *Could it be a possibility?* I'd certainly read articles about children and women who'd been trafficked in Australia, but I didn't know if these incidents were few and far between.

One afternoon as I pulled up at a set of lights near my home, I let my eyes wander absentmindedly, my brain ticking over all that I'd been learning. Then, suddenly, there was a burst of colour from the right-hand side of the road. A red pulsing light that flickered on and off. *Open! Open! Open!* It was a cheap, gaudy sign; the type often used in late-night fast-food franchises. Only, it wasn't attached to anything like that. Instead, it adorned the side of an old Queenslander home. Even more unusual were the windows, each of them covered from top to bottom with newspapers.

The traffic light switched to green and I edged forward, craning my neck as I passed the white wooden house. How many times had I passed by this corner, never really taking notice? Had it always looked this way? As I drove on, I thought again of the small neon sign, and I was instantly reminded of Chong Kim's story. *Could sex slavery be existing right here?* I wondered.

That night I went online and searched for the name of the massage shop I'd seen operating from the old white house. Sure enough, it linked up with an adult forum; a place where men discussed women as casually as objects or Pokémon cards to be collected and then discarded. As I started reading the comments from clients, I thought I was going to vomit.

> *'Oh, I feel soooo bad for them – not. They know the line of work they're in. It comes with the territory. I don't give two shits about them – they're money-hungry whores who are too lazy and greedy to get a real job.'*

> *'Having kids can really fuck up a woman's body. You should have seen her belly – she had a shitload of wrinkly, saggy skin. My stomach is turning just thinking about it!'*

> *'She said she came to Australia to look for work and pursue a good relationship. She sounded so immature – talking about "finding herself", and religion. I tapped her a few times (let's just say she was average) and then made up an excuse and left early.'*

The casual misogyny was so repulsive I could barely stomach reading it. Even worse, though, was the way that they traded the names of the young women without any care for their safety. This meant that an abuser could trawl the forum and discover, with very little effort, exactly how much a certain girl cost, what her vulnerabilities were, and how easy it was to manipulate, coerce, or exploit her into doing certain things.

As I read, I kept thinking about all the things I'd rather be doing with my time; how much easier it would be to close my laptop and push all of this to the back of my mind. And yet, I knew that I couldn't.

More importantly, I knew that it wasn't enough to just read the words on this website.

If I want to find out what's really happening inside these venues, I can't just rely on dodgy forums, I thought. *I'll have to go deeper. I need to visit them and see what's happening through my own eyes – starting with the one near my house.*

It was then that I made my plan.

'This way, please.'

Trying to calm the flutter of nerves within my stomach, I followed the middle-aged Mamasan through the living area, and toward a darkened room in the back of the house. All around me, newspaper-covered windows glared back, their black and white text effectively hiding from view any passing traffic or pedestrians. Internally, I tried my best to act as though all of this was normal – even though it was becoming clear that this was anything but so. A physiotherapy clinic or deep tissue massage centre was one thing, but an old Queenslander house with covered windows and a very suspicious Mamasan (who had only opened the door a few centimetres to speak with me) was another entirely.

From what I'd read through my research of human trafficking, most venues that operated illegally or engaged in human trafficking followed a very reliable pattern: they opened well outside of normal evening hours, their windows were always covered, and the young women who worked inside either struggled to speak English, or couldn't explain the services provided on their signage. It was also common to see these venues in both upper-class and lower socioeconomic areas, most of them blending in amongst everyday shops.

Taking all of this into consideration, it was clear that the only way to find out what was truly going on was to visit these massage parlours in person. Although I wasn't their regular 'type,' I figured that my plan was innocent enough that it may just work. I simply needed to pick a venue, say that I was new to the area, and ask if they had a business card. Once I had their mobile number, I could reverse search it and see where it led. This, it seemed, was the key – because while the names of the venues rarely populated anything online, the phone number instantly connected me to adult forums or social media accounts that immediately revealed the true nature of the business.

Today, however, I was taking things up a notch, because I was no longer just asking for a business card – I was now using my own money to become a paying customer.

From the doorway, a young Taiwanese woman smiled warmly. 'Hi, I'm Chelsea,' she grinned. 'I will be doing your massage today.'

'Thank you,' I replied casually, lying down on the table as she began to expertly massage my back. In any other setting I would have leaned in to the bliss and taken it as an opportunity to rest, but my mind was running at full steam. Now that I was here, I had no idea what to do. I mean, it wasn't as if this young woman was just going to come right out and tell me about the illegal sexual services happening in her own workplace, was it?

'Pressure okay?' Chelsea asked, her voice – soft and peaceful – cutting through the racetrack of thoughts inside my brain. I nodded, trying to think up ways to start a conversation without it feeling forced, before eventually settling on some routine small talk.

'How's your weekend been so far? Do you have much planned?' I asked.

'Not too much,' she offered. 'It's been a busy week. How about you?'

'Probably the same. My boyfriend and I are thinking of going out for breakfast tomorrow, but that's about it,' I said casually.

Silence followed, and I stared at the floorboards wondering if I'd made a mistake coming here. So far, Chelsea didn't seem like many of the young women I'd read about; the types who were being exploited and trafficked. She spoke fairly fluent English, seemed relaxed and happy, and was good at what she did. *Maybe I was wrong?*

As she worked, Chelsea continued chatting, slowly moving from small talk to opening up about the differences between her home country and Australia; the places she'd visited and the ones she still longed to see. Soon, we relaxed into a comfortable rhythm, sharing stories and laughing about our experiences.

The Stories We Carry

'What's been the weirdest thing about living in Australia?' I asked.

'Hmm.' She paused, thinking. 'Probably the accents. Some of you Aussies have this really thick accent… like, I don't know. Very hard to understand,' she laughed.

'Ahh,' I said, knowingly. 'Bogans.'

'Bogans?' Chelsea's hands paused momentarily on my back, her voice rising in inflection. 'What is this bo-gan?' she asked, elongating the word. 'Are they white people?'

An uncontrollable laugh burst from my lips, the question taking me by surprise. 'You want to know about bogans? I can tell you a story or two,' I joked, launching into a visual description of some of the people I'd met while working in various seaside towns. As Chelsea and I eased into a comfortable conversation, she began to share more with me as well, recounting stories of her life growing up in Taiwan and how disgusted she was by Vegemite (our 'national treasure' when it comes to toppings for toast and bread).

Though our conversation was light and friendly, I still felt a buzz of nervousness; an almost prickling sensation that told me there was something deeper I needed to talk with her about. It was the same feeling I'd had many times over the years; the voice of my intuition. A sense that there was something going on in this parlour and that all wasn't right.

The only way to know, though, was to ask – and I was terrified to take that next step. From underneath the table I took a deep breath, forcing the words past my lips.

'So... what's it like working here? Have you been at the parlour for a long time?'

Chelsea suddenly paused, the tone of her naturally light and sweet voice changing. 'Uh... it's... it's okay. I mean, there are a lot of very nice clients, very kind. Like you,' she added quickly. 'But most of my clients are men, and... well...' She paused again, her hands kneading a little harder along my calves. 'Sometimes they ask for things that I don't want to do. *Extras*. Things like that.'

'Oh.'

In the silence, I began cursing myself. Would she regret opening up to me? Had I pushed too far? But then, to my surprise, she continued; almost as if, now that the flow of secrets had started, she couldn't close the valve again.

'I always tell them to stop – that I don't do things like that,' she added, her voice strong and firm. 'But sometimes I don't get a chance, because they don't even ask. They just start touching themselves.'

'I'm so sorry,' I said quietly. 'That must be so awful to have to deal with. It's disgusting that there are men out there who think they have a right to do this to you.'

Chelsea laughed in a way that told me this was all too common; that it was something she tried not to dwell on too much – even though it bothered her. 'There are definitely a lot of creeps,' she noted discreetly. 'I once had a man who phoned and asked for a *Couples' Massage*. I thought it was sweet – that he wanted to book for him and his wife. But no...' She moved around the other side of the massage table, continuing. 'He arrived alone, and when he came in he took all his clothes off and started saying things like,

"Oh you're so beautiful… If I wasn't married I would *love* to take you out."' Chelsea paused, shuddering. 'He'd been married for only three months.'

'Wow.' *What else was there to say?*

'It was really awkward. You know… because I have a boyfriend, too.'

'Were you okay? Did he leave you alone?'

'Yeah. He didn't touch me,' she said, her voice tinged with relief. 'But he kept asking me all these questions. Things like, "Do you think I'm handsome? Am I your type? What do you like in a man?" I just pretended I didn't understand what he was saying. *"Sorry, my English not so good."*' Chelsea tilted her head innocently, playing on her accent.

'These men and the things they're asking you to do – the things they're doing without your permission,' I began, 'it's not okay. It's actually illegal. They shouldn't be asking you for sexual services, and you have every right to report them to the police. If you want to, that is. Also,' I smiled, 'I totally wouldn't judge you if you punched them in the balls next time.'

Without warning Chelsea erupted into a fit of giggles, one palm clasped tightly over her lips. 'Maybe next time I will,' she winked, before regaining her composure. 'Some of the girls here… they're happy to do that – those extra things. I don't think the manager cares. But I don't want to, so thank you.'

And there it was; the thread I'd been searching for. The confirmation that my intuition was right and there *was* far more going on inside this venue than I'd first thought. *And if it's happening here,*

I wondered, *how many of the other regular houses with flashing signs out front are also operating as illegal brothels?*

As I finished up my massage that day and walked down the street toward my car, I took a final glance back at the white Queenslander and thought – once again – about how normal it all looked to the outside eye. How much it blended in. Every day, thousands of cars zipped by – likely without a single thought for what women were experiencing inside, and the types of men who were walking among us. The kind who kissed their families goodbye and then walked up those rickety steps to purchase a woman's body for a mere $30 or $40.

It made me sick, physically and emotionally. For the briefest of moments I considered filing everything I'd learned away in a box in the back of my mind; replacing it with funny memes and pretty pictures on Instagram. But every time I tried, I was reminded of all I'd witnessed in Thailand. The children who'd been sold for $2. The young women who were forced to go against their bodies and minds every day, in order to survive. Women like Chong Kim, who were trafficked in first-world countries as the world moved on, unaware, or worse, unaffected.

Before me lay a gigantic rabbit hole, and just like Alice in Wonderland, I was at a crossroad. I had to make a decision but which way would I turn?

I glanced down at the business card I'd been given – the one on which Chelsea had scrawled her personal mobile number before thanking me for my offer to lend an ear if she ever needed any advice or someone to talk to. 'Sometimes I don't understand things about my visa, or whether I'm being paid the right amount, so thank you', she'd shared. 'It can be hard not being in my own country.'

The Stories We Carry

When I left that day, I was blissfully unaware of the horrors I was yet to encounter. I thought I'd already been shocked to my core, but in reality there was so much more to discover.

I was in my own version of Alice in Wonderland, with two paths before me.

And just like the story, I dove right down the rabbit hole.

Once I started investigating further, I couldn't believe I'd ever been so blind. Even more shocking was the fact that none of it was hidden. In fact, once you knew what to look for, it was all too easy to spot in advance.

On one occasion I walked up to the front door of an old Queenslander house in Brisbane, only to find a sign telling me to go around the back. When I got there – walking through a low-hanging line of clothing – I was confronted by a Lebanese man who walked out from a side bedroom, his face etched into an angry scowl. Just behind him stood a petite Asian girl, no older than 20. Her head was dipped low, her arms wrapped protectively around her stomach. There was no mistaking her body language; this was not a young woman enjoying whatever was happening.

She'd stood in the doorway momentarily, before slowly meandering away into the darkened hallway, leaving another worker to address me. The second woman stared at me warily, and I forced my lips into a smile.

'Hi, I was wondering if you had a price list. For your nail art,' I added.

'Nail art?'

'Yes, you have it listed on the sign out front.'

Her brow furrowed, both eyes narrowing in confusion. Eventually I realised that she couldn't understand me, and I left shortly afterwards with a cheap business card marked with a handwritten mobile number.

On another occasion, I found myself driving through the southside of Brisbane after dinner with a friend, when I noticed a flash of gold from a small, darkened side street. In the glint of my headlights I caught the movement of a woman dressed in a bralette top and mini-skirt, as she sprinted down the alley toward a well-known illegal brothel. It rattled me – particularly at 10 pm at night – and I worried for her safety. Unfortunately, by the time I swung the car around and made it back toward the one-way street, she'd already disappeared.

Then there was another venue – this one tucked in amongst million-dollar homes not far from the city. A quick online search showed me it was well known amongst the local 'punters,' and given that it had already been exposed by police and reported in the news a few years prior, it seemed that most people were happy to turn a blind eye. Even now, it continued operating. When I decided one afternoon to stand on a nearby corner and watch their clientele, I saw that most were well-dressed business men who came and went without a care in the world. Many months later, when I eventually stepped inside, I discovered half a dozen young women dressed in mini-skirts, bodycon dresses, and high heels, as a very stern looking Mamasan by the name of Tam watched on. It would be another year or more before the place was raided and when that finally happened, she would be revealed to be a cruel boss who sexually and financially exploited vulnerable young female students.

The Stories We Carry

All around me were signs of corruption and exploitation, and yet, a bigger issue loomed; the question of what to do with this information. After all, I wasn't an investigative journalist and I didn't have anyone funding me or offering support – and from what I'd seen, the police seemed powerless to do much.

At the same time, I felt it was important to do *something*. So one night, after staking out an illegal parlour with my friend Wolfie well into the evening (during which time we never saw a single woman leave), I decided to put together a comprehensive report of all the places I'd come across, and a Google Drive folder full of screenshots from the men accessing these places. I'd then hand it over to local police and find out what the next step was.

It sounded simple, but in reality, it was harrowing. Every evening was spent trawling through disgusting forums and dragging my cursor around little black and white text boxes full of misogyny and racism – casual conversations about Asian women and their bodies that I then compiled into folders for each location. Then I put together a four-page document containing printed screenshots and details of everything I'd witnessed, after which I made an appointment to speak with a head officer at a local police station.

To be fair, the female constable who was assigned to speak with me (and Chris, who had come along for moral support) was fairly kind, and seemed genuinely shocked by what I'd uncovered. But it soon became clear that nothing much would be done.

'Wow, I'm so glad you put the direct links into the reports,' she said, her nose scrunching into a tight ball of disgust as she read through the men's forum screenshots. 'We wouldn't be allowed to access these, so I'm glad you copied in the images.'

Are you serious? You're a police officer and you're literally telling me that I can access stuff that you can't? How is that even possible? I wondered.

'Look, this is all very helpful,' she continued. 'But the reality is this: if we can't get armed robbers to go to jail, there's not much chance of these men being arrested. We don't help the victims,' she clarified. 'We just send them back to the country they came from.'

I felt myself recoil, her words leaving an invisible mark. *We don't help the victims.* Had she really just said that?

Sadly, I knew the officer meant it. Only weeks beforehand I'd read a news article about a massage parlour that had been raided, and the owners found guilty of sexually and financially exploiting young Asian students, and yet not a single one of those young women were treated as victim-survivors. Instead they were deported. No one assessed them for psychological trauma or physical injuries. No one opened an investigation into whether they had been trafficked, raped, or coerced. Simply put, they were 'bad women' who'd 'broken the law,' and they were to be punished for the actions of the men who, let's be honest, were the only reason they were there.

Now, here in the police station, I felt as though I'd wasted my time.

The officer continued. 'It's unfortunate, but that's the reality. Thank you for putting together this report though, we'll take it from here.'

I sat for a moment, my chest feeling like a deflated balloon – and then I made my way toward the door.

Suddenly, I heard her voice again, calling me back. But as I turned, I saw the warning that flashed from her eyes.

The Stories We Carry

'Jas? Stay away from these venues – you need to leave it alone from here on. We've got this.'

Have you? Have you really? I thought, as I walked toward the front of the station. Though I wished otherwise, it really didn't feel that they did.

I exited into the cool night air, disappointed yet determined. *If they're not going to help me, I'll find another way,* I thought. *I can't let this go…not yet.*

Chapter 25

That's the place.

Standing in a darkened parking lot, I gazed upwards, checking for cameras. It was common for a lot of seedy venues to have surveillance at both the front and rear of their buildings, and though I couldn't tell for sure, I had no doubt that this one was the same. *Anyway, too late to turn back now*, I thought.

With hurried footsteps, I left the safety of my car and walked around the corner to the front entrance, wondering all the while if the steady stream of cars passing by knew what I was up to. A pang of guilt worked its way through me, my brain full of images of the police officer, her warning still fresh in my ears.

Stay away Jas, we've got it from here.

In some ways, I guess you could say that I *did* take the officer's advice. For the most part I stayed away from many of the venues I'd been visiting in person – but I wasn't content to step away completely, so instead, I decided to get creative. My plan? To immerse myself into the world of the men who exploited Asian women around Australia – in particular, Brisbane – and create a fake account with an alias. In just a few clicks, I verified my username and stepped into my role as 'one of the boys.' It was a delicate balance, since the majority of the men on this forum were suspicious and wary of giving out too much information to new users, but fortunately for me, there were some who liked to brag. In no time at all, I knew exactly which men would be more likely to help out and give away clues about what was happening inside the four walls of the venues I'd been keeping an eye on. My usual method was to pretend that I was in town for a few weeks and that I was looking to 'have a little fun' while I was there. I'd then suggest the names of some of the venues I'd been scoping out, after which I'd sit back and wait for the men to take the bait. Sometimes, if I was lucky, they'd give me the precise information I needed to add to my research document by literally telling me what was happening and who the shop's Mamasan was. In some ways it was all too easy.

I'd been content with staying outside of the venues – that is, until I came across 'HS', a new parlour that had just opened down the street from Chris' house. Again, it followed the same pattern that I'd witnessed time and time again. Open until late at night; windows that were completely covered; staff who knew little of the services listed on their brochure. And, of course, when I phoned to ask about booking an appointment, I was told that they were 'full,' only to find – when I called back later and spoke to someone else – that they had appointments available all night.

Guess the other masseuse didn't get the memo about not booking in women, I thought.

There was something about the whole set up that sent chills through me, making my intuition spike up like small hairs along the ridge of a dog's spine – and that was when I knew that I just couldn't stay away. Though I couldn't explain it, I felt there was a reason that I'd noticed it while leaving Chris' house. There was a reason for me to check it out more closely.

The Stories We Carry

Now, though, it was 8 pm on a Wednesday night and I was standing outside the massage shop.

Holding my breath, I pushed through the front door and stepped inside the small reception area, my ears instantly filling with the sounds of trickling waterfalls and relaxation music. In front of me stood a young Chinese masseuse in a tight bodycon dress and a pair of high heels, her slim frame partially hidden by a large desk. I noticed that she was completely alone, despite the fact that it was well into the evening, and all the other shops in the area were closed.

'Hi, my name is Rose.' Her voice was low – almost timid. 'Follow me this way.'

With small, slow steps she led the way to a side room, where I popped my bag onto a spare chair and tried my best to make small talk. I could tell she was incredibly nervous but I wasn't sure why. It was only when Rose began the massage, that suddenly, I understood exactly why she was so anxious.

As the young woman began pummelling my back – swapping from what felt like 'punching' my skin, to aimlessly trailing her fingers along my shoulders – I realised that she had no idea what she was doing. Considering the fact that I had recently torn *both* my hamstrings (and that my back was already in pain before stepping through the doors), I couldn't help but wonder if I should just get up, excuse myself, and leave. I mean, sure, I didn't expect the best massage in the world; but paying $80 to make everything worse, simply so that I could try to find out from the inside what was happening within the four walls of these massage parlours, wasn't part of my plan.

Face-down on the table, I began to think about some of the news articles I'd read about male police officers getting paid to 'test' these venues for themselves – sometimes literally exploiting girls themselves, all in the name of 'research.' And yet, here I was, suffering through this pummelling for no reason other than the fact that I genuinely cared about what was happening to young Asian women in our community.

As I grimaced and gritted my teeth, I suddenly felt Rose's hands begin to tremble. Then she stopped, pulling back. 'I'm sorry,' she stuttered. 'I'm sorry if it's not... is this okay?'

'It's okay,' I lied. 'Maybe just a bit softer?'

"Okay... "

I stared at the floor, my head full of random thoughts and questions as she restarted. Was I reading too much into things, once again? Or had my intuition been right about this place? *Just because she doesn't know how to massage doesn't mean anything bad is happening,* I reasoned.

The thought had barely finished cycling through my head when, once again, Rose pulled back. And that's when I heard it – the unmistakable sound of shuddering breaths.

'Are you okay?'

She swiped a hand underneath her nose, tears springing into the corner of each eye. Quietly, I pulled myself upright and wrapped a towel around myself.

'Rose? Are you okay?'

The Stories We Carry

'I'm so sorry.' She began crying harder, her body folding over itself in a sudden release of pent-up emotion. 'I try so hard at massage, but no one... no one show me how. Manager won't teach me, and the man before you... so angry.' Her words came out as a hiccup of emotion; short, sharp breaths of shame and self-hatred. 'I had to give money back,' she continued miserably. 'I give you money back too.'

I leaned over and opened my arms, gesturing tentatively. *Is this okay? Would you like a hug?* She moved forward, accepting my kindness as she continued sobbing.

'Don't worry, it's all okay,' I said reassuringly. 'You don't have to refund me. Seriously, it's fine.'

I really could have used that $80 for a physio treatment, I lamented. Still, considering how upset this young woman was, I didn't feel right about asking for my money back. So, instead, we sat side by side – Rose continuing to wipe away her tears as I redressed. 'It's not your fault,' I said gently, our eyes briefly meeting in the dim lighting. 'No one can be expected to do something perfectly if they haven't been taught how.'

She nodded mutely. I could tell she didn't really believe me.

Over the next 20 minutes or so, we talked casually, our conversation dipping into comfortable small talk as her nerves began to settle. Just as Chelsea had, she shared a little about what had led her to Brisbane, what she did in her spare time, and what life was like in the massage shop. As I came to learn, Rose didn't have much of a life outside the parlour – like many international travellers and students, she had little financial stability and spent all her time working. When I asked about hobbies or friends, her face clouded, a dull, lifeless expression taking over. 'Sometimes I lie on my bed...

I do "air bicycle" exercise.' She shrugged, trying to fill the gaps between her English and Chinese.

'How are you getting home tonight?' I asked gently. It was so late, and I couldn't imagine how she was going to get to the northern city suburb she lived in.

'I will just try to get bus.'

'Would you like a lift?'

Rose turned from the towels she was folding, her gaze growing nervous. In her eyes I saw hesitation; like she was teetering on a thin rope over a canyon. Then she looked away again, waving off my offer and mumbling that it was too much trouble.

'It's really not any trouble,' I continued. 'I mean, it's so late outside. I'm happy to drive you home if it makes things easier?'

She looked at me nervously once more, then, slowly, her bravado began to waver. 'Okay. But are you sure?' Her voice wavered on the last word, her eyes growing misty.

Together, we walked back to my car and I pulled out into a northbound lane, heading away from the direction of my house. Then, as she directed me through dark winding streets, she suddenly grew tense. 'Just here,' she said, her voice thin and strained.

'Are you sure? I'm happy to take you the full way,' I said. We were just entering her street, and she was still a good 100 metres away.

'My landlord… he will be angry,' she said apologetically.

The Stories We Carry

'Angry?'

'He's a bit crazy. He doesn't like me having people over.' She paused. 'Better that I get out here.'

'Oh. That must be hard for your housemates as well,' I said.

Rose stared out the window, her eyes once again growing nervous. 'No. Just me out here,' she replied quietly.

Suddenly, a memory surfaced of something Rose had shared earlier about the house – a four-bedroom Queenslander that cost only $60/week. Now, I wondered to myself what kind of house she could possibly live in – solo – for less than the cost of a weekly food shop. Who was this landlord? And why was he so controlling?

I pulled the car over, more concerned than ever for this young woman, but feeling powerless to do anything more. At the end of the day, I had to respect her privacy and her wishes. I'd done all I could and it was time to say goodbye.

With a small wave and a thin-lipped smile, she disappeared from my car and out into the ebony night beyond.

What in the world have I stumbled into? I wondered. *What is happening to young Asian women in our city?*

'Jas!'

Like an energizer bunny, Chelsea bounced across the small reception area and wrapped her arms around me in a tight bear hug. Then she stood back, appraising me with a teasing smile. 'Oh my God, how are you so tiny? I mean, I'm Asian... and you are...' Her voice trailed off, both eyebrows darting upwards as I threw back a look of mock-disdain.

'Shut up. As if you can talk.'

'Yeah, but your feet are like *baby's* feet,' she giggled.

'Yeah, yeah, laugh it up.' I rolled my eyes while trying to hold back a smile, causing Chelsea to laugh at me again. Ever since we'd first met, she'd revelled in the delight of being taller than a white Aussie girl and right now, she was wasting no time in reminding me.

It was a Tuesday night and over a month had passed since I'd first met Chelsea inside that dodgy massage house in Brisbane's south. Since then we'd met up for dinner in Fortitude Valley, indulging in sweet desserts as we laughed, talked, and shared about our lives. *Hard to believe that we were strangers only weeks ago,* I thought to myself. Yet, it was true. Despite our different experiences and the fact that I was almost ten years older, we'd formed a close bond that I never could have anticipated, often chatting late into the evening via social media, or texting each other with funny emojis. In the past fortnight Chelsea had begun to open up to me more and more about the challenges she was facing in Australia's corrupt massage industry, as well as her concerns about the agricultural work that she was expected to do as part of her visa requirements, and as the days passed, I found myself learning more about the multitude of ways in which young Asian women could fall into exploitation. Though I'd given her some tips and contacts for people she could connect with – hopefully assisting her to avoid the exploitation that was rife in both industries – there was only so much I could do.

For now, however, Chelsea still had a few more shifts to complete at the massage parlour she worked in, and tonight we were meeting at one of the northside venues. She'd asked me to come visit, and I'd replied asking if I could book in with her for a massage – it was a win-win, particularly with the pain I was experiencing with my hamstring injuries.

Like most parlours, this one was also part of a shopping strip – one that included a bunch of 'everyday' businesses – and to the outside world it appeared normal. In other words, it wasn't hidden away in a skanky part of town. It was an illegal brothel that was operating in plain sight. This seemed to be the way that a lot of these establishments worked; they didn't try to hide the truth. Yet, most people were completely blind to what was happening right under their noses.

I followed Chelsea into one of the massage rooms, putting my shoes aside and climbing onto the table. 'How's this week been?' I asked. 'Any luck with searching for a job out west?'

'I've found a few. But I'm still waiting to hear back. Hopefully soon though,' she smiled. 'How about your week?'

I opened my mouth to reply, but before I could speak a loud noise blasted through the shop, followed by clattering, heavy footsteps and the distinct sound of drunken, slurred speech. Chelsea and I both flinched. We could practically *smell* the alcohol.

Outside, another voice cut through the air – this one long and languid, with sweet melodious tones – as Chelsea's female co-worker tried her best to calm the inebriated man who had just walked through the front door. There was some discussion, and then the sounds of compliant steps as he eagerly followed her into the next room. Chelsea and I exchanged glances, her own voice lowering to a whisper.

'Glad it's her and not me,' she said anxiously.

Though the stranger was technically in another room, we were separated only by a thin, wooden partition. This meant that not only could we hear every drunken word he uttered, but he could also hear us. As I soon discovered, this was not only uncomfortable for Chelsea, it was dangerous.

In an attempt to shake off her nerves, Chelsea began talking with me quietly; but she was barely a few sentences in before the drunk man started up again. This time, though, he wasn't interested in his massage therapist… he was interested in Chelsea.

'Hey!' His voice boomed through the small shop, flooding our skin with small, frightened prickles. 'Who's that girl?'

Instantly, Chelsea froze, her fingers digging into the edge of my shoulder.

'Is he talking to you?'

'I don't know…' She pulled her hands back from my body, clutching the ends of her long black hair and glancing nervously at the thin wall between us and the stranger.

The Stories We Carry

'Maybe he wasn't. Maybe he –.' Before I could finish my sentence, the man's voice pitched up a level, the stench of alcohol mixing with his slurred speech as he turned his attention toward us.

'I heard her!' he yelled. 'Next door. *That's* the girl. God, she sounds so sexy.'

There was an unsettling delight in the way he said the word 'girl'; an almost self-congratulatory tone. For a moment he paused, and then, he grew louder again.

'I want that girl,' he announced. 'That's the one I want.'

Beside me, Chelsea grew more nervous. Her usual happy-go-lucky face was now a canvas of discomfort; her lips turning down at the corners and her eyes flickering nervously toward the thin wall. I raised myself onto my elbows, drawing the massage towel tightly around my chest.

'Maybe if we just keep quiet for a few minutes he'll forget us,' I whispered.

'Maybe.'

Chelsea stayed silent, her fingers nervously working their way over my back as – just a few feet away – her poor co-worker joked, laughed, and flirted in an attempt to placate the drunken beast. For a little while it seemed to work, but the moment Chelsea spoke a word, he was once again on the prowl. Just like a predator, he was intently focused on the sound of her every movement, and now that he had her in his sights, he had no intention of giving up.

'Who is she?'

'I want to know who that girl is!'

'I can tell she's sexy… I can tell from her voice. I just want to see her. Where is she?'

On and on it went, and all the while, I wondered: *How the hell is this happening? How is it that these shops are operating in high socioeconomic suburbs and cities, with men coming in at all hours of the night – some of them drunk or high or looking for violence – and these young foreign women are made to work alone, without even a receptionist or a security guard?* Whilst I knew that exploitation was rife within more disadvantaged communities, I still couldn't get my head around the 'in plain sight' nature of what I was witnessing. *Also,* I thought, *what would Chelsea's co-worker do if she was alone tonight? What would* Chelsea *do, on the evenings where she was rostered alone? There's not a single shop open in this strip… who could she call for help?*

As much as I wished that there was something I could do – that, if things really turned sour, I could help these women – the reality was that I, too, was filled with fear. Here we were, three petite women alone in a shop at night with a thunderously drunken man who 'wanted' a young Asian woman. What chance did we stand if he became violent?

Thankfully, Chelsea's co-worker was a quick thinker. Relying on her charm, she quietened the man with a few playful comments and giggles, and within minutes, he had settled. Next door, we exhaled in relief as our heart rates slowly stabilised.

'Jas,' Chelsea whispered. 'Can you stay? I know you're meant to be finishing your massage now, but…' She paused, looking down at the ground. 'I'm scared. I don't want to be alone here for another thirty minutes while that man is in the shop. Can you stay with me until he goes?'

'Of course! As if I'm going to leave you alone right now,' I said quietly. 'I'll wait and drive you home – it's way too late to take the bus.'

'Okay.' Chelsea exhaled, her features softening with relief. 'But only if you come in and stay for dumplings with my room-mate,' she smiled. 'Her boyfriend makes the best dumplings.'

'That sounds alright to me,' I laughed.

That night, after the stranger had left, we slipped out the front door and made our way to the backpacker hostel where Chelsea lived. True to her word, she introduced me to her friends and we sat around in the kitchen stuffing ourselves with home-made dumplings. *How is this my life?* I wondered, as I glanced around at the people who sat by my side. So much had changed in a month, and it all stemmed from me walking into a random massage shop.

Despite all of the distressing, shocking, and gut-wrenching things I was uncovering about this seedy industry, I was grateful for the magical and wonderful moments that were also revealing themselves. Often, I felt overwhelmed by all that I was trying to take on; it felt too much for one person. But tonight, on the floor of a backpacker hostel room, I felt that I was exactly where I was meant to be; that maybe God had placed me here in this random moment so that Chelsea wouldn't have to face all these things alone.

I couldn't be there for every woman facing injustice, but I could be there for one… and to me, that felt like enough.

Jas Rawlinson

Not long after this eventful night, Chelsea managed to follow through with her plan of leaving the massage industry. As we were about to discover, though, she was simply swapping one corrupt trade for another. Like every other working tourist, she was required by Australian law to complete a minimum of 88 days in a 'specified industry' (such as farming or fishing) in order to stay in Australia longer than 12 months, and the easiest option was to head out west for an agricultural job. Almost a decade on, I still struggle to understand the logic behind this requirement – especially after seeing the ways in which so many young women are sexually exploited and the often isolated locations to which they are sent.

In Chelsea's case, she was hired to work on a tomato farm several hours west of Brisbane, where she had no access to public transport or helpful services. Though she had made friends with one or two other tourists who were living and working on the same farm, I was concerned, particularly given the research I'd uncovered about high rates of sexual abuse, harassment, financial exploitation, and forced labour that were being perpetrated against international workers on these farms. As I later learned, many young women were raped or assaulted by male staff, who would then coerce or threaten them to stay silent in order to have their '88 day' certificates approved. If they refused to submit to the sexual requests, the 'clock' would start all over again on their farm work – taking them back to zero. When I read an article four years later from *The Guardian* – a sobering expose titled '#88DaysASlave: backpackers share stories of farm work exploitation' – I realised that not much had changed.*

---

* https://www.theguardian.com/australia-news/2019/sep/26/88daysaslave-backpackers-share-stories-of-farm-work-exploitation

The Stories We Carry

One night, while Chris was showering and I sat on the couch with his housemate Jack, I opened Facebook to find an unread message from Chelsea in our chat window.

> *Jas, I went tomato picking yesterday. Almost died out there. Lol.*

Along with the text, she sent through an emoji of a squishy face with scrunched eyes and teardrops flying from each corner.

> *We worked from 5 am to 5.pm. 12 hours outside. No break. I wanted to stop to take a drink, but the boss lady yelled at me. And guess how much I earned in the end???*

Underneath her message, she included a photo, her muddy gumboots surrounded by a canvas of cracked, dry soil. Beyond her, lines of tomato vines stretched further than the eye could see. I shook my head, horrified.

> *How much?*

Across my screen, three little grey dots danced as Chelsea continued typing. Then came her reply.

> *36 dollars. BEFORE tax.*

'Shit.' I cursed under my breath, causing Jack to swivel his head toward me from the other end of the couch. He arched an eyebrow and I held up one hand, silently promising to tell him all in a moment. Then I continued typing.

Jas Rawlinson

Girl, what the hell?! That's illegal. Is this the same company that made you come in at 4.30 am the other day?

Yes. We get 9 dollars for one basket.

In my head, I pictured a medium-sized rattan basket; the kind often seen in trendy magazines with little sprigs of lavender and freshly picked tomatoes peeking out from the edges. But when Chelsea sent through a picture of the 'bucket', my mouth fell open.

It was a gigantic white container that came up to her knee. And the tomatoes she was filling it with? They weren't the large Roma variety. They were the size of cherries.

Seeing the look on my face, Jack leaned over one shoulder and began reading my message thread. Then – just as mine had – his mouth dropped open, forming into the shape of the same four-letter curse word that I'd just uttered. 'Those are *not* buckets,' he stated, his eyes fixed on the image. 'Those are drums!'

'I know, right?' I stared at the image, transfixed by the dry earth, dirt-stained containers, and the endless rows of tomato-vines. 'She was there for 12 hours and only filled four of them,' I breathed. 'She didn't get a single break.'

'That's seriously messed up. Who's running these places?'

I shook my head, not knowing how to answer Jack.

The thought of Chelsea spending half a day – from sunrise to sunset – filling these large white tubs under the blaze of a 40 degree Celsius day, as she tried not to vomit from dehydration, was infuriating. Even worse, was that she was getting less money than she'd make in one hour at the massage shop. Here, she was still at risk of sexual harassment, but now it was coupled with hard manual labour and financial exploitation.

Spurred by anger, I began searching online for migrant or community support groups in Queensland, but there didn't seem to be a lot available. Eventually, though, I stumbled across an article on an everyday woman named Margaret, who was well known for assisting migrants and international workers in her community. With kind eyes and silver-grey hair, she was a welcome sight for many who had no one else to turn to, and had even been awarded Citizen of the Year in the rural town in which she lived.

The next morning, while driving into the city for work, I dialled her number and hit speakerphone.

'Hello?'

'Hi, is this Margaret?'

'Yes, speaking.'

I introduced myself – apologising for calling early on a weekday – and filled her in on why I was phoning. After explaining a little of Chelsea's story, Margaret confirmed my concerns.

'Ah, yes – "the tomato contractor."' Her voice took on a knowing tone; one that told me that Chelsea wasn't in the best of hands. 'I'm pretty sure I know exactly who you're talking about. We've had our eye on the owner for a while and have already spoken with Fair Work Australia. If you can give me the phone number of your friend, I'll make contact with her.'

From work, I quickly messaged Chelsea to let her know about the support service, and that, if she liked, I could make the three-hour trip west to help her meet with Margaret that weekend.

She sent through a giant emoji face, tears streaming from its oversized anime-style eyes.

Thank you Jas, that would be wonderful. And it will be so good to see you!

A few days later, as I drove into the small country town, Chelsea and I greeted each other with hugs before making our way down to the local pub where Margaret would be waiting for us. I was so in awe of this woman; an everyday member of her community who simply wanted to help others and found joy in running English classes for international visitors. There was no agenda; nothing to be wary about. Just a kind-hearted, community-focused woman. Though initially nervous, Chelsea grew more confident by the end of the day – simply by knowing that she had someone nearby who was in her corner, and who she could call upon if she ever felt unsafe.

As the two of us walked around the small farming town that afternoon, stopping by the pub for lunch and laughing at the farm boys who wanted to 'add us on Insta,' she suddenly grew serious.

'Why do you care so much, Jas?' Chelsea asked.

'What do you mean?'

'I've never met anyone who cares like you. You're my real life angel.'

'Stop it,' I protested. 'I am not.'

The Stories We Carry

'You are.' She smiled broadly, then looked down at her salad – eyebrows drawing together as they did when she was searching for the right words in English – and paused for a few moments. Eventually, she spoke.

'You are a person with a heart full of justice, Jas.'

I shrugged, trying my best to change the topic and take the focus off myself. Compliments were something I'd always felt wildly uncomfortable with and Chelsea's words felt too much. Deep down though, I couldn't pretend that I wasn't touched – because she saw into my heart. She saw *me*: the highly sensitive and intuitive soul who yearned to create meaningful impact in the world. Since girlhood, I'd often felt that I didn't really belong. My voice wasn't 'girlish' enough. I didn't care about fashion and makeup like the other 12-year-old's. I had long 'horse hair' that the popular girls thought was ugly, and joked that they would cut off while I was asleep at school camp. I cared about things that others didn't really think about. Even after so many years, I'd never forgotten the report card I'd received from my Grade Four teacher; the cutting sentence that read: *Jasmine has a tendency to make mountains out of molehills.* For so many years, I had lived my life feeling ashamed and hateful of this sensitive side of myself. The side that cared and felt deeply.

Now – in the hallway of a humble pub – I realised that not everyone looked at my sensitivity as a flaw. Although I'd never fully appreciated it, I realised there were people who saw me for who I truly was, and all that I could be.

Chapter 26

'Would you be willing to go public?'

From across the table, two piercing blue eyes stared into mine and I felt an instant flutter rise within my stomach. At six foot two, with dark brown hair and an intense gaze, the man who sat before me was intimidating, to say the least. Particularly, given the fact that he was also an investigative journalist.

'Yes,' I replied, trying to sound sure of myself.

'Okay, tell me a little more then. How did you get into this world of illegal brothels?'

I cleared my throat and took a bite of my Moroccan chickpea salad, trying to still my nerves. *Don't stuff this up, Jas,* I pressed silently. *This could be really big.*

It was a Wednesday afternoon, and I was sitting in a cafe in Milton with an investigative journalist named Solomon, who worked for one of the biggest media giants in the world. We'd been connected through a mutual friend who had been inspired by the work I was doing around human trafficking and migrant exploitation, and now we were here to talk about a news feature. Not just about the issue – but more specifically, about my research.

As we talked over lunch, Solomon began to formulate some ideas for a potential TV segment. Very quickly though, we ran up against a roadblock. He wanted to speak to the women I'd met on camera – and he wanted me to facilitate it.

'I don't know about that,' I said uneasily. 'Just getting an appointment at these places can be hard enough. As a woman, they instantly mistrust me. So far there are only two women I've been able to talk with on a deeper level. One of them I'm very close to – she might talk. But the other?' A memory flashed to my mind of Rose, the young Chinese woman I'd driven home, and the fear that had overcome her features when I'd offered to drop her home. The shaking of her hands had told me that there was no way she was going to talk.

'It's really hard to gain their trust,' I continued. 'I don't think they'd open up easily.'

I saw the shift in Solomon's face, the set of his jaw.

'But,' I continued, 'I can ask Chelsea if she'd be open to sharing. She's out west at the moment on an agricultural job.'

'Okay. If it helps, let her know that we'll blur her face to protect her identity.'

'Sure. That would be great.'

'But we'd need you to speak on camera as well,' he added.

I nodded. Though I was a little nervous, I'd been expecting as much. 'You'd blur my face too, yes?'

'Oh.' Suddenly, Solomon grew quiet, taking a bite of his burger and staring out toward the river as he chomped it down quickly. 'No, we couldn't do that. Only for the girls.' He shooed a fly away with his left hand, and I stared at the tiny creature, feeling as though he'd just done the same to me.

'But you just said you could do that for Chelsea… for her safety.'

'Yes.'

'It's just…'

A montage of memories flooded through my brain; all of the disgusting conversations I'd read between men online, as they'd talked about the women they purchased like meat in a butcher shop. The young women who bore the brunt of their harassment and racist or sexist attitudes, and the entitlement of the 'punters' who would stop at nothing to get what they wanted. And then, there were the Mamasans and pimps – the wealthy, cold, calculating individuals who ran these corrupt venues. I'd only seen a slice of this world, but I knew enough to know that exposing my identity to the world had real risks. I couldn't understand why Solomon would offer identity protection to the women, but not to me.

Internally, a war played out between the natural people pleaser who wanted to be seen as agreeable and polite, and my intuition, which told me to stand my ground.

Just say yes – you don't want to lose this story.

No, this doesn't feel right. This could be dangerous.

'What if you filmed me speaking from behind, or in a darkened room?' I suggested, trying to offer a compromise.

'No, we can't do that, sorry. If we don't have you speaking on camera, we don't have a story.' Solomon was firm, and I could tell the conversation was pretty much closed.

I walked out of the cafe and back along the road to my workplace, feeling deflated and unheard. From police, to journalists, to the local prostitution licensing association, there didn't seem to be a single person who was either willing or able to help me fight what was happening in my city. They either didn't care, or wanted to use me for clickbait without any care for my safety.

Back at my desk – swamped with mind-numbing emails about construction jobs, price quotes, and earthmoving equipment – I wondered how much longer I could keep using my own money, time, and resources to fund something that no one seemed to want to know about.

No, I thought defiantly. *I have to get this information out. And if an investigative journalist won't help me, I'll do it myself in whatever way I can.*

That night, I sat cross-legged on my bed with my laptop and thought about the men who walked in and out of these illegal venues as though they were invincible. I saw their puffed-out chests, and the neatly pressed business shirts they wore as they came and went at all hours of the day or night – sometimes after kissing their wives and girlfriends goodbye, or leaving their families at the park while 'Daddy goes to get a massage for his sore back' – without an ounce of shame.

I was done with them being invisible. *It's over, boys,* I thought. *It's time you were outed.*

The Stories We Carry

In a few clicks, I created a new blog site – and then I got to work on revealing the truth. All their despicable conversations where they joked and complained about bruises they inflicted or saw on women's bodies. All the misogynistic, ageist, and racist things they said about these women behind their backs. All the lies and excuses they told to hide the truth from their partners and children, like keeping and using 'boner' phones – yes, that's not a typo, you read that correctly. All the comments where they likened the 'selection' of a young masseuse to 'pointing at the one you want like a customer in a butcher shop,' and then 'forcing' their way or 'raising a hand' when extra intimidation was required.

After all, that is what I pay her for.

60 minutes of HER time to make ME happy doing whatever I want.

I titled the piece, *Men who purchase women for sex – their own words.* It was an exposé into what was happening in our city, often in rich, upper-class areas, and though I didn't know the real names or identities of these men, I wanted them to know that they weren't operating under complete anonymity online. They were being watched, and every disgusting word they wrote was there for the world to see.

Exhausted, angry, and deflated, I hit publish, and then I went to bed.

Shit.

I stared at the large green blocks on my screen, and instantly my fingers began to tremble. Each long rectangle showed the stats for my website, and from what I could see, they were out of control.

Holding my breath, I scrolled down to the little red bubble where my unread comments sat; lying in wait like a predator, eager to be unleashed. I knew, instantly, what was happening – and so did my nervous system. Already, my stomach was doing barrel-rolls and flip-flops.

I've been found out.

Weeks had passed since I'd published my exposé article and in that time, I'd been doing life as normal. What I hadn't realised, however, was that a male punter had come across my little site and decided to share it publicly on the very forum I was investigating. Now, thousands of men were coming to my blog – and they wanted to know who I was.

With a ball of anxiety lodged in the pit of my stomach, I began reading through the comments. Then, I switched to the punter's website where they'd linked to my blog. Some were embarrassingly stereotypical – men lamenting how I was probably an 'ugly, angry feminist' – while others claimed I wanted to be a 'white saviour.' In their opinion, all 'HABs' ('hot Asian babes') were lazy, money-hungry whores, and there was no possibility that the women they were purchasing for sexual gratification could be financially or socially vulnerable.

> **They know what to expect.**
>
> **I don't feel sorry for any of them.**
>
> **If I see a girl that looks upset, I offer her a shoulder to cry on, listen sympathetically to her shit for a while, then I wipe away her tears and ask her to suck my d***k while I pump a load down her throat. If you do it the right way you won't even have to pay.**

The Stories We Carry

Haha! Give 'em something to really cry about, eh?

When I showed Chris, he was livid, wanting to burst into these commenter's lives and tell them exactly how disgusting they were. But we knew there was no point; men like this didn't see any problem with the way they viewed women – or more specifically, *Asian* women.

To be honest, there was a part of me that was nervous about having been brought to their attention; even if they didn't know my name. I wasn't tech-savvy when it came to IP addresses and things like that, and I questioned if anyone could possibly find out who I really was. Friends of mine – one of whom was previously married to a man who was well immersed in Australia's criminal underbelly – were concerned about what I was getting myself into. They begged me to stop; to listen and understand that I wasn't as smart as the people involved in such high-level corruption.

'But how can I just ignore all of this?' I'd reason. 'How can I see, and read, and know all of these awful things are going on, and just walk away?' It felt like a betrayal of myself and my values.

Over the next few months I continued on, trying my best to draw attention to the issue, but it seemed that no one wanted to know. The local government bodies who were tasked with monitoring these types of venues seemed powerless to stop it, and as the local police had told me, they weren't there to help the women involved. As much as I wanted to continue my investigations, I'd hit a brick wall, and with my double hamstring injury, I couldn't afford to continue paying money for bad massages in the hopes of connecting with the women involved.

Instead, I decided to start a project called Operation Kindness, where I put together Easter gift packages (including delicious

Easter eggs, of course!), and hand-delivered them to some of the girls I'd spoken to in local parlours, as well as those I'd never interacted with. For the most part, I was met with mistrust from Mamasans – most of whom literally looked down their nose at me, demanding to know what I wanted – while young women in mini-dresses slunk away in the background. I felt deflated, as though everyone were against me. *Journalists. Police. Government agencies. The men who'd found my blog. The cruel women running these parlours.* No one wanted to acknowledge the exploitation or corruption. No one wanted to help me spread kindness or to check on the wellbeing of these women.

As I walked down a street in East Brisbane toward another parlour, I felt the weight of all I was carrying; how pointless it felt to care about people who didn't care about me. Shoulders hunched, I walked inside the salon and, holding back tears, asked for the manager. Once again, I explained why I was there – that I was delivering Easter packs to women in beauty bars and parlours, because I knew women in the industry, and that it could be lonely when you worked so many hours and knew so few people. This was my small way of spreading some kindness.

I braced myself, waiting to be told – once again – to leave. Instead, the young Asian manager's expression transformed into one of wonder and surprise.

'Oh my goodness, that's so kind!' she beamed. 'Are these really for us?'

I stood in shock, surprised by her warmth and unable to speak. I felt as though the weight of her kindness had rendered me mute; I just couldn't get the words to form.

The Stories We Carry

'Are you okay?' she asked gently, her hazelnut eyes searching mine.

Little streams of salt water began to gather on my cheeks, and I swiped them away. 'Sorry,' I said shakily. 'I've just… not everyone has understood, that's all. You'd think I'm trying to hand out rotten eggs or something,' I laughed.

She smiled again, holding the gift basket close to her body. 'Some people just don't understand random acts of kindness. But I want you to know I appreciate it. So, thank you. The ladies here will be so excited.'

Then she leaned forward and drew me in for a hug.

As I walked back to my car, bags of Easter eggs now gone, I reminded myself of the truth I had always lived by: that life is about being there for those in need, in whatever way possible. Though I'd wanted so badly to do more – to help stop the corruption going on within our city – I was just one woman, and I couldn't fight it alone. It was okay to acknowledge what I had achieved, what I'd learned, and most importantly, to focus on what I *could* do. To make a commitment to always speak out when I saw something that didn't look right and to listen to my intuition.

Sometimes, I catch myself thinking about those 12-18 months that I spent investigating illegal brothels, and I wish I had a nice, pretty, inspiring ending to the story to share. In the months to come I saw that one of the venues I had investigated and reported was eventually raided and closed – but for how long, I couldn't be sure. If history had shown me anything, it was that these places re-opened quickly; sometimes in the same place or somewhere new. That's the thing about life… it's messy. It can be ugly, and disempowering, and unjust. It can hurt and harm people. And sometimes, though we want to solve a problem, we can't do it alone. Sometimes, we need to do what we can, and then pass the baton over to someone else.

If I can share something positive about this time, it's this: there are so many incredible people in the world – many of whom are far more qualified than I, to tackle this issue – who are moving the world in real and tangible ways. Victim-survivors are in good hands with them and I do what I can to support those advocates or charities. Most importantly, I have come to realise that it's okay not to know all the answers and to understand that we are not responsible for fixing every injustice in the world. I rest easy, knowing that I didn't stay silent and I didn't ignore injustice where I saw it.

With all that said, there was something beautiful that came out of this difficult and heavy period of time. On a sunny day in Autumn, with my mother by my side, Chris proposed to me under my favourite childhood tree; the very place where my mother and I had sat when I was a toddler, eating our breakfast together while looking over the beach. It was a place where everything had been right in my world; a patch of earth where I had felt safe, loved, and cared for. And he wanted that to be the very spot where he asked me to marry him.

A few months later, we married in a gorgeous location on the Gold Coast, and as I walked toward the front doors of the venue I stole a quick glance at the hands that supported me down the aisle; the hands of my brother and mother. With each step closer to where Chris stood waiting, I thought of the teenage version of myself; the young girl who had once believed that no one would ever love her. That she had not a shred of purpose. And that's when I realised – with almost disbelief – that I had achieved both of the things I wanted most in the world as a fifteen year old. I had someone who loved me completely and unselfishly; someone who wasn't jealous or abusive or controlling. And just as importantly, I had Jason and Mum by my side – just like the stick figure image I'd drawn in my school counsellor's office so many years earlier.

It was a picture that, once upon a time, I felt would never, ever eventuate. And now, it had come true.

When Chris and I married, Chelsea was one of the first people to congratulate us, and it reminded me again of the serendipity of our friendship; one that could easily have never happened. Somehow, though, a bond was formed between us that continued for many years. When she moved on from the agricultural farms and continued her travels around Australia, she even stayed with my mother in our little mountain home. I thought it was so special that she was able to meet my whole family, enjoying a 'traditional' Aussie meal of sausages and steaks, along with one of my mother's famous coconut and seafood stir-fries. I marvelled at the fact that she sat on the same verandah on which I'd spent so many years staring out across the valleys and wondering if my life was really worthy of living.

During this time, she also spent a few nights with Chris and I in our home, and we laughed with carefree abandon as we dressed up in brightly-coloured wigs and took dumb selfies. Often, I caught myself wondering, *Who could have ever imagined what would come from me deciding to walk up the wooden staircase of an old Queenslander house in my suburb?*

I'm happy to tell you that Chelsea went on to achieve her dream of entering the airline industry, and passed all her exams to become a highly respected hostess, spreading kindness and warmth to those around her while exploring the world. When she returned to

Brisbane in 2016 for an overnight layover, she immediately messaged me for a catch up.

Her first question?

'Hey Jas, can you take me to Aldi? I want to get some of those really awesome BBQ chips.'

I turned to her, deadpan. 'You travel the entire world, seeing places I could only dream of, and all you want is a cheap pack of supermarket chips?'

'Yep.'

'Well, your wish is my command,' I joked.

To this day, our friendship remains in my memory as one of the most wonderfully magical and surprising connections I've ever made; most importantly, one that shows that sometimes, when you step out in courage, you gain unexpected treasures along the way.

Chapter 27

Editorial Assistant wanted for Queensland magazine.

I stared at the job description, my heart almost leaping out of my chest. *Holy shit*, I thought. *That's me!*

It was 2015 and I was still on the hunt for my big break. Five years had passed since I graduated from university, and despite spending my nights and weekends writing volunteer articles for three different music, art, and non-profit organisations and websites, I still hadn't been able to find work in my industry. Though I was grateful for the steady income I had in my current admin job, I knew that there was more that I was destined for. Going to work every day felt like I was walking through a constant 'soul hangover'; my body and mind literally ached, feeling as though I were breaking into tiny pieces. It's something I've spoken with other creatives about in more recent years, and all of us found that this sensation was a common experience. It wasn't an exaggeration when we talked about literally feeling sick; the everyday monotonous routines of filing folders, filling out spreadsheets, answering phones, and checking off tedious tasks was destroying us from the inside out.

Now, staring at the job advert before me, I knew that I couldn't pass up this opportunity. It was now or never.

Please, please, let this be my break, I prayed.

Thankfully, God was listening. Only a few days later I was offered an interview with the magazine editor and while there were a few red flags (such as the extremely low pay, and the company being run from the office of a chemical supplies building!) I jumped at the chance. After all, I didn't have much room to be picky.

At the same time, I'd also been referred to another job by a recruitment agency – an admin position with a construction company – and I'd been promised the opportunity to use my writing skills in the role. For the first time in so long, I felt a profound sense of peace; that no matter which way things went I'd at least have the opportunity to work in some capacity as a writer.

I was making my way out of the building from my second interview, when my phone began to ring.

'Hello? Jas speaking.'

'Hi Jas, it's Laura.'

Instantly my stomach dropped. *Oh my gosh, it's her – the editor from the magazine.* I noticed that my fingers were now trembling as well.

'Is now a good time to speak?'

'Yes, absolutely!'

'We were really impressed with your portfolio and the diversity of your work,' she began.

Oh no... I stopped in the middle of the street, gazing upwards toward the city's train line. *Here it comes,* I thought. *The gentle let*

The Stories We Carry

down. I'd heard it so many times over the years, and I felt – for sure – that it was coming again now.

'Jas, we'd like to offer you the job.'

Wait, what?!

I let my mouth hang open, staring in absolute shock. I couldn't say a single word. Instead, I pressed a hand over my ear to quieten the noise of the passing traffic and walked toward a small park. *I must have heard her wrong.*

Laura continued. 'We'd like you to start next week – but there's just one important thing to check first. I know you applied for the part-time role but we'd like to offer you a full-time contract. Would you be available for those extra hours?'

'Of course! Yes, that would be amazing, thank you so much,' I gushed. 'Thank you.'

Standing in the centre of E. Mccormick Place, surrounded by traffic, I stood beaming. The whole way back to my car I grinned to myself like a complete lunatic. I'd done it. I'd gotten the break I'd been waiting for. Finally, after so many years, I was living in my purpose.

I can't believe this. I'm a real-life writer!

Sitting behind a plain white desk, I stared at the brand-new Apple Mac that had just been set up for me and smiled. Now all I had to do was get to work doing what I did best – telling stories. And I knew exactly where to start.

Jas Rawlinson

Two years earlier I'd attended a panel discussion with various women in the arts, and despite all the incredible female creatives who I'd written about that day while covering the event, I'd remembered one particular quote from a Brisbane writer named Krissy Kneen. 'I think it's really important that when you get a leg up, you bring someone else up with you,' she'd said. 'If you see someone who's struggling and you've managed to get a foothold, don't just run to the top – help them up too. I think that's vitally important.'

Over the next few months, that's exactly what I did. I snuck in editorial features with photographer friends of mine, or those who were doing great things to make a difference in the lives of others. I showcased small businesses and those without a huge platform. Then, I branched out to cover other local heroes, like BACA (Bikers Against Child Abuse). Originally founded in Utah in the USA, but now working globally in countries including Australia, the organisation was comprised of a team of motorbike lovers who worked with authorities to empower and protect child survivors. Whether they were helping frightened mothers to fit new locks and security lighting to their front doors, sitting outside a child's home in the middle of the night so they felt safe enough to fall asleep, or attending court dates with a survivor, these big-hearted, burly humans were genuine angels in leather jackets. *I wonder how many children feel more protected by these bikers than the courts,* I mused to myself, as I scrolled through the website.

Due to the sensitive nature of their work, BACA were very wary of the media and rarely gave interviews. In particular, they were cautious about being lumped in with vigilante groups – something they didn't condone. But after a few discussions, I was granted an interview with Nifty, one of the BACA angels. I remember feeling slightly nervous and intimidated on our first meeting. After all, with his long, scraggly beard, thick Chopper Reid-style moustache, and heavy leather boots and jacket, he was a commanding presence – but then, he smiled, his intense blue eyes transforming into windows of kindness and warmth.

I felt his beautiful spirit; the love and care he took for these vulnerable kids, some of whom were just toddlers. I could only imagine how much it meant to them and their mothers to know that a team of male and female bikers were sitting outside, guarding their door each night and keeping them safe.

I was one of the few digital journalists and writers to gain their trust, and it was one of my favourite features that year.

As the months rolled on, I continued to find incredible local heroes to interview and whenever feedback for the magazine came in, there was always praise for the articles I'd written. They also consistently gained the most traction on social media. Unfortunately, as I discovered in time, my editor wasn't as thrilled as I was about issues of social injustice. For the first few magazine releases she was full of praise, but after a few short months, I noticed the subtle difference in the way she interacted with me versus my co-worker. Amy, a seasoned journalist, loved to write about style, interior design, food and restaurants – and she was great at it. The girl was also a dead-set legend when it came to witty headlines and I'd often ask her for advice on my own features. But instead of seeing our individual strengths and nurturing them both, my editor eventually grew annoyed with my suggestions.

'I want to do something meaty,' I said, as we sat brainstorming one afternoon. 'I was thinking of doing a feature on domestic violence, but specifically amongst Christian women and the church.' I'd recently read a book on rates of abuse within religious spaces and how difficult it often was for women of faith to break away from toxic relationships, and I thought it was an interesting topic.

'Jaaass,' she lamented, her accent drawing out each letter. 'Why do you always have to pick such serious topics? Can't you do something fun?'

Her words stung, pulling at my skin like a small barb. It triggered the part of me that still felt like the odd one out – and now, I was hearing it again.

You are too much.

But you also aren't enough.

I went above and beyond in that role, but unfortunately, my position was made redundant after less than a year. I still remember the way I felt as I arrived home after receiving the news; how I'd sat on the dusty front steps of our shoe-box rental and stared at the ugly industrial buildings while chugging on a cider. I just couldn't believe it. How had I come so far – persevered so long – only to have it taken away from me so quickly?

What if I never again have the chance to do the thing I love most in the world? I wondered.

It was only a few weeks later, while watching a female rock band in the city and waiting for Chris to finish work, that I got chatting to a guy who was sharing a table with me. Somehow – in a purely platonic way – Robbie and I had connected, sharing about struggles in our lives, and I'd opened up to him about my job situation. 'I guess it's time to give up,' I lamented. 'I don't have time to write anymore. I need to put all my energy into resumes. Do you know how many I've sent out? Like, over a hundred! It's insane. It's a full time job in itself.'

The Stories We Carry

In the dimly-lit bar, with the sounds of wailing guitars and drunken laughter raining down on us from all directions, Robbie took a long sip from his beer and then plonked it noisily on the table.

'Fuck that.'

'Excuse me?' I leaned away, shocked by his sudden intensity.

'I said, *fuck* that.' He held me in his gaze, refusing to look away. '*Write*. Forget about the resumes. You have to keep writing, Jas.'

'But...'

'No. *Keep writing*,' he repeated.

His passion – the way he was so sure – felt unfamiliar, yet I knew that he meant every word. It was one of many random and serendipitous moments throughout my life and one that I've never forgotten. His encouragement gave me the boost I needed; reassurance that someone else saw value in the pursuit of what felt, at times, like nothing more than a 'creative hobby.' But he saw it. He saw me.

Little did I know that in less than a year, I would be creating something far bigger than I'd ever imagined – that I'd be the author of a book series that would one day change lives all across the world. Everything was about to change, and I was right on the verge of discovering what that shift would be.

⸺

'One month. Holy shit, can you believe it?'

I stood in the kitchen, prepping dinner with the phone on loud speaker as I talked with my friend, Bonnie. Over the past few months we'd been working in secrecy on a creative project, and now, it was only weeks away from coming true. I poured a can of coconut milk into a frying pan and cranked up the heat, chopping vegetables and tofu as I listened.

'Do you know if the Lord Mayor is going to come?' asked Bonnie.

'Looks like it! I think he's going to make a speech as well.' I pushed some slivers of carrot to the side, and then started on another one. 'Shit, that reminds me, I've still got to chase up the TV station. I'll do that today.'

'Cool, and I'll work on the opening speech,' replied Bonnie.

'Sounds good. Let me know how you go and then flick me an email.'

I tapped the off button on my phone and adjusted the heat on the pan, watching as the coconut milk began to bubble. Since losing my job, one of the main things that had helped me to stay afloat was the work that Bonnie and I were doing in secret – but now, our dreams were about to become reality. We were only weeks away from opening the first permanent domestic violence memorial in our city – and one of the first of its kind in Australia.

The idea had come to me after a horrific onslaught of female homicides in late 2015. In one month, we'd lost several women in our community – at a rate of at least one woman every week. This included Tara Brown, a 24-year-old mother who – after dropping her three-year-old daughter at childcare on a normal September morning – was followed, run off the road, and bludgeoned to death by her ex-partner. Only five days earlier, she had begged for local police to help her, to please keep her safe, and yet, the officers involved failed to listen. It would take six long years and an internal investigation for a Queensland coroner to reveal that police had failed to act appropriately, and to provide the assistance Tara deserved.*

Throughout late 2015 the tally of dead women – all murdered by a current or former partner – continued to rise. In despair we watched as the rate accelerated from an average of one woman per week, to two. Every few weeks there seemed to be another Red Rose rally, or a candle vigil, and over and over, Bonnie and I found ourselves close to tears. *How is this still happening?* we asked. *When is it going to stop?*

Tragically, the murders didn't stop, and so, we began to ask different questions. *What can we do to make sure the victims are remembered, and that they don't just become faceless names and statistics?* While we'd played with the idea of holding a candle-lighting ceremony, I couldn't shake the feeling that it wasn't enough. Candles would all too quickly be extinguished, and posters would disintegrate and disappear inside of rubbish bins. In no time at all, people would move on and forget. *Unless*, I mused, *we create something more permanent.*

'What about a memorial?' I asked, while talking over Facebook Messenger one day. 'It would give these families a beautiful space – somewhere other than a cemetery – to sit and feel the spirit of their loved ones, and we can also raise money for a local DV service.'

Bonnie loved the idea, and so it was that we began a six-month journey to bring our goal to life. Through community support and crowdfunding, we sourced a local company to create the memorial

---

* https://www.abc.net.au/news/2021-01-28/domestic-violence-murder-tara-brown-police-coronial-court/13095862

plaque, liaised with council to have it installed, and arranged for our local Lord Mayor to officiate at the opening of the space. I also reached out to several women who had lost family members to domestic homicide and arranged for them to speak. In a moment that was both beautiful and sobering, one woman revealed to me that the opening of our memorial was also the anniversary of her daughter's last day with her loved ones. 'This date usually hits me like a sledgehammer,' she shared. 'But this will give me a reason to go out and achieve something in her honour.'

While our plans were all unfolding smoothly and everything was coming together, there was one area where everything was falling apart – my mental health. Just as I had during my teenage years, I suppressed and hid the truth, pretending that all was fine when it really wasn't.

Now, as I looked down at the swirling pan of coconut milk atop my stove, I noticed that my insides felt the same. Strange things were bubbling up within the confines of my mind; things that I just couldn't explain. Over the past few months I'd been speaking with more and more survivors of domestic violence, and as they shared about their experiences, I found myself experiencing an almost push-pull sensation. On one hand, something in my intuition told me to lean in; that there were details within my own history of abuse that needed to be addressed. But every time I began to pick away at a layer, the protective part of my brain would slap away all curiosity.

Don't go there. Don't remember. This isn't a puzzle you need to put together.

In hindsight, it was unsurprising. I'd spent ten years mentally pushing away the individual pieces of my trauma so that I could move forward, and in many ways, I'd done a great job. Blake was a

The Stories We Carry

distant memory – someone I rarely thought about, except for when I had to (such as a trip to Coffs, or a new relationship). Once briefly acknowledged, the lid went right back on the box and it was once again time to push it aside. I'd never stopped to think about what I was burying; that maybe, I wasn't actually dealing with my trauma. I was simply ignoring it.

Through the process of speaking to so many other women who were survivors – or who had lost children and family – I realised that my perception of my own abuse history was alarmingly black and white. Though it feels embarrassing to admit this, I was still very unaware of the many different non-physical forms of domestic violence. So often, the images I saw in awareness campaigns were of bruised cheeks and swollen eye sockets; missing teeth and bloody noses. None of those visuals mimicked my lived experience with Blake or my father, and so, when I spoke with survivors, I often marvelled at how lucky I was to have never experienced domestic violence.

What I didn't know just yet, was that I had experienced many other forms of intimate partner and family violence – forms that are not as commonly discussed. It was only when I began to educate myself further, that I realised the truth; and that's when the nightmares, flashbacks, and post-traumatic stress started. I began to remember things from my past that my brain had kept under lock and key, knowing that I wasn't yet able – or ready – to process such memories. This included an experience in my late teens with a boyfriend who had literally forced me to go through with something I didn't want to, telling me, 'Stop pushing me away and just try it.' Unable to escape, my survival response had been to eventually submit – and even worse, to pretend I liked it. In some ways, the humiliation of my own betrayal felt worse than the sex act itself.

Then there was another experience in my mid-twenties, where I was physically restrained by a man I'd known for most of my life, and told: 'Stop pushing me away. It's not like I'm going to rape you.' My response? To go limp and stop fighting as he proceeded to do things that I didn't want. To this day, I still physically cringe and move away when my husband tries to get close to me in certain ways.

Then of course, there had been Blake, and all of the emotional manipulation, gaslighting, and multiple occurrences of non-consensual sexual experiences that had taken place over a period of more than a year.

Through it all, I'd told myself that I had no personal experience with domestic violence – because none of these situations included physical injuries, aggression, or outward displays of gross violence. They also didn't occur within long-term, serious, or stable relationships. In my head, this was essential, because my inner dialogue had led me to believe that abuse could only be labelled as DV in a serious partnership.

Yet, all of those experiences included sexual or emotional abuse. Though the violence wasn't visible in the same way as a bruise, it was still there, and it was still as damaging. Every time it happened, it was enforced through manipulation, coercion, intimidation, and repeated patterns of grooming. It was violence of a kind I'd never understood. Had my abuser been a stranger in a dark alley, there would have been no question about calling Blake's actions out for what they were — *rape*. Had he hit me, I would have automatically known that this was an abusive relationship. But because I considered him a friend, and he'd refused to officially call me his girlfriend (even when we were dating), I labelled the abuse as 'Blake just being a bit mean.'

The Stories We Carry

Now, as I began to learn more about the non-physical aspects of domestic violence, such as financial, religious, emotional, and sexual exploitation, my carefully constructed narrative began to crumble. Soon, the trauma began to flood into my everyday life, tormenting me at home and work (a new job I'd just started), and playing endless loops of negative self-talk and distressing memories inside my brain. During the day it followed me down the bicycle path outside the office, pressing tears into the corners of each eye as I hid away under a leafy tree to eat lunch alone. And then at night, it followed me home – tearing apart my mind with thorny accusations.

Why didn't you stop him?

Why didn't you fight back?

Why did you even go to his house that night?

It wasn't rape. Was it rape? This is all your fault!

The closer I got to the opening of the memorial, the worse it became. *Go away*, I'd think. *Leave me alone, I don't need you.* But instead, it only grew worse.

Then, in desperation, the trauma went after the most important thing in my life – my marriage.

At no point in our entire relationship had I ever feared Chris. I'd always felt that we had a pretty healthy relationship when it came to intimacy, but now, all of a sudden, I found myself reacting as though I were back in that room with Blake. Just a simple touch from my husband sent my body from zero to 'get me the fuck out of this house right now' in less than 30 seconds, and in the moment, I was truly afraid. I didn't want Chris anywhere near me. Not his lips on my lips. Not his hands on my hips. I just wanted to get as far away as possible.

Run. Get out. Get away.

It was as though a floodgate had been opened, and all the fear and pain came rushing out. It began with a gnawing uneasiness in my stomach and a quickening of my breath, and then it grew rapidly, accelerating until I was gasping for air. My husband, immediately sensing that something was wrong, quietly and calmly asked what was happening. But I couldn't answer. I could barely breathe, and the only words I could muster were, 'Don't touch me!' It's possible the sentence never left my lips, but everything in me was screaming these three words. I didn't want to be touched. Instead, my body wanted to transport itself 1,000 kms away. All I wanted was the sensation of soft, warm, baggy fabric around my body; oversized sweatpants and shirts that swam around my limbs and made me feel cocooned.

Invisible. Because to be invisible is to be safe.

It was in this moment that I finally realised the truth: I was experiencing Post Traumatic Stress.

As supportive and understanding as my husband was throughout that panic attack, I knew that I had to get help. I had to find a way to acknowledge and clear the traumatic memories, because if I didn't, I knew they could do real damage to my marriage and my health.

Soon afterwards, I made an appointment with a local GP and asked for a mental health care plan. This was a huge step, as I'd never once had a positive experience with a professional therapist. The counsellor I'd seen after my assault had been so negligent that I'd only lasted two appointments, and the psychologist that I tried three years later left the practice shortly after I began seeing her. I was terrified to try again, but I knew that attempting to ignore the situation meant things would continue to deteriorate.

In many ways I got lucky, because the psychologist I worked with ended up being just the right fit for me. She was professional and empathetic and seemed to genuinely care. Together, we worked on some ideas for how I could begin to process, and then move on from, the disturbing memories holding me back. Through our discussions I discovered that the number one thing that was most traumatic wasn't the assault itself – it was the fact that no one in my abuser's circle of friends or family knew what he had done. Like many perpetrators, he was just living his life as normal, with no one to hold him accountable, and that's what hurt most.

For many of us who have experienced sexual abuse, the thought of going to the police – let alone facing our abuser in court – is an added level of distress that we don't feel prepared to take on. As a result, we lack closure. There is often no sense of justice, and for me, this was certainly the case. I had explained as much to my psychologist, sharing that I just didn't know what to do to get the closure I needed.

'Have you thought of writing a letter with everything you wished you'd had the chance to say to him?' she asked gently.

I took a moment to take in her words. 'I could,' I noted. 'But I don't know that that will give me the closure I need. It's not really about him.' I paused again, struggling to enunciate what was going on inside. 'No one knows what he did to me. *That's* what eats me up. Not his family, not his friends… it's like he gets a free pass in every way.'

She thought for a moment. 'What if you wrote to his family, or to his current partner?'

The silence stretched out between us as I considered what she was suggesting. Could I write to his mother? Was I brave enough to do that? Though I wasn't a mother myself, I couldn't imagine how crushing it would be to receive that kind of information about your child, and I wasn't sure I could do it. The last conversation we'd had had been 10 years prior, at which point she'd asked why Blake and I didn't hang out anymore. I'd given her a shitty excuse about his drug habits – something that wasn't necessarily untrue, but wasn't the real truth. Now, I could see that my lies hadn't just protected her heart – they'd also protected his abuse.

'I think that's what I need to do,' I said. 'I don't want to hurt anyone but I know I'll never get closure until I break the silence.'

My psychologist nodded, an understanding smile spreading across her round, kind face. 'Okay. Let's talk about how you can do that.'

A week had passed since my psychology appointment, and I was still torn about taking the next step. While my therapist had made it clear that I didn't have to send the letters in order to get closure, in a way, I felt that it was this step that was crucial to my healing. At the same time, however, I felt scared. The thought of opening up a portal to Blake's world by emailing his partner, as well as his family, brimmed with unknown danger. *How will they respond? Will I get in trouble? What if they don't believe me?*

I wrestled with each of these fears, until eventually, I found my way to the truth. *This is not about being believed,* revealed my soul. *This is about breaking the silence.*

The Stories We Carry

That afternoon, instead of slinking away to the trees outside my workplace so that I could cry privately, I pulled out a notebook. Then, I began writing. Words tumbled out across the page, forming sentences and paragraphs, and eventually taking the shape of a letter. Every painful thought – all the truths I'd suppressed – were laid bare. Every warning I would want to share, if I could spend a day with his current partner; every difficult memory that I needed his family to know. And when I was done, I tucked it back inside my bag, wiped the tears from each eye, and returned to work.

It was a few days before my nerves began to settle, but once they did, I discovered a newfound sense of confidence. There was a depth of clarity that had been missing in the past, but was now abundantly obvious. One that told me what the next step was – that I needed to contact Blake's family. Would they believe me? Maybe… maybe not. Was it possible that Blake would find out and start harassing me? I had no idea. But no matter the consequences, I knew that this was what my soul needed. This is what *I* needed to do. And once I knew, there was no going back.

Now, sitting at my office desk, I glanced discreetly at my co-workers and quickly opened up Facebook. Then, I typed in the name of Blake's sister.

I stared at her profile image – something I had done occasionally over the years. Like her brother, she had the same wide smile, dimpled cheeks, and squarish teeth. Like Blake, she had the same beautiful blue eyes. But that was where the similarities ended. Because, unlike her brother, she wasn't a cruel, manipulative rapist.

I took a deep breath, glanced around the office again, and then started typing. Overnight I'd spent a lot of time thinking and talking with Chris about who I should contact first, and I'd decided that Emma was the easiest option. We'd been the closest, and I felt she might be the most open. Even still, I thought it best if I contacted her using a separate Facebook account that wasn't tied to my name and personal life.

I put my head in my hands, willing the words to come – but the harder I tried, the less they materialised. *How do you start an email to the sister of the man who raped you?* I thought, releasing a small sigh. There was no textbook for the ideal way to perfectly break the silence around abuse. No guidebook on exactly what to say, and when. (And if there was, I'd be wary about taking their advice.) You simply have to feel it, and allow your intuition to guide you.

In the end, that's what I did. I sat and I thought it over, and then I took an honest approach. I admitted that this was an out-of-the-blue email. That it had been a long time since we'd spoken, but I was hoping she might be able to help connect me with Blake. I was transparent about the fact that it was incredibly personal to ask for his address, but the contents of the letter I needed to send were equally personal.

Then, I pressed send and let the universe take care of the rest.

Not long afterwards, as I was trying to concentrate on the tasks I'd set aside for the day, I noticed that the small window in the corner of my screen was flashing.

Holy crap, is it… did she…?

I scanned quickly, reading the name again; but there was no need. It was Emma! Holding my breath, I started reading.

Jas, it's so nice to hear from you! Wow, time really does fly! We actually don't see Blake very often these days. Every

> **time we try he either doesn't show up or he just makes excuses. It's pretty sad because he has a daughter now and we hardly see her either. Is everything okay with u?**

I re-read her message, pausing on the last sentence: *Is everything okay with u?*

Yeah, just dandy, I thought dryly. *Oh, P.S. Your brother assaulted me ten years ago. Okay, bye!*

That may have been the crazy reply that ran wild inside my head, but it wasn't one I could say out loud. Once again, I wished there was a guidebook to tell me exactly what to say. *If only*, I thought wistfully. *If only I didn't have to figure this all out on my own.*

There were so many challenges to face, as a survivor of sexual assault or abuse… so many roadblocks that were just waiting to trip us up, and steal the wind from our lungs before we'd even had a chance to speak out or seek justice. So far, I had only had to face one of these hurdles (cutting Blake out of my life), and now, I was preparing to tackle the second – telling his family. But there were so many other hurdles beyond where I was now; so many fences and mountains and water-crossings that, for many victim-survivors, proved to be too hard to face. From DNA kits and police statements, to court documents, astronomical legal fees, defamation fears, post-separation abuse, financial vulnerabilities, public humiliation, stalking, threats on your children's lives, and more… Well, only now could I fully comprehend why so few cases made it through to court, let alone resulted in true justice.

For me, I wasn't sure how far I wanted to travel on the 'conventional' route to justice, but I knew that I'd come too far to bow out now. So, instead, I braced myself and continued on.

I've wanted to reach out to you and your mum for years, but opening up about the real reason I cut Blake out of my life was too painful. No one wants to hear horrible things about a family member... But at the same time, I need to feel like my voice matters.

I paused on the last line, and then hit send. I was now well and truly past the stage of no return... but I knew there was no going back. To be honest, I expected that Emma would disappear at this point. *She'll totally freak*, I thought to myself. *There's no way she's going to reply – let alone help me.*

As the minutes passed, I continued to berate myself for sending the message and being so open. But then, to my surprise, I saw the three grey dots at the bottom of the screen begin to move again. Like a little caterpillar, they bounced up and down, taunting me as they stopped, started, and then stopped again. When Emma's reply finally came through, I felt as though I'd been hollowed out – not because she didn't believe me... *but because she did.*

From behind the safety of a screen, she told me her own story. How, when she was still a girl, Blake had chased her up a hill and tried to choke her. 'To this day, I still don't trust him,' she admitted.

I stared at the message, lost for words. The thought of Blake – someone whose laugh was infused with a rare, childlike quality of pure joy – chasing his tiny sister until she was out of breath and wrapping his hands around her throat was... it was too much. How was this the same man who had once picked roses for me, I wondered. How was this the same man who had held me with such tenderness and called me his princess?

The Stories We Carry

How is that not *the same man?* asked my intuition. *That is exactly the same man who raped you. You're so lucky you left when you did.*

That afternoon, Emma and I continued to share with each other about our own life journeys. Not once did she diminish any of my experiences, or blame me for what happened; instead, she was empathetic and encouraging. To my greater surprise, however, I found that she was also adamant that I tell Blake's current partner.

'I know something is going on with him and Sharna,' she shared. 'We never see them anymore. I'm so glad you left him and I hope she does too. One time, she almost did… I can't help but think that if she was to hear your story, she might find the confidence to leave and move forward with her life.'

As I made my way home that afternoon, I thought about the power of this moment and the changes that were happening within me in real time. I could feel some of the shame stripping away; almost as though the chains that had shackled me since that night with Blake ten years ago were finally loosening and falling to the ground. And all because I'd chosen to speak out.

'Emma, there's something else I have to ask you,' I added hesitantly. 'I don't know how to say this, but the night that Blake assaulted me… that was the same night that I found Becca crying in the living room. I think of her from time to time, and I've always wondered if… well… if she remembered that night too.'

I allowed the memory to wash over me, remembering the way I'd padded down the hallway and the feeling of her hot, tear-stained face as I cradled her in my arms. It was almost dream-like, in a way. So far away and distant. Many times over the year I'd wondered: Did that really happen? I knew that it had, but at the same time, it felt surreal – particularly, given that Becca was the only other person who experienced it with me, and we'd never again spoken after that night.

Now, as Emma and I talked, I asked the question that I'd always longed to be answered. I needed to know, did her sister have any recollection of that night in the garden? Was there anything that I'd said – in the midst of my own trauma – that had helped her? I craved an answer; to know if there was a reason for me being there that night. If perhaps, the awful things I'd experienced only hours beforehand had deepened my empathy in a way that allowed me to sit with Becca – cold and shivering under a dark ebony sky – as the pain that could not yet leave my heart, burst out into the world through her shuddering body.

My phone pinged, pulling me from my memories. It was Emma.

'Jas,' she wrote. 'Becca does remember that night. She told me you helped her a lot. Thank you for what you did for her.'

In the tiny living area of our shoe-box Queenslander, I stared at my phone and smiled.

'And Jas? I think you should send the letter to Sharna,' she concluded. 'I really do believe that it's going to help her a lot. Thank you.'

It's going to help her a lot.

I held onto that.

Right now, it was all I had.

Chapter 28

*E*verything was going so much better than I'd expected.

Since reaching out to Emma the day before, I'd not only broken the silence, but I'd also emailed Sharna as she'd suggested. (Blake's sister felt it was the best way to ensure that he didn't interfere with anything I was about to share.) Throughout the day, we continued talking as normal, but then, something shifted. I could feel it – subtle, but also teeming with danger. *Be careful*, warned my intuition. *This doesn't feel right.*

One moment all was fine, and then, suddenly, she disappeared. When I tried to send a message, it bounced back.

What the hell? Has she blocked me?

It didn't make sense – after all, everything had been going so well – so I switched over to my personal profile, where Emma and I had also connected, and mentioned to her that my messages hadn't been going through. I waited to see if she'd acknowledge it, but instead, she simply continued our conversation as if nothing had happened. *Must be my imagination,* I thought. *Why would she block me after being so supportive yesterday?*

Though her messages were kind, I felt the shift in energy; almost, it seemed, as though each of her replies were laced with an underlying feeling of distrust. Then, she began switching topics – ignoring our casual conversation about holiday plans, and instead, circling back to personal questions I'd already answered the day before.

'Hey, I'm so sorry to ask further details but did Blake have sex with you without consent?' she asked. 'So sorry Jas, I do believe you, I just wanted to know what happened,' she added quickly.

Suddenly, a warning bell sounded from deep within. *Something's not right here*, I thought. *Has someone talked her out of speaking to me? Or does she just not believe me anymore?*

'That's okay,' I replied, typing out the words slowly. 'No, I didn't give consent.'

'Omg, I'm so sorry Jas. That's horrible,' she typed back. 'Sorry again, I'm just so disgusted that he could do this. You are so strong getting through all of this.'

See, she does believe you. It's fine, soothed my heart. *You can trust her. This is going to be okay.*

The grey caterpillar dots began dancing again, and another message soon followed. 'Hey, you know how you said you blacked out?' Emma asked. 'I'm just wondering… what did you mean?'

This time, the alarm inside my head rose an octave higher, setting off a swarm of angry bees within my stomach. My muscles clenched and sharp little pains began spiking inside my sternum. *Something is wrong*, they said. *Why is Blake's sister suddenly asking all these questions, after you've already told her in so much detail what had happened?*

My intuition was right – it didn't make sense. One moment she was telling me how glad she was that I had left her brother, and not to call myself stupid for going back to him in the past, and now, suddenly, she was asking for more details? I just couldn't wrap my head around it. All this time, Emma had been the one to voluntarily share her family's details with me; she'd been the one who had pushed me to email Sharna, and told me about her own violent experiences at the hands of her brother. So why, now, did I get the feeling she was suddenly distrustful? Her messages gave me the impression that she was recording evidence, and that through the process, she was… I don't know? Trying to get me to contradict myself so she could catch me out? Was that what was happening?

Emma and I continued talking for a little while longer, but then, later that evening, the conversation trail abruptly stopped. As I sat beside my husband, who was quietly watching TV, I realised that I had been blocked on both profiles.

Why would she do that?

Absolute shock enveloped me. I'd opened myself up so fully, and the betrayal of being believed, validated, and then essentially *deleted*, felt like a bigger wound than if I'd been disbelieved from the beginning.

I glanced over at Chris, wondering if he could sense what was going on, but his eyes were fixed to the TV screen. Filled with anxiety I picked up my phone again and decided that, if everything was indeed going to shit, I would try one last route to get the closure I so desperately needed.

Copying in the phone number that Emma had given me for her mother, I typed out a message and, with a sickening sense of fear and dread, briefly explained why I was texting her after a decade of no contact. Then, hopefully, I asked if she would be willing to speak with me.

Almost instantly, my phone beeped. My heart crashed inside my chest, and I felt as though I couldn't breathe. All the blood seemed to be draining from my head, but I willed myself to read it – to find out, once and for all, if I would get closure from his family.

> *Hi Jas. I've heard from Emma about it all. So very sorry to hear about it. I was very shocked. I'm sorry darl, but I can't talk to you about it. I'm dealing with other stresses in my life. I hope you are well, take care.*

In silence, I stared at the short row of text and the two love hearts – one green, the other purple – that had been added at the end.

Is that it? Is it over?

An emptiness that I hadn't felt in so very long began to seep from within, hollowing me out like an old, dead tree. It inched its way along the frail, brittle branches of my limbs, breaking them down piece by piece until my entire body felt like crumbled pieces of charcoal.

'She blocked me.' I blurted out the words, my eyes still fixed to the screen. Beside me, on the couch, Chris swivelled his head.

'Who blocked you?'

'Emma. And now her mum doesn't want to talk to me either.' I held out the screen, showing him the message.

'Oh babe...' Chris leaned toward me, his eyebrows knitted with concern. So very gently, he tried to pull me into his arms, but like jelly, I melted out from underneath. Suddenly my feet were carrying me through the front door and down the wooden steps, while my body followed numbly. Outside, the night air was calm and cool, the street surprisingly quiet, but there was no space inside my head to appreciate its beauty right now. No space to appreciate or feel or say anything at all.

Without any idea of where I was going, my feet carried me around the corner of the house, toward a hibiscus tree – and there, under its rustling, dark green foliage, I collapsed. I lay motionless on the cool grass, curled into a ball. *I should be crying*, I thought to myself. *Why am I not crying?*

I waited, but no tears flooded my cheeks. No soul-piercing scream sliced through the night.

There was just… nothing.

In the distance I heard a voice; the sound of Chris as he walked down the steps and paused, calling out my name. The concerned note in his voice, as he waited for me to answer.

Just call out, came a voice within. *Get up. Get UP!*

Instead, I lay frozen – just like that night ten years ago, where I lay on Blake's bed, feeling weighted to the ground as I watched him climb on top of me; all the while feeling so confused. Wondering to myself why I couldn't speak. Why I just didn't get up. *Get up, damn it! Get up!*

It was the same feeling now. I wanted to speak, but I couldn't. I wanted to stand, but I was frozen. So instead, I lay by the chain link fence of our yard and stared up at the endless dark night sky.

'Jas? Jas, are you here?'

Chris paced around for a while but slowly his voice faded, eventually leaving me alone. It was just me, the hibiscus tree, and the cloudless, ebony expanse above.

Sometime later, when enough strength flowed into my body to allow me to crawl to my knees, I walked shakily back into the house and collapsed into my husband's lap. As I'd later learn, he thought I'd gone for a walk to shake off the stress; he had no idea I'd been lying just metres away from him outside our bedroom window. It felt futile to try to explain what had happened; to try and justify why my body had taken me to that spot on the lawn and then pressed the deactivate button, rendering me immobile.

I didn't have the strength. So instead, I simply existed.

'It's okay,' he murmured, stroking my hair. 'It's going to be okay.'

Somewhere, deep down, I knew it was true. I knew that eventually this pain would pass. But right now, in this moment, I just felt so very raw.

Revealing the truth to my abuser's family was one of the bravest things I've ever done. It was painful and terrifying, but it was also the catalyst to breaking free from my PTS. I understand that this action may not be one that every victim-survivor can take – and that it may not be safe to do so – but for me personally, it was life-changing and necessary.

Through the process of reaching out I had to let go of any attachment to a specific outcome, and instead, just 'accept'. I had to stay grounded in the knowledge that this was about speaking my truth, regardless of whether it was heard or ignored. That was my only goal, as I worked toward my healing.

One month after that painful night, with the support of a friend, I took a step I'd never thought possible: I reported Blake's act of violence against me to my local police. Armed with photocopies of diary entries from before, during, and after our relationship, including detailed descriptions of how I'd felt after the rape and how it had impacted me, I summoned all my bravery and told the truth. Not *my* truth; *the* truth. 'If he should ever do this to another woman, I want my statement to be on record,' I explained.

That was the day I stepped up for the 20-year-old version of me who was too burdened with shame to speak out. It was the day that I broke the silence, refusing to uphold the façade of Blake's reputation any longer. It was also the day that I finally gave myself the power to move on – regardless of whether a single police officer believed me or not.

I'm grateful to be able to share that – shortly after taking these steps – my post-traumatic stress symptoms disappeared. The flashbacks stopped disturbing me at work, and I no longer walked around with fear inside my body.

You may have noticed that I don't refer to my trauma as 'post-traumatic stress disorder' – that's because, for me personally, I don't view it as a disorder. The symptoms I was experiencing were 'normal', given the trauma I'd been through – they just needed to be acknowledged, and provided with a care plan. As someone once said to me, 'Don't view your post-traumatic stress as a disorder, see it as a well-earned scar.' I recognise that not everyone is able to completely heal from this type of trauma, and you might prefer to call it 'Post Traumatic Stress Disorder' rather than 'PTS.' If this is the case, I honour you for where you're at, and your individual journey. As always, I can only share about my own experiences, and what helped me.

When it comes to Blake and his family, I never again spoke to any of them after that night in 2016. I may never know what truly happened, or what caused Emma to block me, but I did find out that Sharna read my letter. No reply was ever sent, and I'll never know whether I was believed or not, but sometimes all you can do is plant a seed.

Every now and then, I scroll through Facebook and look at her profile, praying that she is happy and healthy. To the best of my knowledge, I believe that has since left Blake.

There's no way for me to know what gave Sharna the strength to do so, but I know that I gave her all the information she needed to make an informed decision about her own relationship. Maybe my letter helped her to acknowledge some of the red flags that she had previously struggled to understand? Once again, I'll never know, but I hope that it planted a seed of courage. A seed that allowed Sharna to know that she didn't have to continue to drown in a rising sea that she hoped would remain calm and stable. She was allowed to swim in a different direction. She was allowed to be free.

Sharna was just one of many women who I thought of when Bonnie and I went on to open the domestic violence memorial in March of 2016, and I pray that she and her child can live free from the abuse that so many women and children experience worldwide. They deserve to grow, laugh, play, and just be. Because truly, the greatest freedom is that in which you can simply exist in the world as you are, knowing that you are safe. We all deserve that. Each and every one of us.

Chapter 29

'You ready?'

'I think so.'

Our voices were full of nervous giggles and excitement, as Bonnie and I moved forward to address the crowd. For the last six months, we'd dreamed, planned, and envisioned this moment, and now the day was finally here: March 30th, 2016. The official opening date for Brisbane's first domestic violence memorial.

Standing in front of a beautiful stone waterfall, with the sun beating down on us, we watched as small groups of people and local TV reporters began to gather and join the growing crowd on the lawns of Emma Miller Place. Their faces were sombre, their gazes fixed attentively to the row of portraits behind us; photographs of women who had once lived vibrant lives, yet at the same time, had lived in fear. Women who had been mothers, aunts, sisters, friends, and valued co-workers – but had had their lives ripped away by a husband, a boyfriend, or a jealous ex-lover who refused to allow them to be free.

In my hand, I clutched a single piece of paper – on it, the words that I would read, as I addressed the crowd. The A4 sheet shook violently and I willed my pounding heart to settle, but there was no time for a case of stage fright. The cameras were all waiting. I stepped up and spoke directly into the microphone.

'Although I've been actively involved in learning about violence against women for a number of years, it wasn't until last year, while writing an article on Australia's domestic violence scourge, that I realised the true extent.' My voice rang out across the crowd, all faces fixed on mine as the assembled news crews filmed. 'I can't even recall how many times I had to edit that article over the period of a month before going to print, because the number of women being killed was rising *that* frequently. Every time I would have the article finished and ready to go, I would have to update it again. By the time the article was published in late September, 60 women had been murdered through male violence – the majority killed by a former or current male partner. I don't want to have to keep asking, "When will this stop?" If I'm honest, I wish a memorial such as this didn't have to exist, but until we change our culture, we can't stop speaking up. We need to keep raising our voices, but we also need our courts to hold to account perpetrators of violence. *The punishment must fit the crime.* Too many times, we hear of women whose abusive partners are let off with nothing but a warning, or simply given another AVO – something which often fails to stop an abuser. The courts must stop failing victims – and that includes men as well.'

As the crowd listened in respectful silence, I spoke of a male survivor who had recently contacted me, sharing the depths of despair he'd reached while waiting on the justice system to help him achieve shared custody of his children. He'd been fighting for 12 years. A survivor of physical abuse, emotional manipulation and control, Gary had often seen his children used as pawns against him, and like many men, had struggled to have his voice heard and believed by courts and police.

'So today,' I continued, 'we are here to honour all who have had their lives destroyed by domestic violence; victims and survivors, families and friends. We are here to demand that our country, our city, our courts, and legal systems do more, and that there are no more light penalties and excuses. We urge each of you here today to raise your voices any time you witness emotional or physical violence against another person. We urge you to write to our government, and demand more when you see victims let down by the court system. Thank you for coming, and thank you for standing with us in solidarity.'

That morning, Bonnie and I stood amongst the crowd as we pulled back the soft pink sash from the top of the newly installed memorial – revealing the plaque that was inscribed with the words "No more violence, no more silence" – and paid our respects to the women, men, children, and LGBTI people in Queensland who had been murdered through family or domestic violence. In one steady stream, community members came forward to gently place a red rose by the memorial – some also placing photographs of their loved ones by the edge of the garden, their eyes heavy with tears that never quite cleared.

All around, survivors stood alongside grieving families, while mothers who had lost their daughters to domestic homicide stood in solidarity, arms wrapped tightly around each other. Muslim women stood alongside men from a local Krav Maga club, and the city's Lord Mayor spoke quietly with survivors. Each person had their own story and their own pain, and yet, each of us were dedicated to ending the silence around domestic violence. It was one of the most powerful moments of my life.

All our hard work had paid off. The memorial plaque and the lush green lilly pilly tree behind it looked beautiful, and we'd also raised vital funds for Women's Legal Service QLD; life-saving donations that would help to keep their phone lines staffed, so more women could access the support they needed.

Jas Rawlinson

As a young teen, I'd often lay in bed at night – heart thundering wildly as I decoded the emotions and threats in my dad's footsteps or voice – thinking about how much I wanted to make sure that no other woman or child ever experienced this fear. Although my childhood dreams of creating a magical device that alerted police every time a victim was in danger might have been a bit fantastical and far-fetched, I realised that in a different way – through my advocacy, fundraising, and writing – I had still achieved my dream of doing something significant to create a safer world for victim-survivors.

Most importantly, though, I'd broken the cycle within my own family. I had married a good man – someone who I knew would never hurt me – and I'd cast off the chains of trauma that Blake had placed on me ten years prior. When I discovered some months later that I was pregnant, I realised, with tears in my eyes, that my dream had come true after all. Because I knew that this child would never go through what I did. This child would never know the agony of being belittled, degraded, and told that he was worthless and stupid. He would never have to run frantically across a field to escape the pounding footsteps of his furious father and the screeching of hot tyres angrily skidding on gravel. He would be safe.

He would be safe because I had broken the cycle.

Opening the memorial was the start of an entirely new chapter in my life; one that I could never have dreamed of. In the months that followed, I was approached by several fellow domestic violence advocates who invited me to share my story in a book they were writing, and although I did so under an alias, it was the beginning of my journey into speaking out publicly about my life experiences.

The Stories We Carry

Slowly, one step at a time, I opened up, sharing my story with the media and writing freelance journalism pieces for News Corp Australia on social injustice issues such as human trafficking and domestic violence. Two of those articles went viral ('Do you think we'll pay for bad things we've done? Revelations of Aussie sex tourists in Thailand', and 'It's not enough to just rescue victims: The Australian taking on South East Asia's paedophile rings'), with one amassing around 100K views in a 24 hour period, and the other trending as the top article for nearly two days. The latter also led to nearly $10,000 of donations in the same period of time for Project Karma – an anti-child exploitation organisation for which I am now proud to be an ambassador.

As always, I found that the response to my advocacy varied wildly. Often, I was praised for having the courage to take on issues that others wouldn't; and at the same time, I was also degraded and belittled for 'vilifying white men' or 'making up sensationalist stories' about the realities of human trafficking. Entire reddit threads were dedicated to discussing me and one of these articles, and it took a lot of mental strength to force myself not to read them. Unsurprisingly, some advocates of the sex industry were also upset with me telling the real stories of South East Asian women and girls who had been harmed within the sex trade, and wanted to ensure I was 'educated' on my 'damaging' advocacy.

No matter what happened though, I couldn't stop myself from speaking out about the issues that I felt most passionate about, and so I continued on.

In 2017, I decided to take a new direction with my advocacy. I'd been reading a report from the ABC about the concerning number of suicides within Australia (over 2,800 people in 2016 according to the Australian Bureau of Statistics) and I was shocked by what

I discovered. *That could easily have been me*, I thought. *Why am I still here when so many aren't? What helped me stay afloat during some of the hardest times in my life, when so many others can't?*

As I pondered this further, I began to wonder if there was still more out there for me to do in terms of advocacy. When I thought about the issues I was passionate about – like child exploitation and domestic violence – I realised that most victim-survivors had been left with immense mental health issues as a result of their trauma. Of course, as a survivor myself, I knew this all too well; mental illness and trauma were inextricably linked.

While I don't want to simplify the mental health crises that we face worldwide, the reality is this: if only we could reduce our global pandemic of childhood trauma and violence against women, so many lives *would* be spared from severe mental illness and suicide.

After learning more about the ever-increasing suicide crisis, I began what was to become a life-changing project – a book series named 'Reasons to Live: One More Day, Every Day.' Combining my skills as a writer, interviewer, and photographer, I searched for inspiring people who had faced severe adversity and found a way through to the other side, and I set to work interviewing them about their journey from pain to purpose. Some of the questions I often asked were, *How did you make it through? What helped you the most, and what* didn't *help? What is life like now, and what would you share with others who are in the deep pit of hopelessness that you once found yourself in?*

I felt it was important for people to hear real, raw, and vulnerable stories from everyday people – not just celebrities. As humans, we need to know that our lived experiences and feelings are valid. That our pain is real, and there is no trauma or adversity that is 'bigger' or 'more worthy' of receiving support than someone else's. Pain is subjective, but if something is hurting you – if it's causing distress in your life – then it's real. You don't need to apologise or belittle your experience by saying, 'It's not that bad,' or, 'Other people have it worse.' Pain is pain.

Originally, the book was going to be a collection of stories from both high profile and everyday individuals, with nothing from myself. Why? Well, I honestly didn't want to be in the spotlight. It just didn't seem important to me – that is, until my co-authors kept asking me, one after another, to share why this book was so important to me. 'What's your story?' they'd ask. 'Why do you care so much about this topic?' Some were curious, while others were wary. They wanted to know what was in it for me – if I might put a 'spin' on their story. But as they came to know me more intimately, and as I mentored and coached them through the process of turning their experiences into an inspiring, powerful, and captivating story of triumph over adversity, I found that – just like my clients – I, too, was beginning to grow in confidence.

Eventually, I realised that there was no way for me to publish 'Reasons to Live' without also including my story – it just didn't make sense. The project needed a leader; someone who would be the face of this issue and conversation, and as the creator of the book series, the responsibility fell to me. Though nervous and fearful of being seen as egotistical, I began to share about my own lived experiences with family violence, sexual assault, and suicide. It was nerve-wracking; not just for me, but also my brave mother who worked with me to ensure the book's introduction was truthful and respectful to our collective experiences. To be honest, I wouldn't have blamed her if she'd said that she didn't want me to speak out at all. That would have been entirely fair. But my mother is and has always been the fiercest, bravest, and most resilient person I know… so she said 'Yes.'

At the time, I had no idea how the book would be received, or if anyone would care, as I did, about stories of hope after hopelessness, and triumph over tragedy. It was a complete experiment, one that I slaved over in my lunch breaks at work, and during the evenings after I'd finished dinner. As I discovered, however, it was something that many people were hungry for. One reader – a young man from the UK named Austen – even reached out to share that 'Reasons to Live' had become his 'mental health bible;' something that helped him to hold on to hope as he lay in hospital recovering from a suicide attempt, and, in time, giving him the strength to find his own reasons to live.

In the years ahead I went on to write, edit, and co-author another two books in the 'Reasons to Live' series, and I found that what had initially started as a passion project was now becoming a movement. Between 2016 and 2021 I worked with almost 30 people from around the globe – from speakers and charity owners to everyday change-makers, millionaires, those who'd grown up in poverty, and everyone in between – and empowered them to bring their story to the world in order to help others feel seen and heard. One rule I had was that (almost) no topic was off-limits, so long as they had a message of hope to share, and were mentally well enough to do so without re-traumatising themselves. Some of the many subjects and stories that I covered as a ghostwriter, editor, and mentor, included powerful tales of rising above childhood exploitation, surviving and thriving despite life-altering injuries and disabilities, escaping religious abuse, recovering from the grief of losing a loved one to suicide, embracing sexuality and identity, overcoming addiction and eating disorders, and recovering from postnatal psychosis.

Many times I wept as I edited or wrote each person's narrative, choking back tears of disbelief and grief for all they'd been through. But every time I got through to the end and saw the journey they'd been on, I was overcome with a deep sense of pride and unfiltered love. Each of the humans in 'Reasons to Live' had such incredible stories to tell; experiences that many of them had never before shared. 'You're the first person I've ever told this to, Jas,' they would say. 'And even though I'm scared, this is honestly the most empowering thing I've ever done.' Each of these people were on the precipice of something completely foreign and out of their comfort zone, and they could easily have given up or run away. But they committed, and through the process, they found freedom, liberation, and a sense of connection with other survivors who understood them.

As one of my co-authors, Lauren Watson (an Australian circus and aerial performer with incomplete paraplegia) recently shared, 'It was the first time anyone asked me to tell my story and it wasn't altered to fit their own narrative. It was the first time I connected with another person whose goal in life was to advocate and connect us all through lived experiences… My heart is full of love and gratitude that I could be a small part of something much bigger than we are.'

Equally as beautiful, though, was the path that this passion project took me on. Because it was through this process that I went on to find my true career calling, becoming a non-fiction book coach for female leaders and change-makers who, like myself, feel called to create massive social and global change through the power of raw, real, and powerful storytelling. In late 2018, while on maternity leave from my job as a magazine editor and content writer, I decided to take the plunge and start my own business. It was here that I learned the *true* meaning of perseverance – because if I'm honest, nothing tests your resilience levels more than becoming self-employed (except, maybe, doing so while also being a stay at home parent to your first child!).

The life I live today is far wilder and more fascinating than anything I could have ever dreamed up, and speaking out about my story has opened the door to many incredible opportunities. I've filmed a documentary, spoken at global summits, been interviewed by leading mental health podcasts, and created a successful business. I've come a long way from the shy, self-loathing girl that I once was – but that doesn't mean that I'm immune to insecurity or self-doubt. Every day, I struggle with imposter syndrome… particularly as an introvert, and someone with a highly-sensitive personality type. But I choose not to give up. My business motto is to focus on *experimentation without expectation*, and when I feel like giving up, I allow myself to rest, and then continue onwards.

My journey from survivor to advocate to leader has been a challenging one, and many times, I've recognised the overwhelming obstacles that many lived-experience advocates and survivors faced. In my first few years of business, I was constantly underestimated, rejected, turned away, and overlooked – not just by media outlets, but also organisations who claimed to care about helping people to move beyond trauma and truly thrive. I've been told by media and major government-funded organisations that 'No one wants to hear about issues like these,' and, 'We can't talk about suicide prevention unless you pay us.' I've also been told by suicide prevention organisations that it's 'too triggering to use words like suicide, when talking about an attempt.' My astounded response to the latter was: 'How can we ever expect to reduce suicide rates, if we're too scared to even use the word?!'

When faced with big players in the mental health space, I often felt intimidated, but I chose to listen to my intuition and my gut. I backed myself when others wouldn't, took any speaking/media offer that came my way, and said Yes to opportunities even when I wasn't sure how I'd make it work. I juggled all of this while managing the round-the-clock responsibilities of being a full-time parent with a husband who was away on deployment, and I spent hundreds of hours building connections, finding ways to stand out from others around me, and making sure that my network knew how much I valued them.

This next phase of my journey has required more courage than I ever expected, and it is something I still work through every single day. I've had to learn to trust myself, and to stand up for myself when faced with people (often, older men) who attempted to take advantage of my sensitive nature or – in the beginning – my business naivety. Over the years I've made amazing friends, and lost friends; I've experienced incredible support from people in my online and personal circles, and I've also had people who just didn't get me. For some, I was (and still am) too outspoken, too opinionated, too raw. I've learned to accept that that's just the way things are. In the words of a blog I once wrote: 'Not everyone will like you, and that's okay.'

Today, I'm proud to be recognised as a highly respected, empathetic, and globally endorsed voice on conversations around domestic violence, mental health, and book writing. Equally as important, I've learned to truly own my story, and to stop apologising for being visible and successful. In the past few years I've shared my story and expertise with hundreds of thousands of people through outlets like ABC, Business Insider, Authority Magazine, and 9 News, and at the time of writing this book, have just been named a finalist for the AusMumpreneur 'Author of the Year' and 'Women Changing the World' awards. I've even swum with sharks on a reality travel TV show to help raise awareness and money to end child sexual exploitation! Who would have ever thought I'd do something like that? Not me!

Best of all, I now empower mission-driven women like myself to create global impact through books that change lives. Mothers and female entrepreneurs with the most extraordinary stories – including one of the bravest women I know, who escaped an abusive relationship with a famous Hollywood star, and is now creating a global movement to stop other women and families from going through what she and her children endured. I've always believed that words have the power to change lives, and I see this in action every day.

Throughout the past few decades, my life has changed in a myriad of ways that I never thought possible, and while there are many factors that have worked together to propel me to where I am today, much of it has come as a result of choosing to trust my intuition and listen to the voice inside that is nudging me towards something new – even when it feels scary. Recovering from sexual assault… choosing to leave behind a safe and stable relationship in pursuit of true fulfillment… fighting for the career that I wanted and backing myself when others wouldn't… and holding journalists accountable when they've been disrespectful with my story… These are all small, yet critically important catalysts that have re-routed the direction of my life. They weren't born from a place of comfort; they were difficult, nerve-wracking, and challenging – especially as a highly sensitive, introverted person who struggles with perfectionism and people-pleasing. But when you really want something – *really*, truly want it – you'll do everything you can to find a way to make it work.

To know that my advocacy and story has helped so many people to find the value in telling their story, and to know that I've been able to empower them to share such intimate and personal experiences in a safe and supported way brings me so much joy. It has been worth every struggle and hardship, and every moment of betrayal or hurt or disappointment, because at the heart of everything I do as an author, speaker, and book coach, is a desire to create true change for others. My work is about enabling people to embrace their own stories, and to use them to create ripples of change for future generations.

In 2021, I was checking social media when I saw a photo of a young man on bended knee, proposing to his girlfriend. As I scanned the image, I realised who it was. Instantly, a smile spread across my face. It was Austen, the young man who had come across my book several years earlier, while lying in a hospital bed recovering from an attempt to take his own life. As I typed out my congratulations, I scrolled underneath to see the comment he'd tagged me in.

> *Jas, I wouldn't be here in this moment right now if it weren't for your help. I hope you know that.*

I couldn't help but feel that after all the pain and trauma I'd experienced in my life, I could finally see the silver lining; the message within the mess, and the light within the darkness. What I had survived and lived through wasn't necessary – in fact, it should never have happened – but I could see, now, that I had used my time wisely. I had not only overcome; I had *transformed*. And through the process, I had been able to provide the gift of hope to someone else.

Not everyone gets to that place. It makes me sad that my dad didn't hold on long enough to find his own reasons to live; that he didn't reach out for help, and keep doing so until he found the right person to support him. But I take comfort in the fact that – through my story – other men have found the courage to stay another day. To find the courage to keep moving forward, one day at a time. Men like Dale; a middle-aged man who told me that my story mattered more than I'd ever know, and that my words had helped him to get through one particular day when he was so close to giving up completely. Men like James; a father who broke down in tears at one of my events, sharing that my story had empowered him to take ownership of his mistakes, and to be a better role model for his family so they didn't have to 'walk on eggshells' any more.

Then, there are all the others… names, faces, and stories I will never know. People who have read my books but will never reach out. But most importantly, dear humans who have found courage and comfort amidst the pages of someone else's story, and as a result, have fought for their right to be in this world.

At the end of the day, that's what matters most, yes?

In every fibre of my being, I believe it: yes, yes, a thousand times, yes.

Chapter 30

'*H*as Jas ever told you the Redfoo story?'

Oh man… the Redfoo story. I laughed – cringing a little at the same time. After seven years I still found it hard to believe that my name and that of a celebrity (if you want to call him that) could be used in the same sentence.

'Redfoo?'

Confused, my brother's partner looked between my family and I, searching for an explanation.

'Okay, let me explain,' I began, holding a lychee cocktail in one hand as I told a shortened version of the story – which included the singer Redfoo going on the Kyle and Jackie O Show back in 2014 to complain about me, because I'd called him out on his misogynistic new song/music clip: 'Literally I Can't.' In its essence, the song and accompanying video was little more than three minutes of Foo and his friends gleefully bragging about sexually harassing, and verbally assaulting, young women who didn't want to perform 'girl on girl' sex acts for their entertainment; all while telling them to 'shut the fuck up' and 'get on that pole.' The premise of the song and video was this: *if a woman doesn't want to be filmed without consent, or act out porn-fuelled fantasies, she's boring.*

In the end, I'd launched a campaign with Collective Shout (the same organisation I'd done some volunteer work with, back in 2012 and 2013) – which ended up being quoted in The Times and most mainstream media outlets – calling on Channel Seven to ditch Foo from his position as X-Factor's mentor for young female musicians. The end result? Redfoo didn't end up returning to Channel Seven. Can't say I'm responsible for that... but if I am? Well, I'm not sorry!

As the night progressed, many other stories were shared. Stories of evenings spent observing and investigating illegal brothels, and my travels in South East Asia where I met and spoke with survivors of sexual exploitation and trafficking. I thought about how odd it was that a girl from the bush who was once so timid and terrified of speaking up about anything, could transform into someone who was the complete opposite.

Twenty years ago, my only wish as a 16-year-old had been for the pain inside to stop. Whether that relief came via death or some other miracle, I didn't really care. I just wanted to be free from the living nightmare that consumed me daily.

I'd been on a hell of a journey over the last two decades, one that had led me from the deepest oceans of depression to the ecstasies of joy and healing. I'd been cut to the core with despair and hopelessness more times than I could count, but with all my injuries and scars, somehow, I'd pushed, run, and at times crawled onwards, until the sting of my past hurts faded enough to allow me to trust in life once again.

Now, seated around the table with my family on New Year's Eve, I looked at the faces surrounding me and thought again of that afternoon in the school counsellor's office at the age of 17, when she'd asked me what I wanted life to look like. The twiggy stick

The Stories We Carry

figures I'd drawn, of Jason, Mum and I. Two decades on, I realised that we were all of those things and more.

Mum, once confined to a life of attempting to keep Dad's moods from exploding while trying to put food on the table, was now running her own business as an art therapist, and brainstorming with me about her plans for the future. My brother, although still tight-lipped about many of his own feelings, was the calmest and happiest I'd ever seen him. Neither of us really liked to talk about Dad much, but if I'd learned anything in life, it was that you can't force or hurry another person's healing. I knew that when the time was right, he'd find the words and courage to begin opening up.

Each of us were on our own journey, and we still carried within our minds hundreds of stories of the traumas and adversities we'd faced. But as time went by, I realised something more important. The stories we carried were no longer ones of hopelessness and despair. Instead, they were ones of strength and courage. The stories we carried were filled with depth and humanity, and the power to change the course of history for others.

I lifted my drink and sipped, knowing that whatever happened in the year ahead, I would never forget the power of my voice.

Cheers to that.

Gratitudes

In a way, I feel that this book has been in the making since the time I was a teen. There are a few people throughout my life who have spoken words over me that were almost prophetic in a way, and though I didn't believe them at the time, I now see that they were correct. It started in my mother's church, when a woman told me that she believed I would one day share my story/testimony with others; and there was also an experience in my mid-twenties when a medical practitioner (who was treating me for a chronic pain disorder) took a leap of courage and told me that she felt that God would make me into a warrior to help others; like David, fighting Goliath. So, I guess I should begin this section by thanking both of these individuals for seeing something in me – and holding a vision – that maybe, just maybe, kept me going through years of uncertainty and despair.

There are so many people who have played a role in my healing, growth, and dreams, but one of the biggest cheerleaders I have had is my mother. Mum, you know I'm not one for soppy conversations, but I hope you also know how much I love, respect, and look up to you. No one personifies resilience the way that you do. No one has fought for me, the way that you often have. You've stood against my bullies, you've argued with medical practitioners to get me the help I've needed, and you were the one to support my dreams by financially supporting me through university. Every time I write or publish a book, I remember what you sacrificed to give me the education I have. I would not be the writer or author I am without you.

Thank you to my beautiful friends, many of whom have stayed by my side for decades. There are too many of you to mention, but in particular, thanks to Rach, Bonnie, Verina, Julz, Han, and Steph for so much emotional support over the years. Amber V – I will never forget the night you put aside everything to listen to me share my story for the first time. As a now mother myself, I can imagine you had so many others things you could have been doing!

Louise – what the hell would I do without you in my life? You are warmth, and empathy, and laughter, and generosity personified. Whether we are horse-riding, laughing about highly-sensitive/empath problems, or doing our favourite thing in the world – eating good food and drinking bubble tea – I always feel at ease with you. Thanks a billion for all the amazing brand photos you've taken of me over the years (including this book cover!).

Courtney Greatrex – it's not often that I think of journalists while writing my gratitudes, but I knew that this list wouldn't be complete without you. I've had some deadset awful experiences over the years, but you have always handled my story with such professionalism and genuine care. You are a wonderful human, and an exceptional writer. Thanks for my New Idea and WHO features!

Thank you to my publicity mentors, Selena Soo and Lynya Floyd, for giving me the tools, wisdom, and knowledge to create global impact with my story. So much of my success has come from implementing what I've learned from you both, and every time I receive a compliment about being 'the media queen', I know that I have you to thank! And on that note, thank you to my other mentor, Denise Duffield Thomas, for helping me to work through my money blocks and understand that it's okay for good things to happen to me all the time!

The Stories We Carry

Thank you to my editing and publishing team for being open to working with me under my insanely short deadlines. Cheers to Natasha Denman and team for listening to all my long-ass voice memos, and Karen Crombie for not only assisting with editing, but also emotional support. Karen, I really appreciate your genuine care for my story.

Thanks to my family, particularly my sister-in-law and parents-in-law. I would NOT have gotten my books done (or at least, not without a complete breakdown) without your support over the years with babysitting.

A thousand hugs and thanks to Linda and the team from Botanical Lab, for your out-of-this-world bubble teas. You have created a space that is so beautiful, and one that I can always feel at ease in. I appreciate the times you've made special orders for me outside of normal hours, particularly when I'm about to travel interstate on a long drive.

To my Big Little Brother, 'Manchild', I am so proud of you and how far you've come. I love our dry, sarcastic jokes and the way that we can laugh about our past traumas. Every time I wear green I think of you and our love of Little Britain. PS. I know you hate reading, but can you finally hurry up and actually *read* one of my books? Like, geez. Get with the program! ILY.

To my love: Chris. As I shared earlier in this letter, you know more than anyone that I'm not a fan of mushy #CoupleGoal posts on social media, but I really do love and appreciate you. I know I am not the easiest person to live with (from my annoying tendency to use a thousand towels per week, to my HSP quirks, and my inability to sleep without white noise apps), but you love me so unselfishly, and with so much patience. Thanks for being an amazing role model for our son, and working so hard to support us. Oh, and thank you for letting me bring my laptop on holiday so I could finish this book! (But please, next time let me choose the holiday destination – no more crazy 4wd trips with crocodiles and eleventy-million creatures that want to kill us!)

There are so many people to thank, and not enough room, so if you're one of my treasured friends or clients, please know that I see, love, and appreciate you. (But if I don't stop adding more words to this book, I think my publisher might kill me haha.) I am so grateful to each and every one of you who have read my books, attended my events, shared my articles, and cheered me on. The celebration of this book is as much for you, as it is for me.

PART 2

Resources to Help You Thrive

HOW TO SHARE YOUR STORY SAFELY

"I want to speak out about my story, but I'm not sure how to begin... Do you have any advice?"

Many times over the years I've received different variations of this question from brave survivors in my network. As humans, I think it's natural to want to use our life experiences to help others, and it can also be cathartic and healing to do so. However, there are some important things to consider before going public.

Firstly, before publicly sharing our stories it's important to work out *why* we want to speak out. For example, what is it that we want to achieve, and how do we hope to feel after doing so? If it's to help others, you can always begin by writing a blog under an alias as opposed to going through the process of writing an entire book. Or, if your motivation for sharing is to aid your own healing, then this is what I recommend: write out your story in full, and spend some time – while practicing self care – really focusing on who you are today and the strong person you've become. List down all the accomplishments you've made, large and small, and allow yourself to reflect on how far you've come.

Secondly, I strongly encourage survivors to create a 'support squad' of people who they know they can speak to openly. If you don't have a safe or supportive family, I recommend choosing a good friend or therapist to talk to instead. Go to the people who will uplift you; the ones who will believe and validate what you've been through. It goes without saying that there is always a risk of backlash, so it's important to have professional support if you plan to go public.

And finally, remember that your story is yours to tell. You have every right to speak out, and to share it in a way that is beneficial and empowering to you.

Sharing Your Story With Media Outlets

First and foremost, I want to make one thing absolutely clear: sharing your story with friends or people in your community is one thing, but going public in the media is another entirely. It should always be a personal and empowered choice, and never one that is done out of obligation and pressure – so please ensure you make this decision for *you*. It may also be worth speaking with a trusted professional or friend, to ensure you are crystal clear on whether this is the right step for you to take.

If you do decide to move forward, I'd encourage you to do the following:

1. **Research the outlet and ensure their values align with yours.**

    Honestly, this is so important! When I first began speaking out, I said Yes to just about anyone/everyone, but I've gotten a lot 'pickier' over the years and I've come to understand the value of my story. For example, recently I was invited to feature in an international news publication with a gigantic audience who wanted to write an indepth article on my work and my life journey – but I said no. Why? Well, personally, I have a rule that if I can't open a website in front of my five year old without exposing him to soft-core pornographic articles (you can probably guess which 'news' sites I'm referring to), then it's a hard no. No matter how great the global 'exposure' might be, I don't want my story lodged in the middle of articles promoting pornographic websites and platforms. I know my values, and I stick to them.

2. **Ask to read/listen to a draft of the article before it goes live.**

A lot of advocates and entrepreneurs are surprised when I share this with them; in fact, many times they don't even know that it's something they're allowed to request. Speaking personally, I probably wouldn't have known either if not for my own negative experiences with the media – and that's why I feel strongly about including this section.

The truth is, you are *absolutely* allowed to ask to review a copy of the article and headline before it goes to print. This is something I began doing after a traumatic experience a few years ago, when a news outlet published my story under an offensive, degrading, and disempowering heading, and I still do it today.

Now I only publish my story through journalists that allow me to review a copy of the article before it goes to print. I also ask them to request that their online team not use inflammatory or sensationalist language in the headline. If I'm pitching a client's story, I ask the same questions. And you know what? Journalists and editors have always been willing to do so.

If you're nervous about sharing your story with the media, and aren't sure how to broach the conversation with journalists, here is a template that you're welcome to use. Note: this is a template for phone conversations but you can adapt it for email threads as well. Just change the bracket section as appropriate and add your name/signature at the end.

> *"Thank you so much for your time today, I really appreciate your support for my story. Before we wrap up our call I had a quick question I wanted to ask. Understandably my story has a lot of sensitive elements to it, and I wanted to check if you could flick me a copy of the draft article before it goes live. As **[a survivor of ___/someone who has experienced___]** it's important to me that my story is handled sensitively, so I'd love it if you could send through a draft so that I can ensure everything is correct before publishing. Would that be okay?*

TOOLS AND TIPS FOR THRIVING AFTER TRAUMA

People talk in grandiose, dreamy ways about 'thriving', but what does it truly mean to do so? If you take a quick scroll through social media, you might come across a cute selfie or a sultry portrait of someone 'living their best life'... but are they really?

Thriving – in its truest essence – is about so much more than a picture of yourself strutting through Coachella in the latest fashion trend, cruising in a sports car, or any other version of the tried and true 'insert vain, fomo-inducing Instagram reel here' that we see everywhere.

So, what does it take to truly thrive? How can you live free from trauma? There are a number of things I do for my mental wellbeing and inner resilience (both daily and weekly), and I wanted to include some of them here.

As always, please be aware that this information is not recommended as a substitute for professional support. These are the tools or resources that have been helpful in my journey, as well as my daily wellbeing, and I hope that they give you some additional ideas for things that may be of help to you as well.

Thriving Tool #1: Gratitude Journaling

Some people think of writing and journaling as something that only high schoolers do for fun, but in reality, it's one of the best things we can do for our mental wellbeing. In fact, a 2016 study (referenced in *Greater Good Magazine) found that participants who wrote letters of gratitude, experienced higher levels of happiness, as well as greater activation and neural sensitivity in the medial prefrontal cortex, an area of the brain associated with learning and decision making. This also showed that people who are more grateful are often more attentive to how they express gratitude.

Speaking from personal experience, I've found that putting aside just a few minutes at the end of the day to list five things I'm grateful for, is really helpful in shifting my mindset from being stressed out and crappy, to being calmer and happier. Think of it as your daily wellness vitamin.

Thriving Tool #2: Digital Detoxing

I'm going to admit, right now, that I spend way too much time looking at my phone. And I know that it's not good for me. Not only does it increase my anxiety and comparisonitis, but it often activates my fight or flight response and creates havoc with my digestion.

Unfortunately, I'm not alone in this struggle. Overuse of technology is one of the biggest battles faced by our young people today, and it's killing our creativity, inner peace, and ability to be present.

If you're looking to improve your wellbeing, one of the best things you can do is choose a day of the week to do a digital detox. It could be a Saturday or Sunday, or you might choose to start with half a day. Whatever you do, I recommend swapping screen time for a physical book, some time in the garden, a walk with a friend, or another hobby that gets you away from technology.

---

* Source: How Gratitude Changes You and Your Brain (Greater Good Magazine, 2017)

Thriving Tool #3: Discovering True Self-Care

I used to think of self care as bubble baths or a nice meal with a glass of wine. But the reality is, these are just short term fixes (and let's be honest, alcohol is not the best treatment for our mental or physical health).

True self care is the type that nourishes you from the inside out, and lasts long after the experience. It's a regular practice that builds upon itself, like lego blocks, to create a strong foundation. For example, in late 2020 I realised that I was experiencing burnout several times per year – mostly, because I never took time for myself. I was always busy, busy, busy, serving everyone else. Change only came when I prioritised myself enough to stop and ask what *I* needed.

For me, I'm happiest when I'm by the ocean. So for the last year, I've rearranged my working week to include beach walks on a Friday. I've also become selfish about this, and no longer schedule work on those days. Thankfully I have wonderful clients who respect boundaries, but if I should ever have someone who doesn't, I feel confident to politely say: "Sorry, I'm not available that day."

Self care isn't selfish – it's essential. After all, how can I serve others if I'm not filling my own cup first?

Thriving Tool #4: Setting Strong and Unapologetic Boundaries

Without a doubt, one of the most important things I have ever done is to learn how to begin setting and implementing boundaries. I'd like to say that I'm a pro, after so many years of experimentation, but I've found that the journey to becoming rock-solid in our boundaries is ever evolving. That said, I'm extremely proud of how far I've come.

In order to thrive, it's vital that you understand three things.

1) You are allowed to set boundaries in your life.

2) You absolutely *must* set boundaries in your life.

3) Setting boundaries does not make you a b*tch – you can still be a kind and empathetic person while putting things in place that make life more comfortable and peaceful.

For those of us with a history of trauma (and in particular, women), it can feel almost painful to prioritise ourselves over others, and to voice what *we* truly want (not what we *think* we should want). As a result, our heads are filled with messages like, 'Be polite. Don't offend. Don't hurt her/his feelings. Be relatable. Be nice. You don't want to lose this opportunity/relationship/job, do you?'

As a sensitive and empathetic person, I know that this compassionate side of my personality is a double edged sword. On one hand, my empathy/sensitivity is one of the main reasons my clients seek me out as a book coach – but it has also led to unhealthy patterns of people pleasing, self sacrificing, and becoming a doormat for other people's bad behaviour.

Whilst I've dealt with a lot of these issues in regard to intimate relationships, I think it's important to note that our ability to stand up for our personal values, body autonomy, or feelings is also important in our work and personal relationships.

The Stories We Carry

Here are a few examples of personal and professional boundaries I've put in place over the years:

- I no longer have notifications turned on for social media.
- Clients are not allowed to have my phone number – I conduct all sessions via zoom.
- When strangers or potential clients ask me to call them so they can 'pick my brain' or 'just have a chat', I politely decline. My time and energy are precious, and I reserve them for myself, my family, and my clients.
- I pull myself back from replying to every stranger who emails, especially those who want to dump their problems on me for a quick fix.
- I choose who – and what – I invest my energy into. For example, sometimes I'll reply to people in my social media community with indepth messages, but I allow myself to be guided by intuition – not guilted into it.
- I have a non-negotiable 'day off' during the week, where I never book clients.
- I decline potential clients or opportunities that don't feel like a good fit (even though, internally, I want to help everyone).
- I don't answer client emails on a weekend (and if I struggle not to, I compose a draft reply and schedule it to send on Monday).
- When strangers contact me asking for mental health advice, I gently let them know that I'm not a professional and that it would be negligent for me to try to assess/fix what is going on for them.

Although boundaries are something I still have to work at, I'm no longer the girl who used to be everything to everyone (including strangers). At times, it's meant upsetting people, and I can sense that there are some within my own circle who aren't happy that 'relatable Jas who always answered everyone's messages at the drop of a hat' is no longer around, but I know that my mental wellbeing is more important.

If you're new to setting boundaries, this is my advice: the next time someone asks you to do something, or wants you to interrupt the flow of your day/energy to help, ask yourself:

- *How does this make me feel energetically? What is the immediate response in my body? (If you learn to tune in to it, your body will often tell you very clearly what it does/doesn't want.)*
- *Is there something I'd rather be doing right now that's more important to me? (Eg. Writing my book, working on my business, spending time with family, walking on the beach, crafting, gardening…)*
- *Do I feel like I have to say yes? If so, why do I feel that way?*
- *If I say no, what's the worst that might happen? (Eg. My friend won't like me anymore. People will think I'm full of myself.)*

Here are a few affirmations you can speak out loud, or internally (if you'd like to):

It's safe for me to have boundaries, and to choose what I do with my body.

It's safe for me to look after my mental wellbeing and energy.

It's safe for me to put myself first and choose who I respond to, and when.

The more energy and peace I have, the more I can pour into the people and things that bring me the most joy.

PS. This is an excerpt from a resource I've developed called 'Creating Strong and Unapologetic Boundaries.' You can download a free copy of the full version from www.jasrawlinson.com/boundaries.

HELPFUL RESOURCES

With each book that I create, it is important to me that people have a list of helpful resources and support services to help them where they're currently at. I recognise that not everyone is comfortable with seeking support from a helpline or large mental health organisation, and for that reason, I have always endeavoured to provide a mixture of grassroots and well-established support options.

Below, you'll find a list of services and resources that I personally support, or which have helped people close to me.

Lived-Experience Advocates and Experts

Custody Peace
Custody Peace is a coalition of more than 100,000 survivor parents and concerned citizens in the United States, advocating for evidence-based policies which put child safety and risks at the forefront of child custody decisions. They are committed to creating a world where all women and children are free from all forms of Coercive Control and Post-Separation Abuse through legal accountability.

W: **custody-peace.org**

Sarah McDugal – Betrayal Trauma Recovery Coach
Sarah McDugal is an author, speaker, abuse recovery coach, and co-founder of Wilderness to WILD and the TraumaMAMAs mobile app – both of which provide evidence-based, trauma-effective resources for women after abuse. She creates courses, community, and coaching for women recovering from deceptive sexual trauma,

coercive control, and intimate terrorism. Her passion is helping mamas heal and rebuild healthy solo-parent families while they protect their children from further harm, and navigate the family court system after escaping abuse. Sarah's tools and resources guide women 'out of the wilderness of abuse, into a wild, thriving, peaceful post-trauma life.'

W: btr.org or traumamamas.app/links

Jess Hill
Jess Hill is a double Walkley award-winning journalist, author and speaker who focuses primarily on social issues and violence against women. She is the author of 'See What You Made Me Do.' She is also the host of the ground-breaking podcast series 'The Trap.'

W: jesshill.net

Movement of Mothers
Founded by Renée Izambard, Movement of Mothers is a US-based coalition of change-makers, with children's safety in custody cases at the core of their ethos. "We support scientific research to formulate legislation in the child's best interest and ensure accountability in the family court system," said Ms Izambard. Join the #MeToo movement of mothers below.

W: themovementofmothers.com

Safe4Kids
Safe4Kids is an Australian-based company specialising in child protection education, with a focus on keeping children safe from abuse. Led and created by Holly Ann Martin (OAM), a child safety

expert of 35+ years, Safe4Kids offers child protection education resources as well as tailor made child protection training for parents, teachers, and educators in Australia and internationally.

W: safe4kids.com.au

Gaggle

Regarded as a pioneer in helping educators manage student safety on school-provided technology, Gaggle's mission is to ensure the safety and wellbeing of all students while supporting school leaders in proactively identifying those who are struggling. Gaggle helps educators see the early warning signs so they can take action to protect students from harming themselves or others – before it's too late. As student mental health concerns have grown in recent years, the need for a digital safety net to support students in the virtual environment has become more apparent. Gaggle's solution uses a combination of artificial intelligence and trained safety experts to provide real-time analysis and review of students' use of the school's online collaboration platforms for email and schoolwork. Gaggle offers administrators, teachers, and parents the peace of mind that students are being protected – 24 hours a day, seven days a week, 365 days a year.

W: gaggle.net

Professional Support Services

Lifeline

For 24/7 crisis support and suicide prevention services, call Lifeline on 13 11 14, or use their online chat every night from 7 pm at lifeline.org.au/crisischat.

W: lifeline.org.au

Women's Legal Service
For Statewide Legal Advice call 1800 WLS (1800 957 957).

W: wlsq.org.au/contact

Beyond Blue
P: 1300 22 4636. **W:** beyondblue.org.au

Kids Helpline
P: 1800 551 800. **W:** kidshelpline.com.au

Suicide Call Back Service
P: 1300 659 46. **W:** suicidecallbackservice.org.au

Mates4Mates
P: 1300 462 837. **W:** mates4mates.org

Mensline
P: 1300 78 99 78. **W:** mensline.org.au

1800 Respect
P: 1800 737 732. **W:** 1800respect.org.au

About Jas Rawlinson

Jas Rawlinson is an award-nominated book coach, resilience speaker, and best-selling author who empowers female change-makers to transform their stories into books that create global impact.

Sought out for her empathetic leadership and unapologetic advocacy for stigmatized issues such as domestic violence and child abuse, Jas has worked with people from all walks of life, from high-profile figures in the music industry to entrepreneurs and everyday people. She is highly respected for her unique ability to lead her clients strategically through the often emotional writing and publishing process, and has been featured in and endorsed by names such as National Center on Sexual Exploitation, Business Insider, Yahoo Finance, news.com.au, Mindvalley and Mamamia. She is also the founder of Brisbane's first domestic violence memorial, and an anti-human trafficking ambassador who has spent time with survivors and investigators in SE Asia. In late 2022 she will feature in front of 100 million+ people on the award-winning TV series Adventure All Stars, as part of her mission to end child trafficking.

Above all, Jas believes that everyone has a story with the power to inspire, impact, and change lives.

www.jasrawlinson.com

Write Your Life-Changing Book with Jas Rawlinson

Are you an emerging female leader and change-maker who wants to create true impact through your story? Have you always wanted to write a book about your life journey and expertise, but don't know where to start?

When you're ready, here are four ways that Jas can support you:

1. Download Jas Rawlinson's free author checklist – 14 Steps to Becoming a Published Author: www.jasrawlinson.com/authorchecklist

2. Access a free recording of Jas Rawlinson's masterclass: How to write, publish, and market your book like a pro (valued at $97): www.jasrawlinson.com/masterclassreplay

3. Enrol in Jas Rawlinson's signature course: Write, Publish, Market Your Memoir Like a Pro: www.jasrawlinson.com/writingcourse

4. Work with Jas privately via her 1:1 program: From Big Idea to Author of Impact: www.jasrawlinson.com/bookcoaching

Book Jas Rawlinson to Speak on Your Podcast or at Your Next Event

Jas Rawlinson is a global resilience, domestic violence, and storytelling speaker who specialises in conversations that inspire, challenge, and change lives. Often sought out for her natural ability to break down difficult topics, Jas has spoken everywhere from global summits and international conferences, to small communities, and major media stations.

Topics Jas can speak on:

- Understanding, addressing, and standing against domestic violence and sexual exploitation
- The power of storytelling as a vehicle for trauma recovery
- Improving mental wellbeing and resilience within the workplace
- Overcoming adversity and creating purpose from pain
- Nonfiction book writing and publishing

Book Jas for your speaking event at jasrawlinson.com/speaking

Authors of Impact – The Podcast

For free tips on writing, publishing, and marketing your non-fiction book, subscribe to Jas Rawlinson's podcast Authors of Impact (available on all major podcast platforms, including Apple and Spotify).

Other books from Jas Rawlinson

Reasons to Live: One More Day, Every Day

Featuring inspiring stories from both everyday and high profile survivors of mental illness and trauma, 'Reasons to Live One More Day, Every Day' is the bestselling, internationally-renowned series changing and saving lives. Through the power of lived-experience storytelling, each book follows the lives of 10 remarkable humans from around the world, who have found the courage to rise above mental pain and adversity. Endorsed by major figures such as Lifeline, Kevin Hines, Livin, News Corp Australia and more, 'Reasons to Live' is more than a book – it's a movement with the power to save lives.

Catch up on the 'Reasons to Live' series at jasrawlinson.com/books

Connect With Jas Rawlinson

📷 @jas_rawlinson

📘 @ jasrawlinsonofficial

in @ jas rawlinson

🌐 www.jasrawlinson.com

www.ingramcontent.com/pod-product-compliance
Lightning Source LLC
Chambersburg PA
CBHW030252100526
44590CB00012B/376